BERNARD MALAMUD
a reference guide

A
Reference
Guide
to
Literature

Ronald Gottesman
Editor

BERNARD MALAMUD

a reference guide

JOEL SALZBERG

G.K.HALL &CO.

70 LINCOLN STREET, BOSTON, MASS.

REFERENCE BOOK
NOT TO BE TAKEN
FROM THE LIBRARY

Library of Congress Cataloging in Publication Data

Salzberg, Joel.
  Bernard Malamud : a reference guide.

  (A Reference guide to literature)
  Includes index.
  1. Malamud, Bernard—Bibliography.   I. Title.
II. Series.
Z8544.57.S24   1985   [PS3563.A4]   016.813'54   85-5499
ISBN 0-8161-8647-2

This publication is printed on permanent/durable acid-free paper
MANUFACTURED IN THE UNITED STATES OF AMERICA

Contents

The Author

Joel Salzberg's academic degrees are the B.A. in English from the City College of New York, the M.A. in English from Indiana University, and the Ph.D. in English from the University of Oklahoma. He has taught at the University of Northern Iowa, and has been an associate professor of English at the University of Colorado at Denver since 1970. His publications, focusing on Poe, James, Melville, and Hart Crane, have appeared in such journals as the <u>Emerson Society Quarterly</u>, the <u>American Transcendental Quarterly</u>, <u>Studies in the Novel</u>, and the <u>Bulletin of the Rocky Mountain Language Association</u>. He is on the editorial board of <u>Abstracts of English Studies</u> and also serves as a reader for <u>English Language Notes</u>. For the summer of 1970, Dr. Salzberg was awarded an English-Speaking Union Grant for the purpose of pursuing postdoctoral study at the University of Edinburgh, Scotland.

Preface

In an undertaking of this kind, one is always thankful for the assistance that others have provided by their earlier research. Previous bibliographical surveys on the fiction of Bernard Malamud gave my project a momentum it otherwise might not have had. I am indebted to the work of Rita Natalie Kosofsky (1969.27) and Morris Sher (1970.23), and to the more recent labors of Donald Risty (1977.33), Robert D. Habich (1978.8), and Joseph Grau (1980.6; 1981.6). Their special contributions to the bibliographical map of Malamud criticism and scholarship are identified in my own annotations of their work.

More general bibliographical sources used in this study are those normally found in the reference section of university libraries. The American Humanities Index, Articles in American Literature, 1968-1975, Arts & Humanities Citation Index, Book Review Index, Combined Retrospective Index to Book Reviews in Humanities Journals, 1802-1974, Combined Retrospective Index to Book Reviews in Scholarly Journals, 1886-1974, MLA International Bibliography, and the New York Times Book Review Index were particularly useful. In an attempt to avoid accidental omissions of potentially useful items, a cross-check of bibliographical sources was done through Computer Literature Search using the MLA, LC, and MARC data bases. Professor Giovanna Franci-Zignani of the University of Bologna, Italy, supplied a number of references to book reviews and articles on Malamud in Italian that I did not otherwise encounter. Luck was always a factor. Bernard Malamud graciously supplied me with a reference to Anthony Burgess's review of God's Grace, which I had not run across in any bibliographical index.

My sources eventually led to the reading and annotating of nearly nine hundred articles, books, chapters in books, doctoral dissertations (primarily abstracts), and book reviews. This Reference Guide also offers a broad representation of international discussion on Malamud in the annotations of German, Italian, French, Spanish, Japanese, Serbo-Croatian, Flemish, and Norwegian commentary. Daily American newspapers and journals that feature only brief reviews and book notices have been used selectively because of their marginal value: these newspapers have been included to provide a geographical cross section of popular critical opinion, and journals that offer very minimal comment have been represented only when they crystallize a critical position or make a relevant observation on Malamud's work.

Support for this project came from a number of sources. I am grateful for the assistance provided by the Interlibrary Loan and Reference staff at the University of Colorado at Boulder and to Connie Whitson of the Interlibrary Loan Department of the Auraria Library, which serves the University of Colorado at Denver. My thanks also go to colleagues at the University of Colorado at Boulder and Denver who translated foreign-language criticism into English. Without the financial aid of the Councils on Research and Creative Work of the University of Colorado at Boulder and the University of Colorado at Denver, and the Seed Money Award at the University of Colorado at Denver, budget constraints might well have been a factor in affecting the progress of this research. Douglas Gunn, a student at the University of Colorado at Denver, was diligent and able in locating additional citations and cross-checking references in the final stages of this work. A very special thanks goes to Professor Melvin H. Buxbaum of the University of Colorado at Boulder for his part in the continuing dialogue related, directly and indirectly, to this book. Finally, my greatest benefactor has been my wife, Kathleen A. Salzberg, whose editorial skills may well have smoothed the way for everyone involved in the editorial process.

Introduction

A book has a bedrock of meaning, and I keep that in mind
when I write, but I would not interfere with imaginative criticism if the critic can demonstrate to me that he has read my
book carefully. I enjoy interpretation wherever it goes and
critical variety up to a point, that point being idiocy.[1]

Much of the criticism cited and annotated in this Reference
Guide might hold for Bernard Malamud some interest, if not pleasure,
insofar as it reveals the kind of careful reading and imaginative
response to his work that he hoped would take place. In the thirty-
odd years that Malamud has been a professional writer of stories and
novels, a growing body of critical discussion has accumulated on the
uniqueness of that work. To a very large extent that discussion has
been short on "idiocy" and long on intelligence and imagination. In
the course of this bibliographical research, my frequent encounters
with the richness and variety of commentary on Malamud's fiction
served as the good angels that lightened the inevitable burdens of
this project over the last two years. I hope that this book in turn
will make critical research on Malamud less arduous by identifying
and elucidating the patterns in his literary carpet that give his
work its special character. Bernard Malamud has been read as the
most Jewish of contemporary Jewish American writers; a practi-
tioner of an older Yiddish literary tradition; a romancer who, in
the manner of Hawthorne, employs myth, symbol, and allegory; a
naturalist; a fantasist; an existentialist; and a humanist out of
place in contemporary society. Ideally, the range and vitality of
discussion on Malamud will not only direct the reader to the widest
possible spectrum of criticism in already established categories,
but also may suggest what yet needs to be written.

Biographical details in the life of Bernard Malamud have the
familiar ring of the twentieth-century Jewish American urban
experiences that one finds in the almost mythic autobiographies of
Alfred Kazin's A Walker in the City or Irving Howe's more recent A
Margin of Hope. Born on 26 April 1914, Bernard Malamud was the
oldest of two sons of Bertha (née Fidelman) and Max Malamud, Russian
Jewish immigrants who settled in Brooklyn in the 1900s and who

earned a meager living working days and nights in their grocery
store. Malamud's early boyhood recollections extend beyond working
in the family store to the frenetic play of the neighborhood street
life and journeys to the exotic worlds of Coney Island and Times
Square made accessible by the El. Other assorted memories of
Malamud's early life include writing stories at the age of eight or
nine, reading Frank Merriwell, discovering Charlie Chaplin films,
watching the Dodgers at Ebbets Field, and witnessing the lingering
illness of his mother, who died early in his life. After graduating
from Erasmus Hall High School in Brooklyn, Malamud completed degrees
at the City College of New York (B.A., 1936), and Columbia
University (M.A., 1942). His marriage to Ann de Chiara, a woman of
Italian American descent, on 6 November 1945, helped to stimulate
Malamud's interest in Italian fictional characters and in Italy as a
setting for many of his stories. Eventually, Malamud's experiences
as a teacher also furnished source materials for his literary
imagination, and indeed that role has run almost in tandem with his
vocation as professional writer. Malamud has taught in Brooklyn and
Harlem high schools (1940-49), in the composition program at Oregon
State College in Corvallis beginning in 1949, and, almost un-
interruptedly since 1961, at Bennington College in Vermont. From
1966 to 1968, he also served as visiting lecturer at Harvard
University. When Malamud and his wife are not at home in
Bennington, they are in residence in their West Side apartment in
New York City.

As a major contemporary American writer, Malamud has received
many honors for his contributions to recent American literature.
Some of his more notable awards may serve to highlight the important
phases of his career. Malamud has received the Partisan Review
Fellowship, 1956-57; the Daroff Memorial Award and the Rosenthal
Award of the National Institute of Arts and Letters for The
Assistant, 1958, the National Book Award for The Magic Barrel, 1959
(the only collection of stories, other than The Collected Stories of
William Faulkner [New York: Random House, 1950], to receive the
award up until that time); membership in the American Academy and
Institute of Arts and Letters, 1964; the National Book Award and
Pulitzer prize for The Fixer, 1967; membership in the American
Academy of Arts and Sciences, 1967; O. Henry Awards for "Man in the
Drawer," 1969; election to the presidency of the P.E.N. American
center, 1979; the American Academy and Institute of Arts and Letters
Gold Medal for Fiction, 1983.

Despite his well-established reputation at the age of seventy,
Malamud has not become the subject of a full-length critical
biography. His own acknowledged reticence in revealing personal
details of his life has probably been the major obstacle to such a
work. In over thirty published interviews, Malamud has often
commented on the tension between life and art, but rarely on the
tensions between his own art and his own life, matters which still
remain largely undivulged. The bare facts of his life are to be
found in the standard biographical reference sources (e.g., 1958.2;

1975.18; 1978.9), and additional insights into the author can be garnered from interviews (e.g., 1958.22; 1975.6; 1975.28). There is also the inevitable speculation (1980.10) nurtured about Malamud by Philip Roth's novel The Ghost Writer (New York: Farrar, Straus & Giroux, 1979). If Malamud is indeed the basis for Roth's character E.I. Lonoff, elder statesman of Jewish American fiction, then Malamud has been absorbed into fiction even before becoming the subject of biography.

With the appearance of The Stories of Bernard Malamud (New York: Farrar, Straus & Giroux) in the fall of 1983, readers new to Malamud were introduced to many of the stories that brought him to the attention of the editors of Threshold, Commentary, Preface, Harper's Bazaar, Partisan Review, World Review, and the American Mercury in the 1940s and 1950s. "The Cost of Living," "The Loan," "The Mourners," and "Angel Levine" not only made their debut in these magazines but also set the pattern for the short fiction Malamud was to write during the next two decades. The most memorable figure in his work is his tragicomic immigrant Jew whose portion in life is failure, sickness, and the loss or alienation of children. Through the Yiddish rhythms and tonality of his speech, Malamud manages to bridge the sorrows of his character's racial past with his fictive present. (Malamud's second generation Jews, or his few non-Jewish characters, supply various permutations of this pattern.) The setting of his trials is a borough of New York City, and the more immediate locale is an imprisoning shop characterized by its atmosphere of unrelieved poverty and gloom. In this context Malamud introduces what have usually been regarded as thematic signatures of his fiction: the mystery and miracles associated with human suffering.

The relatively few readers who were acquainted with Malamud prior to the publication of his first novel, The Natural (1952), must have been surprised when the successful ingredients of his stories were replaced with new materials, a mythical treatment of baseball. While the novel increased Malamud's visibility, the newspapers and magazine reviews were generally cautious. F. Cudworth Flint (1952.3) felt that its allegory was not sufficiently self-explanatory, and similarly John Maloney (1952.4) regarded its symbolism as too private. Norman Podhoretz (1953.1), apart from recognizing the uniqueness of the book, asserted that the hero, Roy Hobbs, lacked the moral stature of a mythic character. Harry Sylvester (1952.7) and Leslie Fiedler (1955.1) were among the most appreciative commentators of the period. Sylvester considered Malamud's alternation between a lyrical and vernacular prose a brilliant achievement, and Fiedler praised the novel for Malamud's ability to rediscover in baseball the same insight into life embodied in the Grail legend. It was not until the 1960s, when Malamud criticism began to achieve depth and breadth, that the mythic patterns in The Natural were discussed in detail, and similar patterns were uncovered in The Assistant, A New Life, and The Fixer. The major studies approaching Malamud through the perspective of myth in this period include the work of Earl R. Wasserman (1965.9), James M. Mellard (1967.34), Edwin M. Eigner (1968.4), and Frederick W. Turner III (1968.24). Their discovery of Arthurian legend, vegetation myth, Jungian archetypes, the Fisher King, and Loathly Lady motifs in Malamud's work added a new richness and complexity to it.

The publication of The Assistant (1957) brought Malamud back to the subject matter and themes of Jewish poverty and suffering. With the momentum provided by the appearance of The Magic Barrel (1958), Malamud was soon regarded as an original voice in contemporary American literature. Perhaps one measure of his originality was his ability to make something new of an apparently exhausted genre. In this connection The Assistant and The Magic Barrel demonstrated Malamud's ability to breathe new life into proletarian or depression fiction; first through blending naturalism with fantasy; and, second, through giving human suffering redemptive value in this life without recourse to militancy or revolution. Although filled with much praise, some of the critical responses to these important books were not without reservations. Alfred Kazin (1957.9) judged Malamud successful primarily as a naturalist rather than as a fantasist. Dan Jacobson (1958.7) was bothered by the inconclusiveness that resulted from mixing the fantastic and the naturalistic. On the other hand, Herbert Gold (1957.4) considered Malamud's Chagallian quality as a lyrical and original part of his work. At a later period the topic of fantasy continued to engage such commentators as Robert W. War-burton (1971.53), Jay L. Halio (1971.16), Elsa Pendelton (1972.31), and Daniel Stern (1973.47). Especially notable is Warburton's iden-tification of three distinct modes of fantasy occurring in Malamud's fiction.

In the 1970s Norman Leer's (1971.22) rereading of The Assistant in tandem with Dostoevski's Crime and Punishment addressed the psychological issues of Malamud's fiction, in particular, the theme of the divided self, which Malamud carried into Pictures of Fidelman (1969) and The Tenants (1971). In this decade Barbara F. Lefcowitz (1970.14), Elsa Pendelton (1972.31), Robert Ducharme (1974.4), Ben Siegel (1977.36), Herbert Mann (1978.16), and Joan del Fattore (1978.4) also emphasized the psychological and oneiric elements in their readings of Malamud.

After The Assistant and The Magic Barrel, Malamud continued to write almost exclusively about Jews--usually post-Holocaust im-migrants and survivors or second generation assimilated Jews. His conscious and perhaps unconscious preoccupation with the im-plications of Jewish identity are revealed in such widely diverging books as A New Life (1961), Dubin's Lives (1979), and God's Grace (1982). In the title story of Idiots First (1963), "The Jewbird" (from the same collection), or "The Silver Crown" (from Rembrandt's Hat [1973]), Jewish identity is a conspicuous part of charac-terization and is conveyed through what have become recognized conventions in the bulk of Malamud's fiction: Yiddish inflections, a

Talmudically inspired reverence for life, and a gratuitous and usually unremitting suffering. In such novels as A New Life or Dubin's Lives explicit associations with Jewish identity tend to be veiled or inferential. That identity is nonetheless registered, as with an S. Levin, through a variety of insinuated cultural cues, apart from Pauline Gilley's single allusion to it, or, in the case of a William Dubin, through recollected Jewish images and memories that occasionally haunt him.

It should not be surprising that the Jewish dimensions of Malamud's fiction have stimulated the greatest body of discussion thus far, and these fall into four broad and often overlapping categories: cultural, religious, literary, and linguistic. Henry Popkin (1958.15) drew attention to the richness of Malamud's Jewish sensibility in comparison to that of Delmore Schwartz, Saul Bellow, or Isaac Rosenfeld. Theodore Solotaroff (1959.3) discussed Malamud's Jewish moralism. Earl H. Rovit (1960.7) examined Malamud's relation to the ironic tradition of Yiddish literature, as well as Malamud's own creative adaptations of it. Gabriel Pearson (1968.18) recognized in Malamud's art a moral preserve for a disappearing Jewish ethos. Robert Alter (1962.2) perceived that for Malamud Jews and Jewishness served a metaphorical purpose. Sheldon Norman Grebstein (1973.11) considered Malamud the focal point of a uniquely contemporary Jewish movement. Sam Bluefarb (1975.2) observed in Malamud's work a synthesis of Jewish themes and motifs with those of American and Western literature. Books by Sanford Pinsker (1971.35) and Ruth R. Wisse (1971.55) studied the role of the schlemiel figure in Yiddish and American fiction and the special uses to which Malamud put him. Marcia B. Gealy (1978.6; 1979.16) reinterpreted The Natural in the light of Hasidic literary tradition and also explored Malamud's reshaping of that tradition in his short stories. Sheldon J. Hershinow (1979.26) commented on the synthesis of Judaic, Greek, and Christian thought in his fiction, and Ida Sheres (1978.26) commented on the influences of Old Testament and mystical themes. Two monographs have compared Malamud to other Jewish writers: Glen Meeter (1968.17) explored the religious sensibility of Malamud and Roth, and Robert Kegan (1976.12) examined Malamud and Bellow's indebtedness to Martin Buber and neo-Hasidism. Among the most perceptive critics of Malamud's Jewish ethos, Leonard Michaels (1973.25) and Kathryn Hellerstein (1980.8) analyzed the interplay between Yiddish and English inflections and its tragicomic evocations. The Jewish aspects of Malamud's fiction have been significantly illuminated by this substantial body of criticism, which is indispensable for serious study of his work.

An especially distinct subcategory related to Malamud's treatment of Jews and Jewish themes is the Holocaust. This subject is latent in such stories as "Take Pity," "The Loan," "The Jewbird," and "The German Refugee" and is historically and symbolically evoked in The Fixer (1966). In these narratives Malamud unobtrusively makes us aware of the Holocaust by capturing the sensibility of its survivors and the residual effects of their incommunicable

experience. Malamud himself, however, has been reluctant to
speculate on the extent to which the Holocaust has had an impact on
his literary imagination, perhaps from awe of the subject: "I am
compelled to think about it as a man rather than as a writer," he
observed. "Someone like Elie Wiesel who had a first-hand knowledge
of the experience is in a better position to write about it than I.
He has become a voice for those people who could not communicate
their personal experience and emotions."[2] These remarks may be
overly modest. Others have felt that he has responded to the
Holocaust as an imaginative writer as well as a man. Michael Brown
(1980.1) suggested that Malamud has attempted to understand the
meaning of the event after the fact, rather than confront its
graphic horror, and therefore approaches it only through allusion,
symbol, and metaphor. Dorothy Seidman Bilik (1981.3), in her book
on post-Holocaust consciousness in recent American literature, has
claimed that Malamud's immigrant survivors possess the same
apparitional quality that Lawrence Langer has perceived in actual
European survivors.[3] This area of Malamud criticism is still
relatively undeveloped, but Brown and Bilik's studies may stimulate
Malamud critics to refine or reinterpret stories in which references
to the Holocaust are introduced.

While the Jewish aspect of Malamud's fiction has been keyed to a
discussion of its aesthetic and thematic richness, some critics have
viewed Malamud as inauthentic as a "Jewish" writer. Irving Fineman
(1967.12) has argued that Malamud's characters lack credibility
because of their failure to have any tangible knowledge of Judaism,
and Charles Angoff (1976.1) regarded Malamud's treatment of his
characters as too cold and cerebral. The issue became even more
complicated when such prominent figures in Malamud criticism as
Leslie and Joyce Field (1975.8) reevaluated their earlier position,
which had considered Malamud's fiction a reflection of the main-
stream of Jewish tradition. In a highly provocative discussion,
Leslie Field (1977.11) has come to regard Malamud as a "hyphenated
Jewish writer" who is artistically disconnected from the two most
important events in Jewish history, the Holocaust and the birth of
the state of Israel. Cynthia Ozick (1980.2) surely adds fuel to
the controversy. In her recent insistence on the ethnic, cultural,
and theological bases of Jewish identity, she implicitly repudiates
Malamud's secular or metaphorical Jew.

In some quarters the very validity of a school or genre that is
inherently Jewish has itself been challenged. According to Wolfgang
Bernard Fleischman (1967.13), if suffering, hope, and charity are
central to Malamud's Judaic moral vision, they are also at the heart
of Christianity. Both Ihab Hassan (1977.15) and Charles I. Glicksburg (1968.8) have argued that our sense of what constitutes a
modern Jewish literature is not clear, since there is no single
vision of a Jew subscribed to by all contemporary Jewish American
writers. Malamud himself (1975.7) has been unhappy with the label
Jewish American writer, fearing that interpretations of his work
might be limited by the reductiveness of such a classification. The

issue remains controversial, if not artificial. One may suspect
that the scholarly convenience of the term for identifying writers
with a common background and a similar subject matter (as is the
case with Articles on American Literature, 1968-1975), has been
wrenched from its original intent.

The possibility of change and growth through an experience with
someone else's pain, usually discussed under the theme of redemptive
suffering, has generally been accepted at face value as the corner-
stone of the humanism in Malamud's earliest work. Redemptive suffering has become, however, a troublesome concept for some critics.
Malamud's treatment of this theme has been judged ambivalent, and in
his later work it is argued that it has disappeared entirely. Nat
Hentoff (1963.12) observed some time ago an inconsistency between
Malamud's benevolent pronouncements on man and lurking undercurrents
of hostility directed toward his characters. Marilyn Michele Fabe
(1976.4) also ascribed to Malamud a latent aggression directed
against those who suffer. Philip Roth (1974.17) has dryly remarked
that Malamud's ethical Jewishness is developed with a vengeance and
speculates that Frank Alpine's conversion to Judaism might have been
conceived of as vindictive rather than redemptive in the hands of
another writer. Irving S. Saposnick (1982.26) considered Dubin's
Lives as the most dramatic example of Malamud's departure from the
theme of redemptive suffering, signaled in Dubin's rejection of his
father as a model of passivity and helplessness. These critics have
introduced a cautionary note in reading the early and later Malamud
through nostalgic lenses. Leslie Fiedler's early observation
(1959.2) that Malamud is "a good deal blacker, more demonic than he
is prepared to admit even to himself" may now seem unusually shrewd,
even though possibly overstated, in the company of more recent
critics who have also read a darker Malamud in his early fiction, as
well as in his more recent work. For some critics, God's Grace may
be seen as the latest confirmation of these somber readings, and
this apocalyptic novel may add a new momentum to the reexamination
of his stories and novels.

The interest in Malamud's fiction as a vehicle for social
criticism has been relatively small among the already established
patterns of criticism on his work. Six commentaries deserve
mention: Utz Riese (1973.40) read The Natural and The Assistant from
a Marxist perspective, asserting that although Malamud is aware of
the perversions of a capitalist society, he is incapable of being
overly critical because of his class perspective. Sandy Cohen
(1974.2), while not focusing exclusively on Malamud's social vision,
underlined the importance of the social factors in his work that
influence the behavior of his characters. Eva Manske (1977.25) and
Tobias Hergt (1978.10) have suggested that Malamud attempts to
represent the American Dream as a grim and nightmarish hoax. Iska
Alter (1981.1) explored the impact of the corrupting influences of
society on ethical behavior. Max F. Schulz (1969.41) united social
criticism with myth criticism and discussed the connections between

the underlying Marxian assumptions and mythic patterns that appear
in Malamud's fiction. Malamud has depicted social ills in his
fiction and referred to them in his public pronouncements, but he
has never expressed social doctrines in either. The most fruitful
approach to his fiction through socio-economic criticism has been,
like Schulz's work, an incorporation of such criticism into the
broader framework of other critical perspectives.

With the new emphasis given to the examination of social
criticism in Malamud's early as well as later fiction, it may seem
odd now to recall Philip Roth's complaint (1961.20) about Malamud's
"spurning of our world." With The Fixer (1966) and particularly The
Tenants (1971), Malamud's fiction introduced subjects that had a
greater immediacy and topicality than those found in his earlier
work. One need not, however, assume a causality between Roth's dis-
satisfaction and the thrust of these new novels. Malamud's
preoccupations with political oppression and social injustice
(1958.22) had been with him for some time, and their fictional
expression may be explained perhaps even more satisfactorily as a
result of a new sense of urgency brought on by the racial and
political turmoil of the 1960s. The Fixer was in conception, if not
in dramatic representation (1966.45), an attempt to fuse in the
symbol of Yakov Bok the sufferings of the Holocaust victims with the
oppression of blacks in America. Some critics faulted the novel for
its failure to locate its subject in the contemporary world
(1966.47; 1967.47).

With the publication of The Tenants, Malamud used the strained
and often hostile relations between Jews and blacks that characterized the 1960s as the backdrop for his story; his novel was not,
however, merely an imaginative footnote to the current journalism
dealing with these relations. In two previously published stories,
"Angel Levine" and "Black Is My Favorite Color," Malamud, with
whimsical pathos, had characterized both Jews and blacks as victims. He explained, moreover, in an interview with Daniel Stern
(1975.28), how his own personal experiences--living at the edge of a
black neighborhood, teaching in a black school in Harlem, and
reading black fiction and history--were preparatory for writing The
Tenants.

Whether Malamud was indeed influenced by critics calling for his
fiction to engage the world more directly is really irrelevant. The
Tenants, as a case in point, must stand or fall on the effectiveness
of its own voice. Anatole Broyard (1971.3; 1971.4) felt that the
flawed conclusion of the novel had to be weighed against the risk of
its subject and the depth of its human concerns. Robert Alter
(1972.1) chose to compare Malamud and John Updike in their handling
of racial issues and distinguished between the private racial nightmare of Malamud's Harry Lesser and the collective racial fears of
society represented by Harry Angstrom. Foster Hirsch (1972.17)
considered the novel impressive in its stylistic experiments but
lacking depth as an imaginative treatment of racial conflict. Jacob

Korg (1972.21) recognized in Malamud's experiments with form, especially in supplying three different endings to the novel, a modern artistic solution to the riddle of existence. Other critics were also sharply divided on the success of the book. Apart from the topicality of its subject, The Tenants employed many of the major themes and motifs of his earlier work--the prison motif, the doppelgänger, the relations between art and life, the insistence on man's humanity even as man displays his inhumanity.

These topics comprise the principal components of Malamud's artistic vision, which inevitably has kept his fictional interests within certain boundaries. As a consequence, it may have bothered some readers that Malamud has never extended his range in the treatment of women. Undeniably his focus on women, or his treatment of the feminine sensibility, with the exception of Kitty Dubin of Dubin's Lives, has not been one of Malamud's priorities. Malamud must be granted his donée; his background, temperament, and ethos have led him to other subjects. Nonetheless, women do have a significant place in his fiction, and his own remarks, as well as his works, suggest the nature of their importance: "The death of my mother, while she was still young," he reflected, "had an influence on my writing, and there is in my fiction a hunger for women that comes out in various ways."[4] The implications of these statements are illuminated by several recent articles, which also explore the male-female relationship in Malamud's fiction. Iska Alter (1981.1) in examining the role of women in The Natural and the subsequent novels noted their nurturing, life-affirming function, whether they are presented as archetypes or individuals. Barbara Koening Quart (1983.18) observed that, despite men's yearning for women, they are inevitably subordinated to male vocation and kept at a distance. Chairi Briganti (1983.3) contended that in A New Life and Dubin's Lives women usually serve as objects of male voyeurism because men are imprisoned in their own subjectivity. Malamud's passive representation of women has not, thus far, generated a fully developed feminist critical response.

Resonances of classical nineteenth-century American cultural and literary themes run through much of Malamud's fiction, and Malamud himself (1975.28) acknowledges the inspiration of such writers as Hawthorne, Twain, James, and Hemingway more than that of any other literary tradition. Malamud's use of themes central to the American renaissance--self-reliance, the Adamic man, the international theme, the conflict between art and life--continues to offer promising leads for critical discussion. Samuel Irving Bellman (1965.2) examined the points of contact between Henry James's "The Madonna of the Future" and Malamud's "Still Life." While David Burrows (1969.7) found Emersonian, Thoreauvian, and Jamesian parallels in A New Life, Charles Stetler (1971.48) observed that Malamud had fused in Pictures of Fidelman various elements of American literary tradition with Jewish themes. Christof Wegelin (1973.49) brought the international theme up to date with a study of Malamud's Italian stories and their representation of the end to American innocence in

Europe. Pierre-Yves Petillion (1974.15) recognized in The Tenants Malamud's connection to the apocalyptic tradition in American literature, and more recently J. Gerald Kennedy (1980.11) considered the imaginative impact of Poe's "The Raven" on Malamud's "The Jewbird."

In his technical experiments, Malamud's resemblances to such twentieth-century writers as Joyce, Kafka, and Gide have become critical commonplaces (1972.21), but as yet no work of substance has emerged that goes beyond passing reference. Along other lines, Malamud's general affinities to Kafka have been the subject of two illuminating studies. Helen Weinberg (1970.30), in outlining the Kafkan mode in American literature, identified connections between Roy Hobbs of The Natural and Karl Rossman of Amerika and between S. Levin of A New Life and the protagonist K of The Castle. Neil Rudin (1975.24) argued that Kafka and Malamud share the same concerns in their depiction of the misery and mystery of life, that both are anchored to the Yiddish literary tradition, and that they ultimately affirm love and responsibility as the only means of surviving in an inscrutable world. In Malamud's relation to contemporary American non-Jewish writers, Evelyn Gross Avery's (1979.4) book-length study of Richard Wright and Bernard Malamud focused on Wright's suffering rebels and Malamud's suffering victims, and Tobias Hergt (1979.25) compared the university as theme and motif in the work of Malamud and John Barth.

Since Malamud's fiction often reminds us of Kafka's, as well as that of other writers who fall within the parameters of existential literature, it would seem a curious omission if the existential qualities of Malamud's work had escaped unnoticed. Malamud's af-finities with modern existential writers have indeed been observed, but it is rare to find sustained discussion of the existentialism in specific works. Two exceptions deserve notice. Alvin D. Alley and Hugh Agee (1968.1) argued that Malamud's Frank Alpine and John Updike's Robert Angstrom create their own personal hells and thereby share in a similar existential characterization. Lucio P. Ruotolo (1973.42), in his study of The Fixer, perceived in Yakov Bok an absence of conviction eventually replaced by existential commitment and regarded the political turn in Malamud's novel as indicative of the direction the existential novel is taking.

Five books on Malamud, written at different stages of his career, supply a partial overview of his work, and one by Hershinow (1980.9) discussed in brief the general influences of existential philosophy on Malamud's work. Malamud continued to write stories and novels after these were published, inevitably making these studies partially dated. Sidney Richman (1966.55) provided the first book-length investigation of his work, which still offers one of the most lucid examinations of individual novels from The Natural through A New Life, as well as an excellent summary of themes and techniques in The Magic Barrel and Idiots First. Sandy Cohen (1974.2) treated the theme of self-transcendence, along with other

recurring themes and techniques through <u>Pictures of Fidelman</u>.
Robert Ducharme (1974.4) traced the recurrence of themes and
techniques from <u>The Natural</u> through <u>Pictures of Fidelman</u>, and Iska
Alter (1981.1) examined the social criticism inherent in Malamud's
work.

Much of the best criticism on Malamud in the 1960s and 1970s has
been gathered in three collections of essays. Leslie A. Field and
Joyce W. Field (1970.5) pioneered this undertaking with their com-
prehensive <u>Bernard Malamud and the Critics</u>, which identified major
critical questions surrounding Malamud's work and supplied twenty-
one critical essays on a variety of topics. The Fields (1975.6)
followed up this book with a collection more modest in size, which
focused on the continuity of Malamud's technique and themes before
and after <u>The Fixer</u>. Complementary to the essays is a detailed
interview through letters with Malamud and the Fields. The third
collection, edited by Richard Astro and Jackson J. Benson (1977.3),
containing papers presented at a symposium at Oregon State University, Corvallis, set about to explore Malamud's relation to classical American writers. In some instances, the papers provided a
spirited and, at times, controversial reassessment of earlier views
held on Malamud's work.

<u>God's Grace</u> is still too new to have received any extended
analyses; book reviews currently are the only sources of available
commentary. Critics seem to be evenly divided on Malamud's accomplishment. Claude Rawson (1982.22) was confused about the
intentions of the book, as was Mordecai Richler (1982.25), and
Joseph Epstein (1982.5) judged it very harshly, summing it up as
artistically and intellectually thin. On the other hand, Peter
Prescott (1982.20) stated that Malamud was never better as a
fantasist, Saul Maloff (1982.18) was convinced that the quality of
its imagination was high, and Edmund Fuller (1982.8) speculated that
the novel might well be Malamud's most lasting work. Other novelists besides Mordecai Richler have also reviewed the book and, unlike him, have found much to admire in it. Anthony Burgess (1983.5)
praised Malamud for his skill and John Updike (1982.32), although
finding the allegory confusing, succumbed to the book's charm.
According to John Hawkes (1982.30), Malamud's attempt at writing a
fable in a period of postmodern cynicism was risky and courageous.
Hawkes's view of the novel echoes sentiments other critics have
expressed with regard to <u>The Tenants</u>, which took similar artistic
risks.

Malamud's success in <u>God's Grace</u> may be at this moment more
problematic than his achievements in his earlier animal fables, "The
Jewbird" and "Talking Horse," stories that also ponder the darker
aspects of what it means to be human. Perhaps even more compelling
than the lingering question of the effectiveness of the novel is
Malamud's vision as a writer at this stage in his career. Acknow-
ledging significant changes in his view of man, Malamud recently
observed: "I have moved from optimism . . . to a new and

serious understanding of how growth and achievement take place. Growth is slow and man must fight for it."[5] In God's Grace Malamud is still preoccupied with the themes that he explored in his earliest fiction, the development of man's moral consciousness and the possibilities for redemption in human life, but there is a sobering change between these themes in The Assistant and The Magic Barrel and their muted appearance in this novelistic fable. Dramatic transformations no longer seem possible within Malamud's moral and imaginative framework. Through the use of talking simian creatures, who are often brutal, as substitutes for human characters, Malamud seemed bent on exploring the bestial potentialities of man; but he had not entirely abandoned his earlier, more positive conception of what is human. Whether that residual idea is the result of nostalgia for his earlier vision, inner conviction, or a recommitment to the theme of redemption through the slow and painful process of evolution, we can only conjecture. Malamud is concerned, however, that the signs of hope in the novel should be noticed: "One of the misreadings of the novel . . . is that it ends in tragedy. Some reviewers have failed to recognize that a gorilla recites Kaddish for Calvin Cohn, and that is indeed a cause for optimism; the prayer itself is a vehicle of God's Grace."[6]

Having produced fiction of recognized importance in twentieth-century American literature, Malamud's position among major American writers is secure. At his very best--one thinks, for example, of "The Magic Barrel," "Take Pity," "Idiots First," and The Assistant --Malamud is profoundly moving and reminiscent of Faulkner in his human sympathies and in the depth of his moral sensibility. Over twenty years ago, Ihab Hassan (1963.11) observed in a review of Idiots First that "the place of Bernard Malamud may be finally defined by the sheer precision of his integrity." While critical estimates of Malamud's work will change, as they do for most authors, Hassan's judgment of Malamud is likely to remain intact.

Notes

1. Bernard Malamud, unpublished interview with Joel Salzberg, New York City, 21 June 1983.

2. Ibid.

3. The Holocaust and the Literary Imagination (New Haven: Yale University Press, 1975), p. 49.

4. Interview of 21 June 1983.

5. Ibid.

6. Ibid.

Writings by Bernard Malamud

NOVELS

The Natural. New York: Harcourt, Brace, 1952.

The Assistant. New York: Farrar, Straus & Cudahy, 1957.

A New Life. New York: Farrar, Straus & Cudahy, 1961.

The Fixer. New York: Farrar, Straus & Giroux, 1966.

Pictures of Fidelman: An Exhibition. New York: Farrar, Straus & Giroux, 1969.

The Tenants. New York: Farrar, Straus & Giroux, 1971.

Dubin's Lives. New York: Farrar, Straus & Giroux, 1979.

God's Grace. New York: Farrar, Straus & Giroux, 1982.

COLLECTIONS OF STORIES

The Magic Barrel. New York: Farrar, Straus & Cudahy, 1958.

Idiots First. New York: Farrar, Straus, 1963.

Rembrandt's Hat. New York: Farrar, Straus & Giroux, 1973.

The Stories of Bernard Malamud. New York: Farrar, Straus & Giroux, 1983.

UNCOLLECTED STORIES

"Benefit Performance." Threshold 3, no. 3 (February 1943):20-22.

"The Place Is Different Now." American Preface 8, no. 3 (Spring 1943):230-42.

"An Apology." Commentary 12, no. 5 (November 1951):460-64.

"Thanks for Nothing." Esquire 56, no. 2 (August 1961):101-12.
Excerpt from A New Life.

"A Long Ticket for Isaac." In Creative Writing and Rewriting:
Contemporary American Novelists at Work. Edited by John Kuehl. New
York: Meredith Publishing Co., Appleton-Century-Crofts, 1967, pp.
70-86 (even-numbered pages). An early version of "Idiots First."

"An Exorcism." Harper's 237, no. 1423 (December 1968):76-89.

"Dubin's Lives: Part One." New Yorker 53 (18 April 1977):38-50.

"Dubin's Lives: Part Two." New Yorker 53 (25 April 1977):36-47.

"Abhorrent Green Slippery City." Playboy 24, no. 12 (December
1977):138-40, 142, 348, 352, 354, 356, 358, 360, 362. Excerpt from
Dubin's Lives.

"Home Is the Hero." Atlantic 241, no. 1 (January 1978):42-49,
52-57. Excerpt from Dubin's Lives.

"A Wig." Atlantic 245, no. 1 (January 1980):33-36.

"Alma Redeemed--A Story." Commentary 78, no. 1 (July 1984):30-34.

"In Kew Gardens." Partisan Review 51, no. 4 (1984) and 52, no. 1
(1985):536-40.

"A Lost Grave." Esquire 103, no. 5 (May 1985):204, 206.

Writings about Bernard Malamud, 1952-1983

1   CROMIE, ROBERT. "'Say It Ain't True'; It Isn't but Could
    Be." Chicago Tribune, 14 September, p. 14.
        The Natural reveals Malamud's fine ear for dialogue. It
    is, moreover, unique in its mixture of baseball lore and
    fantasy, and the author emerges as a novelist of interest and
    promise.

2   FITZGERALD, EDWARD. Review of The Natural. Saturday Review
    35 (6 September):32.
        Malamud's attempts to give mythic dimensions to his
    characters make them seem ephemeral. His move from baseball
    folklore to "mystical and cosmic" levels of meaning is forced.

3   FLINT, F. CUDWORTH. "Fiction Chronicle." Sewanee Review 62,
    no. 1 (Winter):166-80.
        Speculates that Roy Hobbs of The Natural may represent
    human nature untouched by civilization, the male principle in
    search of the feminine, or an archetypal American in search of
    the "American Sterile Dream." Such interpretations, however,
    are not adequately developed in the novel and make the reader
    strive too hard for meaning.

4   MALONEY, JOHN. "Baseball as Folk-Myth." New York Herald
    Tribune Book Review 29 (24 August):8.
        The Natural is a mixture of fantasy and realism, but
    unfortunately its realism is unsubstantial. The narrative is an
    allegory involving the mythological qualities associated with
    baseball, but the allegorial level is encumbered with "private
    and uncommunicative symbolism, and the nightmare happenings in an
    apparently sane daytime world."

1952

5   Review of The Natural. Time 60 (8 September):122.
          Malamud's first novel is a combination of myth, farce, and
tragedy. The narrative is engaging as it explores the sport of
baseball both on and off the diamond. Malamud is less
effective, however, when he "juggles symbolism and cloudy
language to suggest the tragic limitations of the average
American dream."

6   SWADOS, HARVEY. "Baseball à la Wagner: The Nibelung in the
        Polo Grounds." American Mercury 75, no. 346 (October):104-6.
        The Natural is a mixture of comic fantasy, Wagnerian
mythic drama, folk legends, and newspaper headlines. Its style
alternates between a tough, romantic prose and the idiom of the
language found in sports magazines. Unfortunately, the generic
and stylistic shifts confuse Malamud's allegorical intention.
Flawed as it is, the novel must be credited for its excitement
and imaginative daring.

7   SYLVESTER, HARRY. "With Greatest of Ease." New York Times
        Book Review, 24 August, p. 5.
        The Natural is the first serious novel about baseball, but
the narrative goes well beyond its ostensible subject. Through
his native ability, Roy Hobbs becomes the symbol of natural man
at his best until he is corrupted by society. Alternating between a lyrical and vernacular prose, "Malamud has written a
brilliant and unusual book."

1953

1   PODHORETZ, NORMAN. "Achilles in Left Field." Commentary 15,
        no. 3 (March):321-26.
        As a serious novel about baseball, Malamud's The Natural
is unique. This popular American sport contains resonances of
the Young Man from the Provinces Story and of Achilles' heroism
in the Trojan war, but Malamud's hero, Rob Hobbs, does not
embody the moral stature of his mythic counterparts. Instead of
being guilty of hubris, Hobbs is merely guilty of an excess of
appetite in either sex or food. Thus Malamud's novel does not
achieve depth despite its mythical associations.

1955

1   FIEDLER, LESLIE [A.]. "In the Interest of Surprise and
        Delight." Folio 20, no. 3 (Summer):17-20.
        Malamud, in The Natural, happily escaped the pitfalls of
many young writers who impose symbols or myths on their work for
lack of imagined detail. Through his use of baseball as subject,

the Grail legend emerges from the game as a logical mythical extension, without any sacrifice to the verisimilitude of contemporary
life, and is thus the source of the reader's "surprise and
delight."
Reprinted: 1960.4.

1957

1   BAILEY, ANTHONY. Insidious Patience." Commonweal 66 (21
     June):307-8.
         An atmosphere of normality pervades The Assistant, a
     result of author understatement. Malamud's moral tone,
     considering the plight of his characters, is equally
     understated.

2   BOWEN, ROBERT. "Bagels, Sour Cream and the Heart of the
     Current Novel." Northwest Review 1, no. 1 (Spring):52-56
     passim.
         The Assistant is more authentic in its depiction of Jewish
     America than Seize the Day. Malamud's ability to introduce
     humor into the inherent sadness of his story is a measure of his
     talent. As a novelist of the urban poor, Malamud has rendered
     his world in a tight, economical, and colloquial prose unrivaled
     by Bellow or any other contemporary.

3   ELLIOT, GEORGE [P.]. "Fiction Chronicle." Hudson Review 10,
     no. 2 (Summer):288-95 passim.
         The Assistant provides an authoritative portrait of the
     poor Jews of New York. In his characterization of Frank Alpine,
     a would-be convert to the "mystic society" of the Jews, Malamud
     is not really convincing. Despite this flaw in credibility, the
     novel is ultimately more satisfying than most of the well-made
     but wooden British novels now being produced.

4   GOLD, HERBERT. "Dream to Be Good." Nation 184 (20 April):
     350.
         Appraises The Assistant as an intense, lyrical, and
     original work, reminiscent of Dostoevski and Chagall.

5   "The Good Grocer." Time 69 (29 April):100-102.
         The Assistant, like other Malamud narratives, contains
     individuals who suffer but also confront their problems. Frank
     Alpine's self-inflicted injuries will no longer occur once he
     struggles to achieve self-discipline and begins to master his
     own life. Malamud may take pity on his characters, but his
     novels are never sentimental.

1957

6   GOYEN, WILLIAM. "A World of Bad Luck." New York Times Book Review, 28 April, p. 4.

The Assistant will be a renewed source of pleasure to Malamud readers for its lucid narrative, its taut yet lyric representation of characters and place, and its philosophical unpretentiousness. Malamud's world will not easily be forgotten.

7   HAYES, E. NELSON. "Fiction and Criticism." Progressive 21, no. 7 (July):29-30.

Evaluates The Assistant as convincing, compassionate, and harmonious in form and content, unblemished by any touches of slickness or insincerity.

8   HICKS, GRANVILLE. "A Note on Literary Journalism and Good Novels by Moore and Malamud." New Leader 40 (29 April): 21-22.

Although The Assistant does not have the humor and the extravagance of The Natural, it is insightful and meticulously written; despite its evocation of the thirties, social issues are ignored in favor of psychological, ethical, and religious concerns. Reprinted: 1970.9.

9   KAZIN, ALFRED. "Fantasist of the Ordinary." Commentary 24, no. 1 (July):89-92.

Finds the celebration of the Jew merely for the sake of being a Jew a dubious affirmation in The Assistant and considers the moral impact of the novel forced. Malamud's major achievement as a writer is in his vivid characterization of his suffering schlemiels.

10   KILBY, CLYDE [S.]. "In a Dark Time These Hearts Are Good." New York Herald Tribune Book Review 33 (28 April):8.

A proletarian novelist of an earlier decade would have made The Assistant, a novel about poor Jews, an attack on capitalism. Malamud's focus is on character. Frank Alpine's "lacerating self-examination . . . and long and intense penitential discipline are perhaps the best of many good things in this novel."

11   LEVIN, MEYER. "Growth in Brooklyn." Saturday Review 40 (15 June):21.

The commonplace world of Malamud's The Assistant is unforgettable. Grocer, wife, daughter, and outsider are highly individualized and yet carry symbolic weight. The impact of the novel comes from its taut, spare narrative.

12   POORE, CHARLES. Review of <u>The Assistant</u>. <u>New York Times</u>, 9
      May, p. 29.
         This is an unforgettable book about the poor in an urban
      wasteland, who communicate in a racy, idiomatic prose. Rich in
      characterization, <u>The Assistant</u> belongs to the great tradition
      of nineteenth-century European novels.

13   RIBALOW, HAROLD U. "A Genuine Jewish Novel." <u>Congress</u>
      <u>Weekly</u> 24 (13 May):16.
         <u>The Assistant</u> reveals Malamud both as a brilliant stylist
      and as a thoughtful moralist, a writer committed to the
      discipline of his craft and to the humanity of his characters.
      "This is, in its deepest sense, a 'Jewish' book . . . because
      Malamud creates Jews who live and have lived, and he knows them
      to their very marrow."

14   SINGER, BURNS. "Fantasies and Sobrieties." <u>Encounter</u> 9, no.
      4 (October):77-79.
         Despite Malamud's intelligence, integrity, and sincerity
      in the writing of <u>The Assistant</u>, the result is simply drabness
      and boredom.

15   SULLIVAN, RICHARD. "Alive, Moving Story of Struggling
      People." <u>Chicago Tribune: Books Today</u>, 19 May, p. 7.
         The <u>Assistant</u> may not convey tragedy, heroism, or intense
      drama. It is, in essence, a religious novel, whose special
      quality is embodied in the goodness of one of its main
      characters, Morris Bober. Goodness made credible is, in its own
      way, a "rare fictional achievement."

                              1958

1   BLACKMAN, RUTH CHAPIN. "Jewish Stories from Malamud."
      <u>Christian Science Monitor</u>, 15 May, p. 13.
         The stories of <u>The Magic Barrel</u> are unified by their
      complex tone which combines humor, resignation, compassion, and
      wisdom. While Malamud's characters are often in a hopeless
      condition, they somehow manage to continue with their existence
      "infused with a kind of New World vitality." Unlike the writing
      of many of his contemporaries, Malamud's is marked by a
      refreshing simplicity.

2   CADLE, DEAN. "Bernard Malamud." <u>Wilson Library Bulletin</u> 33,
      no. 4 (December):266.
         Supplies a concise biographical account of Malamud's life
      and career, and takes special note of his concern with honesty
      in fiction. Reprinted in <u>Current Biography Yearbook</u> (New York:
      H.H. Wilson Co., 1958), pp. 271-73 (updated periodically).

1958

3   FIEDLER, LESLIE A. "The Commonplace as Absurd."
Reconstructionist 24 (21 February):22-24.
      Although reminiscent of Dostoevski's Notes from the
Underground and Ellison's The Invisible Man, The Assistant is
"the least melodramatic of all possible versions of the absurd:
a vision of the commonplace as absurd." Malamud's sense of
absurdity is centered in Frank Alpine's ritual conversion to
Judaism when merely living as a Jew is problem enough.
Reprinted: 1960.4.

4   FOFF, ARTHUR. "Strangers Amid Ruins." Northwest Review 2,
no. 2 (Fall-Winter):63-67.
      The stories of The Magic Barrel are primarily organized
around the relationship of two men, one older and one younger,
and are set in a literal or symbolic wasteland. These
characters are Jews--the poor, the dispossessed, the
suffering--who stand for all mankind. Malamud's attitude
towards them is sacramental.

5   HICKS, GRANVILLE. "The Uprooted." Saturday Review 41 (17
May):16.
      Carrying legendary and biblical overtones, the stories of
The Magic Barrel are concerned with man's responsibility to man,
and this problem is explored through the use of humor, pathos,
and fantasy. "The more faithfully Malamud renders Jewish life,
the wider his meanings are." Reprinted: 1970.9.

6   HURLEY, DORAN. Review of The Magic Barrel. Sign 38
(October):73-74.
      This collection does not subscribe to the contemporary
vogue of formlessness; rather Malamud's stories, especially in
their endings, are characterized by the kind of careful
organization and control reminiscent of O. Henry. Although
Malamud's fictional world seems to deal with the ordinary if not
the banal, it is nevertheless imbued with an ethnic rather than
a religious mysticism that lurks just beneath the surface.

7   JACOBSON, DAN. "Magic and Morality." Commentary 26, no. 4
(October):359-61.
      Malamud's The Magic Barrel is the work of a highly
talented writer whose use of Yiddish cadence is neither quaint
nor ornamental but a subtle form of communication to the
sensitive reader. The most humble characters in his stories
continually strive for some form of moral purification.
Unfortunately, his "fantastic" and "naturalistic" tales seem
incomplete: "the force and logic of the stories tend to fail."

8   KAZIN, ALFRED. "Bernard Malamud: The Magic and the Dread."
     Reporter 18 (29 May):202-7.
         While Dostoevski was able to embody the ethos of
     nineteenth-century Russia within the boundaries of realism,
     Malamud and his contemporaries evoke their world through an
     over-eager use of symbolism when the expressive language of
     Malamud's Jews exists by itself as a cultural symbol. Although
     resembling the great Yiddish writers, Malamud falls into
     abstractness under the modern influences of, for example, Kafka,
     Joyce, and Eliot. Reprinted: 1962.10; 1964.17.

9   KLEIN, MARCUS. "Imps from Bottles, etc." Hudson Review 11,
     no. 4 (Winter):620-25.
         Malamud's strength in The Magic Barrel lies in his
     profound knowledge of "suffering and pity" rather than in
     Judaism itself. While Malamud is narrow in his range of mate-
     rials, "it is still his intimate and fabulous image of grace
     that makes him the exciting writer that he is."

10   MERRICK, GORDON.   "The Attachment to Misery." New Republic
     139 (21 July):20-21.
         Questions the richness of the short story as a genre in
     comparison to the novel, but finds The Magic Barrel rich in
     lyricism and imagination. Occasionally, Malamud's humor is
     excessive, uncontrolled, and tasteless.

11   "Old Men of the Sea." Time 71 (12 May):102, 104.
         The Magic Barrel rivals Sholom Aleichem's fiction in its
     earthiness and humor, but in his concern with the moral impact
     of one individual on another, Malamud resembles François
     Mauriac.

12   PEDEN, WILLIAM. "Dogged by a Sense of Grief and Injustice."
     New York Times Book Review, 11 May, p. 5.
         The Magic Barrel again reveals Malamud's individuality as
     a writer in the variety of characters that populate this
     collection of stories. Each character has in common the sense
     of his own personal suffering which, in some cases, comes from
     memories of the Holocaust. Despite the element of fantasy in
     these stories, Malamud's authentic human beings capture our
     attention and feelings.

13   PODHORETZ, NORMAN. "The New Nihilism and the Novel."
     Partisan Review 25, no. 4 (Fall):589-90.
         Malamud's Jews seem highly authentic in their external
     characterization, yet their spiritual identity appears to issue
     out of Malamud's imagination rather than from models in history
     or literature. As a writer, his vision of life is strangely
     untouched by the corrosiveness of modern existence. Reprinted:
     1964.26.

1958

14   POORE, CHARLES. Review of <u>The Magic Barrel</u>. <u>New York Times</u>,
      10 May, p. 19.
           The stories in this collection are notable for their range
      and depth. Although they do not deal with the Holocaust, an
      occasional word or phrase will evoke in Malamud's older
      characters the bitter memories of that period, as they spend
      their lives remaining in the "frontiers . . . of the past."

15   POPKIN, HENRY. "Jewish Stories." <u>Kenyon Review</u> 20, no. 4
      (1958):637-41.
           While Malamud's Jewish sensibility is indelibly stamped on
      his fiction, the Jewishness of Delmore Schwartz, Saul Bellow,
      and Isaac Rosenfeld seems, by comparison, hardly visible in
      their own writing. The stories in <u>The Magic Barrel</u> invariably
      involve a confrontation between Jews, some of whom fill the role
      of <u>Doppelgänger</u> or <u>Luftmensch</u>. Through them Malamud develops
      his themes of pity and compassion, but, unlike William Saroyan,
      he avoids sentimentality through objectivity, irony, and
      ambiguity.

16   RUGOFF, MILTON. "Making Every Day Life Glow." <u>New York
      Herald Tribune Book Review</u> 34 (25 May):3.
           <u>The Magic Barrel</u> is a result of Bernard Malamud's highly
      personal vision of life, and in this collection of stories the
      ordinary is converted into the extraordinary. Their most
      compelling feature, however, is Malamud's brilliant grasp of
      American Jewish types. "The Lady of the Lake" is especially
      illustrative of Malamud's success.

17   STEGGERT, FRANK X. Review of <u>The Magic Barrel</u>. <u>Critic</u> 16,
      no. 8 (June-July):23.
           The stories in this collection are largely comic, oriented
      to Jewish experience, and unique in their special imaginative
      qualities.

18   SULLIVAN, RICHARD. "13 Small, Individualized Works of Art."
      <u>Chicago Tribune: Books Today</u>, 18 May, p. 7.
           Each story in <u>The Magic Barrel</u> is a unique work of art
      written in a low-keyed, unsensational style. The characters of
      this short-story collection are exquisitely rendered, and
      through them Malamud engages in a celebration of life.

19   SWADOS, HARVEY. "The Emergence of an Artist." <u>Western
      Review</u> 22 (Winter):149-51.
           The world of the Bober family in Malamud's <u>The Assistant</u>
      seems, at first, to be a revival of Yiddish and early Jewish
      American ghetto fiction, but Malamud's characters take on a sym-
      bolic richness not found in this genre. His novel, moreover,

has as much mystery and drama in it as Dostoevski's <u>Crime and Punishment</u>. The publication of <u>The Assistant</u> underscores the importance of Malamud as an emerging writer in the fifties.

20   WEALES, GERALD. "The Sharing of Misery." <u>New Leader</u> 41 (1 September):24-25.
      Although a sense of Jewishness permeates all of Malamud's stories in <u>The Magic Barrel</u>, at their core they are ultimately about mankind. The two elements which most noticeably stand out in this collection are the shared suffering of Malamud's characters and the sense of wonder or mystery associated with collective experience.

21   WERMUTH, PAUL C. Review of <u>The Magic Barrel</u>. <u>Library Journal</u> 83 (15 June):1933.
      The stories in this collection are marked by Malamud's humane treatment of his failed and downtrodden characters. His ability to render the cadences of their dialect is an important measure of Malamud's talent.

22   WERSHBA, JOSEPH. "Not Horror but 'Sadness.'" <u>New York Post</u>, 14 September, p. M2.
      An interview with Malamud in New York City. "Jews are absolutely the very stuff of drama," he observed. Instead of writing about "the drama of personality fulfilling itself," contemporary writers, he felt, were overly preoccupied with human depravity. Occasionally misunderstood, his own writing, influenced by a European tradition, was intended to convey "sadness" rather than "horror." The destruction of six million Jews, he continued, is a tragedy that has been insufficiently treated, but Malamud felt this was also the case with the destruction of six to ten million Chinese when the Yellow River flooded in 1936. Although his work is meant to be apolitical, it is nevertheless influenced by two "political" forces: the barbarism of the Hitler years and the Great Depression. Writing, he concluded, should be an assertion of what is human against what is nihilistic.

1959

1   "Character and Crisis." <u>Times Literary Supplement</u>, no. 2973 (20 February):93.
      <u>The Assistant</u> is an effective fusion of psychological, spiritual, and even biological crisis. The novel carries in it a tension between life's potential and opportunities missed. Despite its questionable ending, this is a work that is defined by its sincerity.

1959

2   FIEDLER, LESLIE [A.]. <u>The Jew in the American Novel</u>.
    Pamphlet, no. 10, New York: Herzl Institute, pp. 57-58.
        Concludes his critical survey of American Jewish novelists
with the observation that Malamud is "a good deal blacker, more
<u>demonic</u> than he is ever prepared to admit--even to himself."

3   SOLOTAROFF, THEODORE. "Philip Roth and the Jewish
    Moralists." <u>Chicago Review</u> 13, no. 4 (Winter):87-99 passim.
        Perceives a basic affinity between Malamud and Roth,
especially apparent in Malamud's <u>The Assistant</u> and Roth's "Eli,
The Fanatic." In both works a non-Jew and a marginal Jew,
respectively, discover the essence of Judaism through "acts of
striving, sacrificing, and suffering." Although both writers
share a similar moral earnestness, it is quietly subsumed within
the aesthetic of their fiction. Reprinted: 1964.32; 1973.46.

4   TUCKER, MARTIN. "A Pluralistic Place." <u>Venture</u> 3, nos.
    1-2:69-73 passim.
        The milieu that the reader experiences in Malamud's <u>The
Magic Barrel</u> differs substantially from that created by John
Cheever in <u>The House-breaker of Shady Hill</u> and James Purdy's
<u>Color of Darkness</u>. Malamud's universe is composed of "the
tender and adolescent of all ages, Purdy's with souls who are
lost in hell, and Cheever's with self-conscious, sophisticated
people of the upper-classes." Throughout Malamud's stories, we
find a maturation process and an emphasis on the importance of
love.

5   "A Vocal Group: The Jewish Part in American Letters." <u>Times
    Literary Supplement</u>, no. 3010 (6 November):xxxv-xxxvi.
        Malamud supplies the best dramatic expression of Jewish
consciousness and the meaning of Jewishness of anyone on the
contemporary literary scene in <u>The Assistant</u> and <u>The Magic
Barrel</u>. "His essentially comic mode of moral analysis, his
faith in the power of the human heart and will to discover and
re-create the self . . ." make him an effective translator of
Eastern European morality into American terms.

<u>1960</u>

1   BRYDON, RONALD. "I, Cincinnatus." <u>Spectator</u> 204 (3 June):
    810.
        Although Malamud's <u>The Magic Barrel</u> may have its sources
in hackneyed Jewish wit and humor, Malamud does have "a trick
of leading his simple O. Henry anecdotes to suddenly complex,
reverberant endings."

2   "A Correct Compassion." <u>Times Literary Supplement</u>, no. 3031
(1 April):205.
     In this review of <u>The Magic Barrel</u>, Mary McCarthy is cited
as regarding Malamud as "one of the most interesting young
writers of the American <u>avante garde</u>." Malamud's designation as
avantgarde belongs to "material and mood" rather than literary
technique, and the title story of this collection best illustrates his originality and subtlety.

3   FIEDLER, LESLIE [A.]. <u>Love and Death in the American Novel</u>.
New York: Criterion Books, pp. 469-70. Reprint. 1966; 1969;
1975.
     In brief remarks on <u>The Natural</u>, <u>The Magic Barrel</u>, and <u>The
Assistant</u>, Fiedler relates Malamud to the Kafkaesque mode.

4   _____. "Three Jews: III Malamud: The Commonplace as
Absurd." In <u>No! In Thunder: Essays on Myth and Literature</u>.
Boston: Beacon Press, pp. 101-10. Reprint. London: Eyre &
Spottiswoode, 1963; New York: Stein & Day, 1972.
     Combined texts of 1955.1 and 1958.3.

5   MALAMUD, BERNARD. "The Writer's Task." In <u>Writing in
America</u>. Edited by John Fischer and Robert B. Silvers. New
Brunswick, N.J.: Rutgers University Press, p. 173.
     States that the mission of the writer is to rediscover the
humanity of man, to envision a new world, and to reflect the
mystery of man's limitation and glorious potential. (From an
address delivered by Malamud as the winner of the National Book
Award Prize, 1959, for <u>The Magic Barrel</u>.)

6   NYREN, DOROTHY, ed. "Bernard Malamud." In <u>A Library of
Literary Criticism: Modern American Literature</u>. New York:
Frederick Ungar, pp. 315-18.
     Offers excerpts from previously published reviews on
Malamud's <u>The Natural</u>, <u>The Assistant</u>, and <u>The Magic Barrel</u>.

7   ROVIT, EARL H. "Bernard Malamud and the Jewish Literary
Tradition." <u>Critique</u> 3, no. 2 (Winter-Spring):3-10.
     The need for a clearly defined cultural past has forced
many American writers to substitute their own subjectivity for
it, and the problem is even more troublesome for the minority
writer who must decide what aspects of his own cultural past he
wishes to incorporate into his work. Although Malamud finds his
orientation within the ironic tradition of the Yiddish tale, he
goes beyond it in order to establish a personal vision whose
tragic character is undercut by ambiguous and symbolic
resolutions. Reprinted: 1970.5.

1960

8   WATERHOUSE, KEITH. "New Short Stories." New Statesman 59
      (14 May):725-26.
         Each story in The Magic Barrel, although emerging out of
      Jewish experience, has a universal appeal. It is perhaps for
      this universality that Malamud and Faulkner share the unique
      distinction of being the only writers to receive the American
      National Book Award for a volume of short stories.

9   WHITBREAD, JANE. Review of The Magic Barrel. Good
      Housekeeping 150, no. 3 (March):55.
         Finds the stories in this collection interesting in short
      doses, but becomes annoyed at "long exposure to his [Malamud's]
      relentless image of pathetic, deprived, heartless, and totally
      self-absorbed man."

10   WIDMER, KINGSLEY. "The American Novel: The Contemporary
      Road." University of Kansas City Review 26, no. 4
      (June):309-17 passim.
         The hero or bum as an archetypal American figure, a
      "naturalistic American Joe," can be identified in Malamud's The
      Natural and The Assistant. In the former, Roy Hobbs is an orphan
      and a drifter who remains detached from society; in the
      latter, Frank Alpine, also a drifter, finally achieves community
      and identity, but only through self-abasement. The essential
      naturalistic characterization of these figures has been masked,
      however, by Malamud's tendency to allegorize.

11   WYNDHAM, FRANCIS. Review of The Magic Barrel. London
      Magazine 7, no. 6 (June):72-73.
         The uniqueness of Malamud's sensibility is carried through
      this collection of stories. The laws of his fiction allow his
      characters to leave their individual prisons. In the best of
      his stories, Malamud is a visionary.

1961

1   ADAMS, PHOEBE. "The Burdens of the Past." Atlantic 208, no.
      5 (November):184-85.
         Despite the fact that A New Life is well written, it fails
      to add anything new to the "pictures of spiritual progress"
      supplied by other novels in its genre. Unlike Malamud's
      previous books, this one seems "conventional in subject and
      attitude."

2   BOWEN, ROBERT O. "The View from Beneath." National Review
      11 (2 December):383-84 passim.

Low-keyed in its narrative style, A New Life is a lucid and highly readable account of academic life, only occasionally marred by stiff dialogue and dull pastoral description. Happily, it does not overstate the Jewishness of its hero, S. Levin.

3   CHARLES, GERDA. "Elizabethan Age of Modern Jewish Literature--1950-1960: Decade of the Great Break-Through." World Jewry 4, no. 7 (July-August):15-17.

Malamud's The Assistant and the stories of The Magic Barrel seem so unusual in the context of American Jewish literature that the work of Saul Bellow appears conventional beside them. The richness and vitality of Malamud's short fiction must be, in part, accounted for by his successful adaptation of the Yiddish folk tale. In commenting on Malamud and other Jewish writers, Charles observes: "There is in the best of our writers a peculiarly Jewish mode of vision and a consequent morality of purpose which is both unmistakably Jewish and also of remarkable value in the creation of an ordered society."

4   DE MOTT, BENJAMIN. "Fictional Chronicle." Hudson Review 14, no. 4 (Winter):628-29.

Considers the allegorical level in A New Life existing at the expense of novelistic fact, and finds its meaning inflated.

5   ELMAN, RICHARD. "Malamud on Campus." Commonweal 75 (27 October):114-15.

Regards A New Life as a less accomplished work than either The Magic Barrel or The Assistant, two of the best fictional products of the fifties. The central issue of plot in A New Life, the appropriation of another man's wife, captures our attention at the expense of S. Levin's characterization.

6   FRANCIS, H.E. "Bernard Malamud's Everyman." Midstream 7, no. 1 (Winter):93-97.

This review praises The Assistant for its lyricism, fantasy, and compassion, but finds Malamud overusing his plot for the sake of moral impact.

7   GOODHEART, EUGENE. "Fantasy and Reality." Midstream 7, no. 4 (Autumn):102-5 passim.

Malamud's ability to evoke lyric, romantic, and mythic resonances from the actual world in A New Life is impressive. These fictional elements are, in their own way, a form of fantasy which is used to redeem the world from its banality. When reality inevitably intrudes, these elements of fantasy are dissipated, and the conclusion to the novel results in irony rather than in celebration.

1961

8   GROSHONG, JAMES W. "Trouble in the West: Malamud's New
       Book." Corvallis Gazette Times, 5 October, p. 4.
       A New Life is a complex book that should be read carefully
on several levels: literally, it is about a failure called S.
Levin; allegorically, it is about Everyman who demonstrates the
capacity to overcome the afflictions of life; as cultural
satire, it probes American intellectual life. The rich and
resonant art of this novel will invite other perspectives.

9   HALLEY, ANN. "The Good Life in Recent Fiction."
       Massachusetts Review 3, no. 1 (Autumn):190-96.
       Compares Malamud's A New Life to Roderick Thorpe's Into
the Forest, May Sarton's The Small Room, and Clara Winston's The
Hours Together. All of these novels involve characters leaving
old lives behind and starting new ones. Halley is even handed
in her praise, but S. Levin in A New Life is possibly more
engaging to the reader than his counterparts in the other novels
because of his comic-heroic conception.

10   HARTT, J.N. "The Return of Moral Passion." Yale Review 51,
       no. 2 (December):300-308 passim.
       If S. Levin in A New Life is intended to function as a
moral agent, a man of conviction and truth, then Malamud's comic
handling of him creates an ambiguity that undermines his moral
stature.

11 HASSAN, IHAB. "The Qualified Encounter: Three Novels by
    Buechner, Malamud, Ellison." In Radical Innocence: Studies in
    the Contemporary American Novel. Princeton: Princeton
    University Press, pp. 153-79. Reprint. New York: Harper & Row,
    1966.
       Claims for Malamud an undeniable excellence. A sly form,
ambiguous irony, and painful humor nourish a preeminently moral
vision. The focus of the Malamud commentary is on The
Assistant, which illustrates the author at his best: through
incredible twists of plot, ironic play, and a capacity to convey
both hope and agony in the rhythms of Yiddish speech.
Reprinted: 1970.5.

12   HICKS, GRANVILLE. "Hard Road to the Good Life." Saturday
       Review 44 (7 October):20.
       Although S. Levin in A New Life is a hero, Malamud has not
allowed him to behave in the manner of a conventional hero. A
blunderer and a clown, Levin nevertheless gains the respect of
the reader by becoming a man of action and conscience despite
the constraints of his past. Reprinted: 1970.9.

13   HYMAN, STANLEY EDGAR. "A New Life for a New Man." New
      Leader 44, no. 34 (October):24-25.
         Despite minor flaws of style and syntax, A New Life is a
      tightly woven novel that reveals Malamud's technical control
      over his materials. Hyman finds the humor especially rewarding,
      reminiscent of the bittersweet humor of Yiddish literature, and
      its handling of suffering expressive of a new maturity.
      Reprinted: 1964.14; 1966.35.

14   KIRSCH, ROBERT R. "This Wise Fool is a Real Schlemiel." Los
      Angeles Times Calendar, 15 October, p. 18.
         Like Bellow, Malamud seems intent on distilling the
      essence of what is Jewish into his characters for the sake of
      translating that Jewishness into a universal condition.
      Although S. Levin of A New Life is technically Jewish, that
      identity never becomes an issue in the novel. Rather, his
      character expresses his Jewishness: in his introspectiveness,
      his insecurity, and his willingness to compromise. He emerges,
      finally, as the wise fool of Jewish folklore, the schlemiel.

15   MADDOCKS, MELVIN. "Malamud's New Novel." Christian Science
      Monitor, 5 October, p. 7.
         A New Life succeeds in making drama out of moral conflict,
      but it fails when it neglects to identify and develop the
      substance of S. Levin's new life. Levin seems to abort the
      quest for order and meaning which he strives for in the first
      half of the novel as he surrenders to love in the second half:
      "The effect is a little as if Don Quixote had given up the
      windmills in a singular obsession for Dulcinea." At its best,
      the novel is a dramatization about goodness in a world alien to
      it.

16   MALOFF, SAUL. "Between the Real and the Absurd." Nation 193
      (18 November):407-8.
         Asserts that A New Life is especially accomplished in its
      description of nature and landscape, its characterization of
      women and sexual feeling, and its satiric treatment of academic
      life. Malamud is a distinctive voice in contemporary fiction.

17   MILLER, LETIZIA CIOTTI. "L'arte di Bernard Malamud." Studi
      Americani (Rome) 7:261-97.
         A general discussion of The Natural, The Assistant, and
      The Magic Barrel. While Roy Hobbs of The Natural tries to
      maintain the innocence of his youth, the characters in The
      Assistant and The Magic Barrel confront the world as it is in
      the present. The metaphoric use of language in The Natural is
      weak because of its irrelevance to characterization. In the

1961

later works characterization and language are more closely
coordinated: Malamud's characters are mainly Jewish and they
are rendered through the Yiddish vocabulary and syntax. His
moral vision, annoyingly obtrusive in The Natural, comes through
more effectively in The Assistant and The Magic Barrel.

18   "Passions and Dilemmas." Newsweek 58 (9 October):105.
        Malamud's A New Life may seem initially depressing, but
the novel possesses a vitality which offers the reader some
compensation. The irony is tempered with compassion, and S.
Levin's final achievement of a new life, complete with wife and
children, is "true tragi-farce."

19   PICKREL, PAUL. Review of A New Life. Harper's 223, no. 1338
        (November):120.
        The strangeness of Malamud's S. Levin should, one would
suppose, have a major impact on the academic community of
Cascadia, but Levin's Jewishness remains undeveloped and has
little impact on the plot. Malamud has not developed the
potential available to him in this novel.

20   ROTH, PHILIP. "Writing American Fiction." Commentary 31,
        no. 3 (March):223-33 passim.
        The Jews of Malamud's The Magic Barrel and The Assistant
are not really mimetic representations of urban Jews but rather
metaphorical conceptions for certain kinds of human potential
and possibility. Reprinted: 1969.39.

21   SPENCER, DAVID G. Review of A New Life. Critic 20, no. 3
        (December-January):78-79.
        This novel is not altogether academic satire or fictional
autobiography. Questions of genre are less important to Malamud
than exploring the subtle dynamics of human behavior. A New
Life "is an artistic and perceptive investigation of the human
comedy, a wise, tender, and amusing novel of real stature."

22   STEVENSON, DAVID L. "The Strange Destiny of S. Levin." New
        York Times Book Review, 8 October, pp. 1, 28.
        A New Life once again reflects the seriousness of
Malamud's art, but it is art in a minor key. The limited
stature of Malamud's work may be a consequence of his failure to
confront the secret recesses of character in the Faulknerian
manner for the sake of his thematic interests. At times
Malamud's ironic and sympathetic treatment of S. Levin intimates
an interest in his complexity, but the novel never fully
explores it and often retreats into social commentary. One can
only conclude that Malamud's intentions are divided.

23   "A Talk with B. Malamud." New York Times Book Review, 8
        October, p. 28.

1962

A brief biographical sketch. Bernard Malamud does not wish to be confused with S. Levin, the hero of A New Life, although Malamud himself has lived and taught at a college very much like Cascadia, Oregon State College at Corvallis. Brooklyn, Rome, and Bennington, Vermont, where Malamud now teaches, are places that have also figured in his life. Unlike S. Levin, Malamud has never grown a beard.

24   WEST, JESSAMYN. "The Awakening of S. Levin." New York Herald Tribune Book Review 38 (8 October):4.
      Although A New Life is an academic novel, Malamud avoids both the abrasiveness and the sentimentality often associated with the genre. The central issue of the narrative involves the hero's attempt to free himself from the debilitating habits and customs of his own personality. Levin is ennobled and the reader is inspired by the struggle.

25   "The Wild Man from the East." Time 78(6 October):96.
      As a work of realism, A New Life is not convincing, but in its "Chekhovian qualities" of humor and pathos, also features of his previous work, Malamud's novel succeeds masterfully. However, S. Levin's potential for redeeming himself from his role as victim remains ambiguous.

1962

1   BERMAN, R.S. "Totems of Liberalism." Modern Age 6, no. 2 (Spring):212-14.
      Finds A New Life obsessive in its attempt to make Jewishness "a talisman of spiritual energies" and S. Levin an inarticulate spokesman for liberal ideology. The novel is an example of the fashionable "cult of the vital" in its commitment to sexual fulfillment and ideas, which are never conveyed beyond the level of platitudes. "The book is full of small allegiances to great ideas, yet it is shamefully barren of their eluci- dation."

2   BLOOMFIELD, CAROLINE. "Religion and Alienation in James Baldwin, Bernard Malamud, and James Powers." Religious Education 57 (March-April):97-102, 115 passim.
      Malamud's view of life is essentially tragic, but this label does not deny the values of love and hope to which Malamud has committed himself as guiding principles of his fiction. The Assistant embraces the essential value of life as well as the recognition of man's imperfection. The conversion of Frank Alpine to Judaism is both a recognition of suffering and a commitment to endurance, two of the fundamental qualities of tragedy.

17

1962

3   CHARLES, GERDA. "Bernard Malamud--the 'Natural' Writer."
        Jewish Quarterly 9, no. 2(Spring):5-6.
            Like his own character Roy Hobbs, Malamud himself,
        suggesting the title of his novel, is also a "natural"--a writer
        for whom the writing of fiction seems to come effortlessly. The
        absorbing element in his fiction is the mystery of suffering.
        In A New Life Malamud relates this theme to the social and
        sexual adventures of a schlemiel who, nevertheless, evokes
        tragic overtones. This novel is a much more poignant version of
        Kingsley Amis's Lucky Jim, the result of the hero's
        self-denigrating Jewish humor. "A New Life is a beautiful,
        poignant, disturbing book."

4   "Il commesso." Il Mondo (Rome), 4 September, p. 14.
            Although The Assistant has been acclaimed in America and
        England, the monotonous and banal plot makes for tedious
        reading. Malamud is better as a short story writer than as a
        novelist, and it is in this genre that he is reminiscent of
        Steven Crane, but without Crane's spontaneity and vitality.

5   DANIELS, SALLY. "Recent Fiction: Flights and Evasions."
        Minnesota Review 2, no. 4 (Summer):546-57.
            This review asserts that Malamud is the first significant
        American writer to have written an academic novel, A New Life,
        whose importance is less consequential aesthetically than it is
        historically.

6   HASSAN, IHAB. "After the Grotesque." Shenandoah 13, no. 3
        (Spring):62-65 passim.
            Identifies the grotesque as a manifestation of man's
        inner-self revealed in a state of deformity. In Malamud's
        fiction that deformity is connected to humiliation. A New
        Life, however, reveals another dimension to Malamud's sense of
        the grotesque. S. Levin, the hero, becomes "ruled by an idea of
        beauty and goodness that both cramps and liberates him for
        life."

7   HOLLANDER, JOHN. "To Find the Westward Path: A New Life."
        Partisan Review 29, no. 1 (Winter):137-39.
            Considers A New Life one of the best academic novels
        written thus far and free of clichés in its treatment of sex.
        The novel may be faulted, however, in its use of point of view:
        "there seems to be some inconsistencies of identification and
        fictional distance between Mr. Malamud and his protagonist [S.
        Levin]."

1962

8   HRUSKA, RICHARD J. "My Grandfather and Morris Bober."
     CCC: Journal of the Conference on College Composition and
     Communication 13 (May):32-24.
         Perceives points of contact between his Polish Gentile
     grandfather, an unlucky farmer in Michigan's Upper Peninsula,
     and Morris Bober of Malamud's The Assistant. In reading
     Malamud's novel, Hruska discovered in Bober the same commitment
     to honesty, hard work, and independence reflected in the life of
     his grandfather, but Bober's life was without humor and hope.

9   JEBB, JULIAN. "As Good as the Blurbs Say." Time and Tide 43
     (29 March):40.
         Malamud's S. Levin in A New Life is handled with
     ambivalence, and the hero does not have sufficient depth to
     withstand such treatment. The novel would have been more
     successful had Levin been more fully realized.

10   KAZIN, ALFRED. "Bernard Malamud: The Magic and the Dread."
     In Contemporaries. Boston: Little Brown & Co., pp. 202-7.
     Reprint of 1958.8.

11   KERMODE, FRANK. "Bernard Malamud." New Statesman 63 (30
     March):452-53.
         Malamud's early stories received immediate approval from
     English readers, but his novels have not had the same success.
     Part of this problem lies in the reader's inability to know just
     how far to take Malamud's irony, and this is especially true for
     the foreign reader. In addition, Malamud's alternation from
     realistic to symbolic scenes has contributed to the uncertainty
     of his intent illustrated, for example, in his movement from
     plausible incidents to highly stylized tableaux in his
     conclusions. One can see this pattern at work in "The Magic
     Barrel," The Assistant, or A New Life. Reprinted: 1968.16.

12   LEER, NORMAN. "Three American Novels and Contemporary
     Society." Wisconsin Studies in Contemporary Literature 3,
     no. 3 (Fall):67-85.
         Examines Bernard Malamud's The Assistant, Wright Morris's
     The Field of Vision, and Jack Kerouac's The Dharma Bums with
     regard to their common assumptions about postmodern society.
     All three novels involve the hero in a search for fulfilling
     relationships. The Assistant differs from the others in its use
     of an impoverished socioeconomic environment as a barrier to
     love, union, and community.

13   LOMBARDO, AGOSTINO. "Malamud e la realtà." Il Mondo
     (Rome), 9 October, pp. 13-14.
         Jewish writers like Malamud are especially fortunate in
     having a rich cultural tradition available to them which
     nourishes in their work a graphic sense of reality. In order to

19

1962

achieve a similar fictional density, many American writers are
forced to exploit their memories of childhood. Malamud's The
Assistant is a world that is anchored in American Jewish ghetto
life.

14   LUDWIG, JACK. Recent American Novelists. Pamphlets on
      American Writers, no. 22. Minneapolis: University of
      Minnesota Press, pp. 39-40.
          Malamud's The Assistant should be compared with the work
      of James T. Farrell, John Steinbeck, or the early John Dos
      Passos in the use of the thirties depression as the enveloping
      setting.

15   MALCOLM, DONALD. "The Grooves of Academe." New Yorker 37
      (27 January):105-7.
          A New Life suffers from an excessive preoccupation with
      uninteresting detail. Such material, although it slows the
      movement of the novel, reinforces Malamud's vision of the
      tediousness of academic life in the provinces. Unfortunately,
      S. Levin, Malamud's hero, suffers from an inarticulateness which
      also makes him tedious.

16   MANNING, OLIVIA. "Under the Influence." Spectator, 208 (30
      March):421.
          A New Life is a disappointment after Malamud's The
      Assistant, primarily because its hero lacks substance. The
      meaningless of S. Levin's former life is not adequately
      registered through his characterization.

17   MARCUS, STEVEN. "The Novel Again." Partisan Review 29, no.
      2 (Spring):171-95 passim.
          Compares Malamud's "The Magic Barrel" to the stories in
      Joyce's Dubliners. The prose style of Joyce's stories is spare
      and mean and, in their impact, unpoetical. In contrast,
      Malamud's prose "is spare in a lyrical way" and carries in it a
      poetry that issues from the author's intentions.

18   PRICE, R.G.G. Review of A New Life. Punch 242 (9 May):
      732-33.
          This novel is unusual in that it presents an idealist who
      is weak and inept but yet capable of change. It "is nearer to
      Nabokov's Pnin than to the routine cry of horror at the sexual
      and aesthetic shortcomings of American higher education."

19   PRITCHETT, V.S. "That Time and That Wilderness." New
      Statesman 64 (28 September):1107-14.
          Offers brief observations on Malamud's position in post-
      Faulknerian literature. Malamud, like his literary predecessor,
      is preoccupied with pain, but Faulkner's concerns with time and

the wilderness are for Malamud problems residing within the self
rather than within the world.

20   ROMIJN MEYER, HENK. " 's Werelds loon" [The world's
        reward]. Tirade (Antwerp) 16:580-88.
            In Flemish. Observes that academic novels are written by
        writers in residence at universities and are inevitably
        satiric. Their works often juxtapose what the university claims
        to be with what it ought to be or what people have made of it.
        Such is the thrust of Malamud's novel, a work that is sustained
        more by irony than satire. While S. Levin may perceive himself
        as a spokesman for humanism, he lacks the moral persuasiveness
        that might give him credibility. Malamud does not use him as a
        persona for his own views, but Levin is nevertheless invested
        with the author's sympathy.

21   RUBIN, LOUIS D., JR. "Six Novels and S. Levin." Sewanee
        Review 70, no. 3 (July-September):504-14 passim.
            A New Life is considered to be the most compelling among
        the seven novels discussed. Although its setting is in
        academia, that setting is, in essence, a metaphor for life. As
        a man who is human, perceptive, and disarmingly honest, S. Levin
        emerges as the only truly heroic figure in contemporary fiction.

22   SIEGEL, BEN. "Victims in Motion: Bernard Malamud's Sad and
        Bitter Clowns." Northwest Review 5, no. 2 (Spring):69-80.
            In Malamud's fiction, man is the primary agent of his own
        destruction. Like his Yiddish predecessors--I.L. Peretz,
        Mendele Mocher Seforim, and Sholom Aleichem--Malamud renders the
        ambivalence and capriciousness of human nature. "Where many
        contemporary American-Jewish writers search for the human being
        in the Jew, Malamud . . . seeks the Jew in the human being."
        His characters are neither great sinners nor great saints but
        rather small, sad figures, usually tangled in their own
        emotions. Despite the shocks they undergo, some part of them
        remains intact. Reprinted: 1963.39; 1970.24.

23   SOLOTAROFF, THEODORE. "Bernard Malamud's Fiction: The Old
        Life and the New." Commentary 33, no. 3 (March):197-204.
            The tension in Malamud's fiction is expressed in the
        hero's quest for a new life and the drag of the old with all its
        former misfortunes and human error. A New Life is an example of
        this tension and dramatizes S. Levin's difficulty in fully re-
        solving it. Although Levin escapes the setting of his former hu-
        miliations and defeats, his new life at Cascadia College is only
        a qualified success and brings with it unanticipated burdens and
        restrictions to his freedom. Reprinted: 1970.5; 1970.25.

1962

24   VOSS, ARTHUR W.M.   Review of A New Life.   Books Abroad 36
     (Winter):79.
          An academic satire, this novel is consciously less witty
     than similar fictions by Mary McCarthy and Randall Jarrell.   It
     is, nonetheless, a powerful work thanks to its ironically
     conceived hero and its muted prose, "a low-keyed almost flat
     style suited to his [Malamud's] material."

25   WEISS, SAMUEL A.   "Notes on Bernard Malamud."   Chicago Jewish
     Forum 21, no. 2 (Winter 1962-63):155-58.
          Malamud's vision of life is shaped by three traditions--
     the Hebrew, Greek, and Christian.   His characters undergo
     Job-like suffering and through it learn virtue.   Ultimately
     these characters discover, or rediscover, what it is to be truly
     human.

                              1963

1   ADAMS, PHOEBE.   Review of Idiots First.   Atlantic 212, no. 5
     (November):159.
          Through his resources of "wit, intelligence, and
     understanding," Malamud takes the misfits of the world and
     endows their struggle with dignity.

2   ADELMAN, GEORGE.   "Idiots First."   Library Journal 88 (1
     November):4238.
          The reviewer admires the pathos, comedy, and fantasy
     Malamud displays in the eleven stories making up this volume.

3   ALTER, ROBERT.   "Out of the Trap."   Midstream 9, no. 4
     (December):88-90.
          Such stories in Idiots First as "Black is My Favorite
     Color," "Life is Better than Death," and "The German Refugee"
     repeat Malamud's themes of entrapment and suffering.   At the
     same time, they add a new tone, complications of plot, and
     narrative technique to Malamud's work.   In "Still Life" and
     "Naked Nude," the reappearing Arthur Fidelman is enhanced in
     characterization.

4   BAUMBACH, JONATHAN.   "The Economy of Life: The Novels of
     Bernard Malamud."   Kenyon Review 25, no. 3 (Summer):438-57.
          Claims that Malamud's novels are a continuation of the
     American romance tradition as defined by Richard Chase, and goes
     on to examine The Natural, The Assistant, and A New Life within
     the parameters of that tradition.

                              22

5   BOROFF, DAVID. "Losers, but Not Lost." Saturday Review 46
     (12 October):33.
         One of the sources of appeal in Idiots First is Malamud's
     imaginative ability to redeem failure. The Italian stories in
     this collection have another appeal: "the Italian blend of
     gusto and self-pity . . .en rapport with the Jewish
     personality."

6   BROOKE, JOCELYN. "New Novels." Listener 69 (9 May):801.
         The relation of the Grail legend to the literal plot of
     The Natural is unintelligible, and the hero of the novel, Roy
     Hobbs, is singularly undistinguished.

7   DAVENPORT, G[UY]. "Idiots First." National Review 15 (19
     November):450, 452.
         The wit of Idiots First has its origins in Jewish humor
     and its American parallels only in the work of Mark Twain and
     Henry Mencken.

8   EDELSTEIN, J.M. "Binding Variants in Malamud's The
     Natural." American Notes and Queries 1, no. 9 (May):133-34.
         Observes that the first edition of the novel (New York:
     Harcourt, Brace, 1952) was published in three different
     bindings: "maroon, blue, and gray." Edelstein speculates that
     the first printing was larger than originally planned,
     necessitating the use of those colors of binding cloth available
     at the time.

9   GROSS, JOHN. "Oy!" New York Review of Books 1 (17
     October):14.
         Idiots First is an effective blend of naturalism and
     fantasy, legend and folklore; even the supernatural is
     utilized. The conventions of Yiddish literature are also
     absorbed in his stories, but Malamud has given them new
     meaning. This collection is equal in quality to The Magic
     Barrel.

10   HASSAN, IHAB. "The Hopes of Man." New York Times Book
     Review, 13 October, p. 5.
         In reviewing Idiots First, Hassan observes that the writer
     may respond in a variety of ways to the human condition.
     Malamud's choice is that of "irony and compassion." In probing
     the problems of human endurance and victimization, this
     collection sustains an ironic but yet a compassionate vision
     which is seen at its best in the story "The German Refugee."

11   _____. Letter concerning omission within his review of
     Idiots First. New York Times Book Review, 27 October, p. 65.

1963

Malamud's position as a writer "may be finally defined by the sheer precision of his integrity." The condition of the world may oblige the writer to move beyond "the limits of conscience or art" in defense of life.

12   HENTOFF, NAT. "Bernard Malamud." Commonweal 79 (6 December):328-29.
Idiots First reveals Malamud as a much angrier writer than has generally been acknowledged, and the stories in this collection almost invariably end in defeat and frustration. There is a fundamental disjunction between the latent hostility of Malamud's fiction and his compassionate public pronouncements.

13   HICKS, GRANVILLE. "Generations of the Fifites: Malamud, Gold and Updike." In The Creative Present: Notes on Contemporary American Fiction. Edited by Nona Balakian and Charles Simmons. New York: Doubleday & Co., pp. 217-37.
Briefly surveys the themes of Malamud, Gold, and Updike's fiction and concludes that the most important point of contact these writers have with each other is in their concern with redemption.

14   _____. "His Hopes on the Human Heart." Saturday Review 46 (12 October):31-32.
Offers a brief synopsis of Malamud's life and career, noting his early life in Brooklyn; his distrust of radical causes at City College; his reading in Russian, Yiddish, and modern literature; the impact of The Magic Barrel on the reading public; the status of his other novels; and his personal philosophy in which man, contrary to prevailing attitudes, is celebrated rather than devalued.

15   HOFFMAN, FREDERICK J. The Modern Novel in America, 3d ed. Chicago: Henry Regnery Co., Gateway Edition, pp. 245-46, 251.
Through the skillful management of the ordinary details of life in The Assistant, Bernard Malamud achieves highly successful "comico-pathetic" effects from the life of a struggling Jewish family. The reader is not confronted with the author's didacticism but rather "suffering and hard luck and venality and ironic understandings based on coincidence or accident."

16   HOGAN, WILLIAM. "Bernard Malamud's 'Gallows Humor.'" San Francisco Chronicle, 25 October, p. 43.
Idiots First is much closer to Jewish immigrant literature than Philip Roth's Goodbye Columbus. The stories in Malamud's collection almost seem as though they had been translated from Yiddish. Attached to the grimness of his tales is a sardonic humor. "A less accomplished craftsman would rely on a wail."

17   HYMAN, STANLEY EDGAR. "Bernard Malamud's Moral Fables." New
      Leader 46 (28 October):20-21.
          The collection, Idiots First, illustrates the American
      short story at its best, especially in "The German Refugee," a
      narrative involving "frenzied redemptive sacrifice, like The
      Assistant and "The Magic Barrel." Because of an occasional
      inconsistency in tone or genre, such stories as "The Jewbird"
      and "Naked Nude" fail to achieve their proper impact. "At his
      best, [Malamud] . . . blends comedy, pathos and melodrama, and
      perfectly sustains that mixture throughout." Although his
      material is often Jewish, it always carries a universality.

18   IGOE, WILLIAM [J.]. "Master Watchmaker of the Short Story."
      Chicago Tribune, 17 November, p. 8.
          The humor of Idiots First reflects Malamud's paradoxical
      imagination: "Pain he finds funny; he satirizes agony." The
      twelve perfectly crafted stories in this collection will be a
      renewed delight to his readers.

19   IGOE, WILLIAM J. "More Than One America." Tablet 217 (11
      May):513-14.
          Roy Hobbs in Malamud's The Natural is a distinctly
      American archetypal figure--a lonely, isolated idealist who
      seeks fulfillment only through realizing the purity of his own
      self-image. He is an American version of Don Quixote or a
      variant of the western hero, Shane. Ironically, instead of
      achieving completeness through the heroic American sport of
      baseball, he discovers the corruption and materialism of
      Nathaniel West's America. This novel is charming but minor
      Malamud.

20   Interview with Bernard Malamud. New York Times Book Review,
      13 October, p. 5.
          The author touches on the following topics at his home in
      Bennington, Vermont: the unlikelihood that man will destroy
      himself; the need for continual optimism; the transformation of
      social issues into art; his attraction to Arthur Fidelman as a
      character; and his great affection for the stories in which
      Fidelman appears.

21   JOHNSON, RICHARD A. Review of Idiots First. Studies in
      Short Fiction 1, no. 2 (Winter):171-72.
          This collection of short stories illustrates Malamud's
      variety of technique and subject matter. While it is possible
      to construct the general outlines of Malamud's fictional world,
      the conflicts besetting his heroes are always individualized as
      illustrated by "The Maid's Shoes," "Still Life," or "Naked
      Nude." Malamud's success is, in part, a result of "a style that
      comprehends a great deal and is surprised by almost nothing."

1963

22   LEIBOWITZ, HERBERT. "Malamud and the Anthropomorphic
      Business." New Republic 149 (21 December):21-23.
      Draws attention to the stylistic and psychological
qualities of the stories appearing in Idiots First. Malamud
sounds like a "waggish minstrel of misery," who also speaks as a
"homolist," offering essential truths. Even while affirming the
sanctity of human life, a brooding sadness persists, the result
of what the stories have been a witness to.

23   LODGE, DAVID. "Home Run." Spectator 210 (10 May):608, 610.
      The failure of the British reading public to have access
to Malamud's The Natural until recently, presumably because it
deals with American baseball, is an assumption of British
naiveté. The uniting of baseball with the Grail legend may
reflect "a gifted young writer's exhibitionism," but this union
does, in fact, lend new meaning and drama to the sport.

24   MALIN, IRVING. "Some Recent Fiction." Reconstructionist 29,
      no. 15 (November):25-28.
      Malamud examines suffering and exile in the context of
family life, but in Idiots First, he extends his exploration to
the academic community. "The German Refugee" asserts the need
for a greater participation in and understanding of suffering
and exile. In this story the uninitiated narrator comes to know
the meaning of these conditions in his tutorial relationship
with Oskar.

25   MILLER, KARL. "Sporting Life." New Statesman 65 (19
      April):602.
      Malamud has effectively incorporated into The Natural the
texture and quality of baseball, while creating a resonant
parable that allows the reader to transcend its narrow
designation as sports novel. This book is graceful and
enchanting, "the wonderful inauguration of a very gifted
writer."

26   MITGANG, HERBERT. "Fiction Fantasies by Malamud (and
      Chagall)." New York Times, 14 October, p. 27.
      Malamud and Chagall share several points of contact:
"both are fantasists, sensualists and humanists." In comparing
Idiots First to Chagall's painting, the central quality common
to their work is compassion.

27   MURRAY, JAMES G. Review of Idiots First. Critic 22, no. 3
      (December-January):77-78.
      Malamud's Jewishness--an aspect of style rather than
ideology--contributes to the strengths and weaknesses of this
collection. The world of the ghetto Jew that Malamud depicts is

now a tired literary stereotype, and in continuing to use that stereotype, Malamud deprives Jews of their individuality. "To put a Jew in a ghetto, whether in Warsaw or in fiction, is to condemn him to death."

28   PHILLOPSON, JOHN S.   Review of Idiots First. Best Sellers 23
       (15 October):253-54.
       Throughout this collection of stories, Malamud illustrates the Thoreauvian statement, with specific application to Jews, that "most men lead lives of quiet desperation." Rich in their symbolic suggestions, the stories lend themselves to a variety of interpretations and reflect the richness of Malamud's talent.

29   PICKREL, PAUL. "Selected Shorts." Harper's 227, no. 1362
       (November):130, 132.
       Although the stories in Idiots First often resemble each other through the use of a poor but struggling Jewish victim, they are really distinctive for their variety of subjects: for example, a poor bankrupt grocer, an unwilling forger, and a Yiddish talking bird.

30   PRICE, R.G.G. Review of The Natural. Punch 244 (1 May):
       645-46.
       The cultural significance of baseball for Americans in Malamud's novel seems foreign for this British reviewer, despite the explanatory appendix in the Eyre and Spottiswoode (London) edition. Furthermore, the Grail quest "does not impose itself naturally, easily or importantly."

31   "Realistic Fabulist." Time 82 (15 November):123, 126.
       This review of Idiots First considers Malamud's adaptation of the Yiddish folk tale to naturalistic material inappropriate. In this collection, "The Jewbird" is too facile a parable about anti-Semitism but is nevertheless rewarding.

32   Review of Il commesso [The Assistant]. Contemporaneo, nos.
       56-57 (January-February):187.
       At its best The Assistant evokes the customs of family life among poor Jews who are incapable of entering the frantic rhythms of American life around them. The touching pathos that arises at the beginning is not maintained throughout, and the novel turns into an abbreviated love story between Frank Alpine and Helen Bober. Its greatest weaknesses are reflected in the unconvincing characterization of Frank Alpine and in the use of a street language that seems artificial.

33   RIBALOW, HAROLD U. "A Collection of Malamud Stories."
       Congress Bi-Weekly: Journal of Opinion and Jewish Affairs 30
       (18 November):18-19.

1963

      Idiots First reflects one of Malamud's greatest strengths, his ability to create intense drama out of his Jewish characters. Whether it is the title story of the collection, "Black is My Favorite Color," or "The Jewbird," the author seems deeply interested in Jews. In their successful mixture of fantasy and realism, these stories will be counted among the most important in contemporary American literature.

34   ROSS, ALAN. Review of The Natural. London Magazine, 2d ser. 3, no. 3:86-87.
      Malamud's remarkable baseball novel seems to have been influenced by Nathaniel West's The Dream Life of Balso Snell and A Cool Million. While no English novelist has written of sport with Malamud's explicitness and authority, the narrative, nevertheless, "alternates between poetic fantasy and Cubist banter." Given its intense, almost lyrical quality, the novel should be read as a kind of poem.

35   RYAN, STEPHEN P. Review of A New Life. Best Sellers 21 (15 November):342.
      This work really embodies the plots for two separate novels: the first is a satire on the academic community in Cascadia; and the second concerns the personal relationships of S. Levin. Malamud's narrative manner is reminiscent of Joyce's Ulysses, but the Joycean echoes are wisely muted.

36   SALE, ROGER. "The Newness of the Novel." Hudson Review 26, no. 4 (Winter):601-9.
      The Italian stories in Malamud's Idiots First leave the reader with a sense of excessive ingenuity and strain. One must look to "The Death of Me" in order to discover the ease with which Malamud is able to incorporate sympathy and understanding in his characters. The success of these characters is partially due to the mystery surrounding their behavior. When characters are too fully understood, as in "Life is Better than Death," the story does not sustain reader interest.

37   "Schwartz, the Bird." Newsweek 62 (7 October):112.
      In Malamud's collection of stories, Idiots First, "The Jewbird" is, perhaps, the most representative of the group, revealing a seriocomic quality that is present throughout. As a stylistic feature of his fiction, Malamud often uses fantasy, which, in his hands, intensifies rather than obscures reality.

38   SHEPPHARD, RONALD. "About Bernard Malamud." Washington Post & Times Herald Book Week, 13 October, p. 5.
      Briefly reviews Malamud's personal life and professional career and concludes that the author's primary concern is to reveal the potential for strength and growth in the lives of ordinary people.

39   SIEGEL, BEN. "Victims in Motion: Bernard Malamud's Sad and
       Bitter Clowns." In Recent American Fiction: Some Critical
       Views. Edited by Joseph J. Waldmeir. Boston: Houghton
       Mifflin Co., pp. 203-14.
           Reprint of 1962.22.

40   SOLOTAROFF, THEODORE. "Showing us 'What It Means Human.'"
       Washington Post & Times Herald Book Week, 13 October, pp. 5,
       12.
           Malamud is a valuable resource for those who look for
       literature that offers a sense of renewal. The force of the
       title story in Idiots First comes from an instinct of what being
       human is all about. Some of the stories in this collection move
       out of Malamud's over-used metaphorical ghetto and join the
       actual world. They are, for example, "The Maid's Shoes," "Life
       is Better Than Death," and especially the Fidelman stories.
       "The main thing about Idiots First is the new possibilities it
       reveals about Malamud's art and the achievement it promises."

41   STALEY, THOMAS F. "The Core of Life." Pittsburgh Press 10
       November, sec. 5, p. 11.
           Idiots First supports the generally held view of Malamud's
       importance and originality on the American scene. He is capable
       of appealing to a wide diversity of groups because of the
       universality of his themes.

42   STERN, MILTON. "All Men Are Jews." Nation 197 (19
       October):243-44.
           As a Jewish writer and a fantasist, Malamud is the Marc
       Chagall of contemporary fiction, and his mixture of fantasy and
       Yiddish sensibility is sustained in Idiots First. In his
       depiction of suffering Jewish figures, Malamud synthesizes the
       character of the schlemiel with that of the saint. When
       Malamud's schlemiel loses his Jewishness, as in the case of
       Arthur Fidelman, his character undergoes a loss of dignity and
       reader sympathy. The best of the stories in this collection are
       "The Cost of Living" and "The German Refugee."

43   STEVENSON, DAVID L. "'The Activists.'" Daedalus: Journal
       of the American Academy of Arts and Sciences 92, no. 2
       (Spring):238-49 passim.
           Considers Malamud's A New Life an example of the
       "activist" novel, although a variant of the genre. This novel
       is defined by energetic, self-conscious heroes "who are in-
       tellectual migrants from the norms of domestic morality and
       ambition in a closed, money making society." Malamud's S. Levin
       continually tests himself to see whether he is a shaping force
       in the lives of others or merely a person subject to external
       manipulation.

1963

44   "The Sustaining Stream." Time 81 (1 February):84.
      Malamud's modification of reality in The Natural and The
Assistant is not dependent on imaginative extravagances; indeed,
the works reflect his subtlety and lucidity.

45   WAGNER, MARY HEGEL. Review of Idiots First. America 109 (26
      October):488, 490-91.
      Varying in their success, the stories in this collection
are always vigorous and controlled. "Black is My Favorite
Color" and "A Choice of Professions" are worthy of special
mention: the first is concerned with racial hatred and the
second is a study in moral responsibility. Both explore the
obstacles facing love between people.

46   WHEILDON, LEONARD. "Short Story Master at His Peak." Boston
      Sunday Herald, 20 October, sec. 4, p. 3.
      Praises Malamud's new collection of stories, Idiots First,
for its simplicity of style, complexity of character, and successful mixture of comedy and tragedy. "The variety is endless,
the quality uniformly high."

47   WHITE, ROBERT L. "The English Instructor as Hero: Two
      Novels by Roth and Malamud." Forum (University of Houston)
      4, no. 3 (Winter):16-22.
      Bernard Malamud's A New Life and Philip Roth's Letting Go
are complementary academic novels that explore realistically the
idea of psychological if not physical marginality in American
life. Malamud's S. Levin and Roth's Gabe Wallach resemble each
other initially in their desire to remain detached from the
entanglements of relationships. While Malamud's novel eventually dignifies the values of love and responsibility, Roth
seems to depict them as too fragile a defense against the chaos
and horror of life. Indeed, Malamud is capable of extending
sympathy and compassion even to those abrasive characters marked
by their pettiness and dogmatism; in contrast, Roth is always
more angry with such figures and less charitable than Malamud in
their treatment. "A New Life may be more pleasing to the reader
because of its 'verve and wit,'" but Letting Go "is a more
challenging and insistently demanding book."

48   WIESEL, ELIE. Review of Idiots First. Hadassah 44, no. 3
      (November):18.
      Considers this collection an important illustration of
Malamud's treatment of outcasts. In his fictional universe
Malamud allows for the miraculous as a protest against a
universe indifferent to man's needs. Malamud's conception of
reality amounts to an act of love for those in his fiction who
are insulted and injured. "Miguel de Unamuno writes that to be
Spanish is the gravest matter in the world but to be Jewish is
to be even more so."

1964

1   ALLEN, WALTER. The Modern Novel in Britain and the United States. New York: E.P. Dutton & Co., pp. 330-32.
Ranks Malamud and Bellow as the best young contemporary American writers, and considers both heir to the Jewish and Russian literary traditions. The Assistant, a work of "moral beauty," carries with it a Chekhovian irony.

2   BELLMAN, IRVING SAMUEL. "Women, Children, and Idiots First: The Transformation Psychology of Bernard Malamud." Critique 7, no. 2 (Winter 1964-65):123-38.
Perceives three central themes through Malamud's work: the transformation of non-Jews into Jews and Jews into Negroes; a world that is poisoned and deteriorating; and the possibility of a new life. A feature of his fiction that has become a critical commonplace is "his imagination of disaster." Bellman ponders Malamud's need to change his pace, style, and even his subject matter. Reprinted: 1970.5

3   BISOL, GAETANO. Review of Il commesso [The Assistant]. In Letture: Rassegna Critica del Libro, March, pp. 202-4.
Considers The Assistant undirected, probably as result of Malamud's attempt to incorporate too many issues in the novel which remain undeveloped. Malamud's hero seems childish in his idealism and too self-conscious in his dialogue, as though he were acting out a role. The incompleteness of the other characters and the simplistic plot construction are other flaws in the novel.

4   _____. Review of Una nuova vita [A New Life]. In Letture: Rassegna Critica del Libro, May, pp. 360-62.
A New Life is organized around three main components: (1) the psychological, which registers the hero's loneliness; (2) the ethical, which dramatizes the compromise of moral principle for easy accommodations to life; (3) and the social, which involves the author's satiric treatment of America. S. Levin, like other Malamud heroes, is characterized by his spiritual poverty, and although the title offers hope, that hope is dimmed by the sadly ironic ending.

5   BLUEFARB, SAM. "Bernard Malamud: The Scope of Caricature." English Journal 53, no. 5 (May):319-26, 335.
Although Malamud's stories may begin with figures who are caricatures, his characters invariably transcend their initial appearance and are used symbolically or allegorically. In this

1964

respect, his fiction reflects a tendency also found in the
fiction of Henry James, the playing off of one level of reality
against another in order to raise moral questions. Reprinted:
1970.5.

6   DEBENEDETTI, ANTONIO.   "La sorte di Levin."   Avanti (Rome),
     23 January, p. 3.
         Although there is an autobiographical element to A New
     Life, Malamud writes alternately with the eyes of the poet and
     the eyes of the journalist. He has a sixth sense about the
     nature of his hero whose life has its brushes with tragedy and
     madness. Malamud's journalistic vision, however, is subordi-
     nated to the vision of the poet, and it is thus difficult to
     locate Levin in the context of his own human history. Levin
     remains a rebellious but shadowy figure, shut off from the
     reader as well as from conventional society.

7   DUPEE, F[REDERICK] W[ILCOX].   "The Power of Positive Sex."
     Partisan Review 31, no. 3 (Summer):425-30.
         Dupee's observations are, in part, a reaction to Leslie
     Fiedler's reservations about Malamud's fiction on two issues:
     Malamud's dilution of sexuality and his indifference to the
     Gothic mode. Both in sexual and in religious matters, Malamud's
     non-Jew eventually identifies with normative Jewish values.
     Insufficiently grim for Fiedler, Malamud's vision is positioned
     somewhere between the dark imagination of Kafka and the
     "whimsical affirmations of Paddy Chayefsky." Idiots First and
     The Magic Barrel are especially accomplished works, primarily
     because of the immediacy with which their characters are
     rendered. Reprinted: 1965.3.

8   FIEDLER, LESLIE [A.].   "Jewish-Americans, Go Home!" Waiting
     for the End. New York: Stein & Day, pp. 89-104 passim.
     Reprint. 1970.
         The Assistant is an evocation of the thirties, "a last
     expression of the apocalyptic fears and Messianic hopes of those
     terrible but relatively simple times." Malamud thus seems
     somewhat incongruous in the company of such contemporaries as
     Saul Bellow and Norman Mailer.

9   GE[BSATTEL], J[EROME] V[ON].   Review of The Assistant. In
     Kindlers Literatur Lexicon. Vol. 1. Zurich: Kindler Verlag,
     p. 1034.
         Observes Malamud's sharp ear and eye for daily life and
     the linguistic features of Morris Bober's speech which identify
     him as a foreigner in America. Bober's failure to achieve
     success in America is tantamount to a crime. The Assistant is
     regarded as one of the most impressive novels of the new
     American literature. Reprinted: 1974.7.

1964

10   GEISMAR, MAXWELL. "The American Short Story Today." Studies
      on the Left 4, no. 2 (Spring):21-27 passim.
         Considers Malamud, and virtually every other contemporary
      American writer of the short story, too preoccupied with
      technique and insufficiently concerned with the social system
      and its institutions.

11   GOLDMAN, MARK. "Bernard Malamud's Comic Vision and the Theme
      of Identity." Critique 7, no. 2 (Winter 1964-65):92-109.
         Malamud dramatizes the denial of the essential self as a
      form of comic hubris. Suffering is the consequence, which
      eventually leads the comic hero back to the origins of his
      identity and to self-knowledge. Although the problem of
      identity is a theme especially compelling for the American
      Jewish writer caught between memories of the past and his
      assimilation in the present, Isaac Babel's Soviet Jew also
      reflects similar tensions and ironies in another cultural
      context. Like T.S. Eliot, Malamud perceives the past as part of
      the present. Fittingly, Malamud as comic artist attempts to
      reunite the past self with its newer counterpart as the means
      whereby a renewed sense of life is to be achieved. Reprinted:
      1970.5.

12   HIGGINSON, J.P. "Recent Fiction." Minnesota Review 4, no. 4
      (Summer):561-70.
         Idiots First illustrates that once again Malamud's
      originality finds its best expression in short fiction. The
      stories in this collection are all of equal value. Malamud
      balances them off with a scene from a play, Suppose a Wedding,
      which is more direct in its treatment of character relationships
      than the stories.

13   HOYT, CHARLES ALVA. "Bernard Malamud and the New
      Romanticism." In Contemporary American Novelists. Edited by
      Harry Thornton Moore. Carbondale: Southern Illinois
      University Press, pp. 65-79.
         Malamud's romanticism is evidenced in the determination of
      his characters to change their lives. The schlemiel-hero effec-
      tively expresses this romanticism because of his continual ef-
      forts to make new starts despite repeated insults and injuries
      that thwart his enterprises. S. Levin of A New Life is a fully
      representative Malamud hero in his attempt to achieve personal
      fulfillment. In addition, A New Life reveals, through charac-
      ter, theme, setting, and symbol, other aspects of romanticism
      closely resembling those in D.H. Lawrence's Lady Chatterly's
      Lover. Both books "protest against the forces in the modern
      world which operate so as to separate man from man and man from
      woman." Reprinted: 1970.5.

1964

14 HYMAN, STANLEY EDGAR. "A New Life for a Good Man." In On
    Contemporary Literature. Edited by Richard Kostelanetz. New
    York: Avon Books, pp. 442-46. Reprint. Freeport, N.Y.:
    Books for Libraries Press, 1971, pp. 442-46.
        Reprint of 1961.13.

15 JONES, WILLIAM G. "Current Novelists 'Entering the World.'"
    Southwest Review 49, no. 1 (Winter):91-96.
        A review essay of current fiction, including Malamud's
    Idiots First, which finds a common thread, the quality of
    pathos, in two books. In Jack Schaefer's Monte Walsh, the
    changing world in which the hero finds himself becomes the basis
    for pain and the evocation of pathos. In Malamud's collection
    of stories, pathos is an inescapable condition of life; his
    characters are born misfits, incapable of thriving in any
    world. For Malamud, to be human is to enter life "with
    sensitivity, passion, and painless self-revelation," but
    paradoxically these very qualities make his character vulnerable
    to the brutal elements around them. Malamud's Jews, who are all
    too human, inevitably suffer as a consequence of their own
    humanity.

16 KATTAN, NAIM. "Deux écrivains américains." Écrits du Canada
    Français 17:87-135.
        Discusses in the first half of this essay the dynamics of
    Jewish immigrant life in America and their influence on
    Malamud's work. Judaism for Malamud was neither a refuge nor a
    quest but an integral part of his sensibility and his past from
    which he was able to draw truths about the human condition.
    Since Jewish values incorporate those of Christianity, in
    Malamud's fiction the Jew becomes the true Christian; his
    fiction, however, focuses on the Jew as a man or artist rather
    than on Jews as a people or a community. (The second part of
    this essay deals with James Baldwin.)

17 KAZIN, ALFRED. "Bernard Malamud: The Magic and the Dread."
    In On Contemporary Literature. Edited by Richard
    Kostelanetz. New York: Avon Books, pp. 249-60. Reprint.
    Freeport, N.Y.: Books for Libraries Press, 1971, pp.
    437-41.
        Reprint of 1958.8.

18 LEHMANN-HAUPT, CHRISTOPHER. An Interview with Malamud
    Concerning The Fixer. New York Times Book Review, 4
    September, p. 8.
        Malamud revealed that in planning this book he wished to
    convey the timelessness of injustice rather than a story
    emerging from a historical event. The accomplishment of this

end necessitated three artistic changes from the original
source: "first, to throw out the real Beiliss and replace him
with Bok; second, cut down the cast to a few people; third, to
mythologize--that is, to make metaphors and symbols of the major
events and characters."

19   LEVINE, NORMAN. "Stockpot." Spectator 212 (12 June):
      802-3.
         The stories in Idiots First are full of stereotyped
characters, and the plots lack dramatic intensity. Malamud's
elongated prose style is more suitable for the novel than it is
for the short story, and his talent would be better served in
the former.

20   MALIN, IRVING, and STARK, IRWIN. Breakthrough: A Treasury
      of Contemporary American-Jewish Literature. New York:
      McGraw-Hill Book Co., pp. 20-21. Reprint. Philadelphia:
      Jewish Publication Society of America, 1965.
         Although suffering is a preoccupation of all Jewish-
American writers, Malamud develops it more fully than the rest
and links it with the meaning of Jewishness.

21   MANDEL, RUTH [B.]. "Bernard Malamud's The Assistant and A New
      Life: Ironic Affirmation." Critique 7, no. 2 (Winter
      1964-65):110-22.
         The continued suffering of Malamud's heroes despite their
achievement of personal redemption is an expression of Malamud's
ironic vision. In The Assistant this vision is reflected in the
aspirations of the characters and the repeated denial of their
fulfillment. In A New Life the irony may be counterproductive
insofar as S. Levin, as a moral hero, seems to be undercut by
Malamud's sustained comic treatment, thereby diminishing his
intended significance. Reprinted: 1970.5.

22   MEIXNER, JOHN A. "Morrison, Kirk, Malamud." Sewanee Review
      72, no. 3 (Summer):540-42.
         Considers "Still Life" in Malamud's Idiots First
brilliant, but despite the pleasure this collection affords, it
is marred by an overreliance on well-established character types
and well-worn themes and situations.

23   NATHAN, MONIQUE. "Écrivains juifs d'Amérique." Preuves, no.
      165 (November):74-78 passim.
         In utilizing the conventions and themes of Jewish
experience, Malamud differs completely from both Roth and
Bellow. For Malamud such material transcends its folkloric
character and embodies meaning for mankind. While Malamud has
imprinted on his consciousness the memories of Hasidic legends,
contemporary Jewish fiction, Malamud's included, belongs to
world literature and has its own autonomous existence.

1964

24 PEDEN, WILLIAM. The American Short Story: Front Line in the
    National Defense of Literature. Boston: Houghton Mifflin
    Co., pp. 147-49.
        Considers The Magic Barrel among the best collections of
    short stories in American literature, primarily because of
    Malamud's highly individualized characters. Malamud's continued
    productivity in the short story is discussed in 1975.20.

25 PERRINE, LAWRENCE. "Malamud's 'Take Pity.'" Studies in
    Short Fiction 2, no. 1 (Fall):84-86.
        Recognizing the locale for the story is crucial for a
    correct interpretation of the plot. Eva and Rosen should be
    viewed within the context of a symbolic rather than a literal
    setting, a kind of purgatory which suggests their flawed human
    nature.

26 PODHORETZ, NORMAN. "The New Nihilism and the Novel." In
    Doings and Undoings: The Fifties and After in American
    Writing. New York: Farrar, Straus & Co., pp. 176-78.
        Reprint of 1958.13.

27 RAPHAEL, FREDERIC. "Stealth and the Outer Life." Sunday
    Times (London), 31 May, p. 39.
        Observes that while no story in Idiots First is original
    to the collection, the book does represent Malamud as a unique
    voice in contemporary literature. His achievement lies in the
    effectiveness of portraiture, mood, atmosphere, and the inter-
    twining of fantasy with reality. The only failing in his
    stories is in their lack of unity and developing intensity that
    one finds in a novel.

28 RATNER, MARC L. "Style and Humanity in Malamud's Fiction."
    Massachusetts Review 5, no. 4 (Summer):663-83.
        Although Malamud's fiction is concerned with the value of
    suffering, his ironic and comic treatment of this theme
    mitigates any sense of sentimentality. The collection of
    stories, Idiots First, is a representative of Malamud's artistic
    strengths. In addition to his facility with irony and comedy,
    these stories reveal his technical ingenuity, reflected in the
    use of first person narration, omniscient narration, drama, and
    fable.

29 Review of Una nuova vita [A New Life]. Mulino, no. 140
    (June):738.
        Admires Malamud's novel for its fine introspective quality
    which is reminiscent of the nineteenth-century Russian novel.
    Malamud does not violate its meditative mood by incorporating a
    conventional happy ending.

30   SICILIANO, ENZO. "Il segrego di Malamud." Il Mondo (Rome),
21 July, p. 10.
    Malamud is obsessed with the lives of Jews, and in The
Magic Barrel his obsession with Jewish characters carries over
into their portraiture: they seem to lead a spiritual more than
a physical existence. Malamud himself appears to function as a
witness to their faith and spirituality.

31   _____. "La tecnica di Malamud." Il Mondo (Rome), 21
January, p. 11.
    This review of A New Life sees Malamud's novel as a
continuation of an American cultural myth that found its most
explicit expression in John F. Kennedy's conception of the new
frontier, a conception which distinguishes Americans from
Europeans. For Siciliano, Europeans live in history while
Americans live in space. In Malamud's novel, the emptiness of
S. Levin's past makes it necessary for him to forge a new
personal history in a new physical setting. Unfortunately,
Malamud's novel does not do justice to this myth. His
characters are sketchily drawn and contribute to the pam-
phletlike quality of the narrative. When the novel succeeds, it
is a result of Malamud's lyric description of nature or his
sense of place.

32   SOLOTAROFF, THEODORE. "Philip Roth and the Jewish
Moralists." In Breakthrough: A Treasury of Contemporary
American-Jewish Literature. Edited by Irving Malin and Irwin
Stark. New York: McGraw-Hill Book Co., pp. 354-66 passim.
Reprint. Philadelphia: Jewish Publication Society of
America, 1965.
    Reprint of 1959.3.

33   TAUBMAN, ROBERT. "People of the Law." New Statesman 67 (5
June):883-84.
    Despite their darkness, the stories in Idiots First are
not the products of a despairing vision. Rather they stress the
ability of the human spirit to challenge the unfeeling laws of
the universe supported only by Malamud's unmistakable love. "I
doubt if unaccommodated man has had a fairer or better defense
by any other modern novelist."

1965

1   BAUMBACH, JONATHAN. "All Men Are Jews: The Assistant by
Bernard Malamud." In The Landscape of Nightmare: Studies in
the Contemporary American Novel. New York: New York
University Press, pp. 101-22.
    Considers The Assistant the most Dostoevskian of Malamud's
novels. In seeking expiation for a crime, Frank Alpine is only

1965

capable of extending and intensifying his own sense of guilt.
He becomes the "Gentile-Jew," the victimizer and victim.
Alpine's purification comes only through pain and suffering, and
his redemption is made possible only through his love for
Helen. His capacity to love becomes a measure of his grace.

2   BELLMAN, SAMUEL RIVING. "Henry James's 'The Madonna of the
    Future' and Two Modern Parallels." California English
    Journal 1, no. 3:47-53.
        Key story elements in Henry James's "The Madonna of the
    Future" have their correspondences in Bernard Malamud's "Still
    Life": an American traveler in Italy interested in art, an
    encounter with an American would-be artist living in Italy,
    discussion involving pictorial art, the psychological problems
    of the artist, and the conflict between the real and the ideal.
    Like James's Theobald, Malamud's Arthur Fidelman is an American
    painter in Italy whose idealized portrait of his Italian model
    is at odds with her actual sordidness.

3   DUPEE, F[REDERICK] W[ILCOX]. "Malamud: The Uses and Abuses
    of Commitment." In The King of the Cats and Other Remarks on
    Writers on Writing. New York: Farrar, Strauss & Giroux, pp.
    156-63.
        Reprinted from 1964.7.

4   FINKELSTEIN, SIDNEY. Existentialism and Alienation in
    American Literature. New York: International Publishers
    Co., pp. 268-69.
        In Malamud's fiction both the victim and the victimizer
    are made helpless: first, by the alienating forces in American
    life that make them outsiders; and, second, especially when they
    are Jews, by their remoteness from Judaism.

5   KLEIN, MARCUS. "Bernard Malamud: The Sadness of Goodness."
    In After Alienation. Cleveland: World Publishing Co., pp.
    247-93.
        While possessed of social satire, A New Life, according to
    Malamud, is a romantic love story. This half of the novel
    carries with it a cumulative melancholy associated with its
    hero. For S. Levin, love changes from joy to moral
    responsibility and principle, and his commitment to Pauline
    Gilley, her adopted children, and his own idealism are presented
    in a somber key. Yet the conditions of Levin's new life are the
    source of Malamud's emotional and moral impact. Reprinted
    1970.5, 12.

6   MALIN, IRVING. Jews and Americans. Crosscurrents: Modern
    Critiques, edited by Harry T. Moore. Carbondale and
    Edwardsville: Southern Illinois University Press, pp. 25-28,
    51-54, 75-78, 99-103, 119-21, 134-35.

Various topics involving Malamud appear throughout Malin's book: Malamud's dissociation from traditional Judaism, the father-son relationship, the obsession with time, the conflict between head and heart, occult experience, and the use of irony.

7   SHRUB, PETER. "About the Love and Pity--The Stories of
     Bernard Malamud." Quadrant 9, no. 6 (November-
     December):66-71.
         The uniqueness of Malamud is immediately felt in his
     style, partially in his terse use of simple sentences,
     which are an appropriate medium for dealing with
     death. Beyond this Hemingway-like characteristic, Malamud's
     stylistic stamp is felt in other ways. In "Idiots First,"
     Malamud unites the most poignant of particulars: for example,
     "Isaakil," with the cold abstraction of death, evoking
     in the reader feelings of love and pity.

8   ULANOV, BARRY. The Two Worlds of American Art: The Private
     and the Popular. New York: Macmillan Co.; London: Collier-
     Macmillan, pp. 232-33.
         While The Natural is faulted for its artificiality, The
     Assistant and A New Life are praised for their effective
     evocation of pathos. The Assistant, moreover, is closer to the
     feeling of Yiddish theater than it is to the art of Chagall with
     whom Malamud has been compared.

9   WASSERMAN, EARL R. "The Natural: Malamud's World Ceres."
     Centennial Review 9 (Fall):438-60.
         Malamud's The Natural uses the cultural rites of American
     baseball, and many historical incidents associated with the
     sport, as the vehicle for expressing man's moral potential. The
     literal story of Roy Hobbs, baseball hero, merges with Arthurian
     legend, as does comic melodrama with spiritual quest. The Grail
     vegetation myth, complemented by Jungian archetypal images,
     carries a thematic tension involving death and rebirth.
     Malamud's thematic patterns, human relationships, and symbolic
     resources help to elucidate The Assistant and A New Life.
     Reprinted: 1970.5.

10   WEINTRAUB, BENJAMIN. Review of A New Life. Chicago Jewish
     Forum 24 (Winter):165-66.
         Malamud's characters are well conceived, and his analysis
     of moral questions probing. A curious omission in the book,
     however, is the lack of more than an oblique reference to S.
     Levin as a Jew.

1966

1 ALEXANDER, JAMES E. "Sordid Testimony of Man's Inhumanity to Man." Pittsburgh Post-Gazette, 24 September, p. 19.
        Malamud has always used human suffering and misery as the prerequisites for man's spiritual elevation, and The Fixer offers another example of this theme in his fiction. Once again human degradation serves as the basis for Malamud's affirmative statement about the human spirit. And it is through Yakov Bok's commitment to life and to truth that the novel achieves its power.

2 ALTER, ROBERT. "Malamud as a Jewish Writer." Commentary 42, no. 3 (September):71-76.
        Represents Malamud as the first important American writer to use the immigrant experience as a source for literary fantasy. The fantasylike figures of his stories are united with the schlemiel-schlimazel figure of Jewish folklore in the protagonists of A New Life and The Fixer.

3 ARIMOND, JOHN. "Of Jews and Injustice." Extension: Catholic Church Extension Society of America 61 (November):50.
        As a tale of injustice and suffering, The Fixer brings new meaning to these themes through Malamud's craftmanship and artistry. Although the fate of Yakov Bok is never brought to a clear resolution, the character is less important as an individual man than as a representative of mankind. In this symbolic role, Bok reveals not only the abyss of human degradation but also man's capacity for enoblement.

4 BALLIETT, WHITNEY. "Rub-a-Dub-Dub." New Yorker 42 (10 December):234-35.
        Finds The Fixer a repelling novel because of the repeated brutalities unleashed on Yakov Bok.

5 BAUMBACH, JONATHAN. "Malamud's Heroes: The Fate of Fixers." Commonweal 85 (28 October):97-98.
        Regards The Fixer as original, but a novel that is anachronistic in the context of the cool, dispassionate fiction produced in the 1960s. Baumbach sees Malamud moving from the irony of his earlier novels to a tragic vision culminating in The Fixer.

6 BELLMAN, SAMUEL I[RVING]. Review of The Fixer. Los Angeles Times Calendar, 21 August, p. 16.
        Malamud's book is more of a mood picture than a novel, and consequently it leaves the reader with little to remember. The one exception is the impressive sermon which Yakov Bok delivers

to the investigating magistrate "on justice, law, Russian
history and the Jews."

7   "Bernard Malamud Tells about The Fixer." Literary Guild
     Review, September, n.p.
         Discusses the genesis of the novel. Pondering the use of
     a black hero or figures like Sacco and Vanzetti, Malamud
     eventually settled on an undistinguished man unjustly
     imprisoned. Such figures as Caryl Chessman and Dreyfus were
     considered until Mendel Beiliss, the eventual prototype for
     Yakov, came to mind. Through Bok, Russian injustice of over
     fifty years ago was intended to illuminate injustice in
     comtemporary America.

8   BRESLER, RITA. Review of The Fixer. Library Journal 91, no.
     13 (July):3470.
         Philosophically, The Fixer is reminiscent of Camus's The
     Plague in its concern with freedom, commitment, and respon-
     sibility. The novel is superb in its analysis and drama.

9   BROYARD, ANATOLE. Review of Pictures of Fidelman. New York
     Times Book Review 74 (4 May):5.
         Malamud seems uncomfortable when he writes about a milieu
     distant from that of The Assistant or The Magic Barrel. Perhaps
     this is the reason that the thematic intentions underlying
     Pictures of Fidelman are obscure, its prose glib, and its plots
     contrived.

10   CEVASCO, GEORGE. Review of The Fixer. Sign 46, no. 5
     (December):66-69.
         Utilizing the legend of Jewish ritual murder of Christian
     children, Malamud's novel explores anti-Semitism from a Jewish
     perspective. The impact of the book arises from the inextri-
     cable plight in which Yakov Bok has been placed, and the
     rendering of his personality as he struggles with his fate.

11   COOK, DON L. "Malamud's Scapegoat Novel: Its Factual
     Basis." Louisville Courier Journal, 25 September, p. D5.
         Unlike The Fixer Malamud's earlier novels may at times
     possess brilliance, but they are always uneven; in this most
     recent book, all of his technical facility and imaginative gifts
     come together in a sustained, coherent structure. Even the
     graphic details of Yakov Bok's suffering, which might have
     easily been glaringly obtrusive, are a logical part of
     Malamud's overall design.

12   DAVIS, ROBERT GORHAM. "Invaded Selves." Hudson Review 19,
     no. 4 (Winter 1966-67):659-68.

1966

        Despite Malamud's departures in The Fixer from the
historical account of Maurice Samuel's Blood Accusation, Malamud
has managed to maintain the external fidelity to many of the
facts connected to the Beiliss case. Malamud, however, achieves
a sense of universality by focusing on Yakov Bok's unjust imprisonment and suggests that, like him, the unoffending reader
is also vulnerable to the injustices of life.

13   DEGNAN, JAMES P. "The Ordeal of Yakov Bok." Critic 25, no. 2
      (October-November):102-4.
        Praises The Fixer for its ability to entertain as well as
instruct while communicating as a philosophical novel and a
novel of ideas. Although Malamud's prose is restrained, Yakov
Bok comes through as a dynamic "hero of almost Promethean
spirit, a revolutionist in the tradition of atheistic humanism."

14   EDELMAN, LILY. Review of The Fixer. Jewish Heritage 9, no.
      2 (Fall):3-4.
        Emphasizes that Malamud's novel is more about Yakov Bok's
becoming a "mentsh" than it is about anti-Semitism. "Yakov Bok's
story is the story of all of us, human pygmies in confrontation
with mammoth injustice, giant evil."

15   EHRMANN, HERBERT B. "The Beiliss Case Viewed by Malamud."
      Boston Sunday Herald, 18 September, Showguide, p. 21.
        Based on the 1911 trial of Mendel Beiliss in Kiev, Russia,
The Fixer is first and foremost a novel rather than "a sociological treatise." Because the point of view is restricted to
Yakov Bok, Malamud inevitably avoids a close examination of a
corrupt justice system administered by corrupt officials. His
novel is, nevertheless, a reminder of man's continuing inhumanity to man.

16   ELLIOT, GEORGE P. "Letters to the Editor." New York Times
      Book Review 71 (2 October):46.
        Attempts to clarify his dissatisfaction with Malamud's
equation of suffering with Jewishness (Elliot, 1966.17). Elliot
claims that such a remark is as offensive to non-Jews as a
devout Christian's assertion that only Christ can save is
offensive to Jews. See also Yevish 1966.73.

17   _____. "Yakov's Ordeal." New York Times Book Review 71 (4
      September):1, 25-26.
        Malamud's almost mystical notion that Jewishness is
"latent in all men but manifested in Jews" is unpleasantly
chauvinistic, and there is the potential that his implicit
equation of suffering with Jewishness may be offensive to
non-Jews. Fortunately, The Fixer does not rely on the flippancy
of this equation. As a novel about political terror, it holds

its own with Koestler's <u>Darkness at Noon</u> and Orwell's <u>Nineteen Eighty-Four</u>. It is also, however, a philosophical novel that is concerned with the human condition. At its best, <u>The Fixer</u> is filled with particularized Jews, not merely a vague, sentimental Jewishness. At its weakest, the political and philosophical elements come into collision at the very end. See also Elliot, 1966.16 and Yevish, 1966.73.

18   ELMAN, RICHARD. "Imaginary Crimes and Real Villains." <u>Congress Bi-Weekly: A Journal of Opinion and Jewish Affairs</u> 33 (12 September):10-12.
      While Maurice Samuel's <u>Blood Accusation</u> examines the problem of Russian anti-Semitism, more than it concerns itself with its nondescript victim, Mendel Beiliss, Malamud focuses on character, developing Yakov Bok as "modern Everyman." Bok exists as the heroic transformation of the uninspiring Beiliss and compels the attention and admiration of the reader.

19   FANGER, DONALD. "<u>The Fixer</u> in Another Country." <u>Nation</u> 203 (17 October):389-90.
      Through the sustained use of Yakov Bok's point of view, Malamud generates a pathos and heroism that seem truly authentic. In addition, Bok is the only character in Malamud's fiction who is able to recognize and confront the forces of history. In its concern with the relation of innocence to evil and the problem of God's existence, <u>The Fixer</u> must be read in relation to the work of Dostoevski and Tolstoy.

20   FINEMAN, IRVING. "The Image of the Jew in Our Fiction." <u>Tradition</u> 9, no. 4 (Winter):19-47 passim.
      Examines the image of the Jew in American fiction from an Orthodox Jewish perspective. Bernard Malamud, among others, creates characters who find their Jewish identity an encumbrance. Despite a variety of conflicts with Cascadia's academic community, S. Levin of <u>A New Life</u> functions as a perfectly assimilated Jew in a Gentile community, amazingly free of anti-Semitism or any inner compulsion to make allusion to his Jewish past. Malamud's image of the American Jew is somewhat of a distortion and obscures the reality of those American Jews who consciously live as Jews.

21   FRANKEL, HASKEL. "Bernard Malamud." <u>Saturday Review</u> 49 (10 September):39-40.
      In this interview, Malamud focuses on the Negro's desire for freedom in American history as a historical base for <u>The Fixer</u>, a book dedicated to freedom and the human heart.

22   FREEDMAN, WILLIAM. "So What's the Big Deal?" <u>Chicago Review</u> 19, no. 1:90-107 passim.

1966

      Identifies the three central qualities found in Jewish
fiction: "the patent emotionalism . . . ; its interest in the
problem and experience of suffering; and its almost habitual
embodiment of history and myth." Freedman briefly comments on
The Assistant and The Magic Barrel relative to these qualities.

23   FREMONT-SMITH, ELIOT. "Yakov's Choice." New York Times, 29
       August, p. 27.
      Malamud's The Fixer expresses "the Judaic factor" within
the Judaic-Christian tradition--that is, the continual
affirmation of life against the brutal array of forces that make
suicide seem an acceptable choice. Yakov Bok's magnificent
endurance against physical and spiritual pain loses some of its
impact when we recall that Mendel Beiliss, on whom Bok was
modeled, was acquitted in the actual trial documented by Maurice
Samuel in Blood Accusation. The Fixer is, nevertheless, a rich
and important novel.

24   FRIEDBERG, MAURICE. "History and Imagination: Two Views of
       the Beiliss Case." Midstream 12, no. 9 (November):72-76.
      Compares and contrasts Maurice Samuel's Blood Accusation,
a historical account of the Mendel Beiliss affair, with
Malamud's fictional rendering of it in The Fixer. Malamud, when
appropriate, reconstructs the events surrounding Beiliss to
serve the purposes of his narrative and confines himself only to
those incidents preceding the Beiliss trial itself. In the
novel the dramatic focus is on Yakov Bok's suffering. Samuel's
treatment of the Beiliss story is calm, detached, and
matter-of-fact. Both writers conclude that pity and terror
should be instilled in us by the suffering of the victims apart
from their attractiveness as individuals. Reprinted: 1970.5.

25   FRIEND, JAMES. "Malamud's Heroic Handyman a Symbol of
       Universal Woe." Chicago Daily News, 10 September, Panoramic
       sec., p. 7.
      The Jewish world of The Fixer (like that of The Assistant) is a
microcosm of humanity comparable to Joyce's Dublin or Faulkner's
Yoknapatawpha County. Yakov Bok thus emerges as a symbol of
suffering mankind in any time or place. The guttural language
which Malamud gives his hero is a profane but appropriate medium
for crying out against the injuries and insults which assault
him.

26   FULLER, EDMUND. "Malamud's Novel Aims High but Falls
       Short." Wall Street Journal, 9 September, p. 12.
      Malamud's The Fixer, for all of its force, is a flawed
work. Its impact comes, in part, from its double perspective:
its backward glance at Christian anti-Semitism and its forward
look to the Nazi annihilation of the Jews. In his treatment of

his hero, Yakov Bok, Malamud is guilty of an excess of realism.
He invents superfluous atrocities and obscenities to the extent
of alienating some of his readers. Another defect in the book
is the ending. The anticipated trial scene never materializes,
and instead we have Bok's vision of confronting and
assassinating the Czar. "The obligatory climax of this book had
to be the trial, with Yakov's embracing of his final fate. . . .
Malamud failed the challenge."

27   GELTMAN, MAX. "Irrational Streams of Blood." National
      Review 18 (1 November):1117-19 passim.
          Malamud's imaginative elaboration of Mendel Beiliss's
history (from Maurice Samuel's Blood Accusation) adds an
unneeded dimension of horror and brutality to The Fixer.
Although the book is highly dramatic for the reader, Malamud
makes an unnecessary fetish of suffering.

28   GLANVILLE, BRIAN. "Speaking of Books: Anglo-Jewish
      Writers." New York Times Book Review 71 (17 April):21, 40
      passim.
          The American-Jewish novel as represented by Malamud (or
Bellow) is declining into nothing more than "pastiche," and is
reflected in Malamud's metaphorical statement that all men are
Jews, an assertion that Glanville rejects.

29   GORMAN, THOMAS RICHARD. Review of The Fixer. Today:
      Catholic Student Magazine 22 (November):30-31.
          Although Malamud's book is effective drama, it is flawed
in two areas: the flatness of Yakov Bok and other characters,
and Malamud's excessive treatment of Jewishness and historical
events.

30   GREENFELD, JOSH. "Innocence and Punishment." Washington
      Post Book Week, 11 September, pp. 1, 10.
          The best Jewish writers reflect the unresolved tension of
their dual identity. In The Fixer Malamud has been able to
overcome this problem by committing himself to Yakov Bok's point
of view and thereby centering his novel in the hero's
self-conscious Jewish identity in pre-World War I czarist
Russia. Once again Malamud is the master of an unsentimental
poignancy, but The Fixer has its limitations. With the
exception of Yakov Bok, the other characters are clichés, and
Malamud's failure to develop his plot with sufficient breadth
and depth results in an overly narrow focusing on Bok. The
novel, nevertheless, registers Malamud's characteristically
muted eloquence which partially redeems its flaws.

31   HARDWICK, ELIZABETH. "The Fixer: 'Novel of Startling
      Importance.'" Vogue 148 (1 September):208.

1966

The novel is "brilliant," and "harrowing," a skillful
mixture of history and imagination which, at the same time,
touches on questions similar to those raised by Hannah Arendt
and Bruno Bettelheim concerning the behavior of the Jews under
Nazi persecution.

32   HICKS, GRANVILLE. "One Man Who Stands for Six Million."
        Saturday Review 49 (10 September):37-39.
        The Fixer is a novel of power and universality, and is
among the best in recent American fiction. Originating in the
long history of injustice against the Negro, the persecution of
social martyrs and civil rights activists, and the persecution
of Mendel Beiliss, Malamud's novel tried to represent these
concerns symbolically in Yakov Bok, a man who learns to resist
as well as endure. Reprinted: 1970.9.

33   HOGAN, WILLIAM. "Malamud's Crime and Punishment." San
        Francisco Chronicle, 7 September, p. 39.
        If The Fixer is about anti-Semitism in Russia and moral
resistance to injustice, it is also about the victimization of
the innocent by bureaucracy. An important, powerful novel, it
establishes its hero, in "a nightmarish world of Dostoyevskian
proportions."

34   HOLLIDAY, BARBARA. "A Prisoner of the Czar: Yakov Bok's
        Ritual Torture." Detroit Free Press, 11 September, p. 5B.
        Although The Fixer is centered in czarist Russia, the
narrative is ultimately directed to the problem of suffering in
every generation and in every place. As strong and as well
crafted as this novel is, it is spoiled by what seems to be a
gratuitous use of violence. The tragic sense of the novel is,
as a consequence, deflected by the reader's growing sense of
revulsion.

35   HYMAN, STANLEY EDGAR. "A New Life for a New Man." In
        Standards: A Chronicle of Books for Our Time. New York:
        Horizon Press, pp. 33-37.
        Reprint of 1961.13.

36   JACKSON, KATHERINE GAUSS. Review of The Fixer. Harper's
        233, no. 1397 (October):127-28.
        Malamud's convincing rendering of Yakov Bok's private
suffering and moral growth reflects his "genius." Consequently,
the reader achieves a vicarious self-esteem in identifying with
his hero. "The book is a remarkable creative achievement."

37   JAFFE, DAN. "Crime and Punishment of Innocence." Kansas
        City Star, 11 September, p. 7E.

The Fixer may not possess the dazzle of a best seller, but it is a novel that will have lasting significance: it is the kind of book that a reader will return to when he hungers for a spiritual renewal. To his credit, Malamud has created a prose that is lucid and a style that is free of technical complexities. Although the book is anchored in historical fact, Malamud distills imaginative truth from history. Indeed, he is so adept in re-creating the time, character, and place of czarist Russia that one soon forgets that this is the work of a contemporary writer.

38   JOHNSON, BROOK. Review of The Fixer. Negro Digest 16, no. 1 (November):52.
        Praises this novel for Malamud's ability to synchronize character and story line and for the universality of its theme. With a few changes in details, this story might take place anywhere and be true to the experience of a representative of any minority group.

39   KENNEDY, WILLIAM. "The Frightening Beiliss Case in Fictional, Scholarly Perspective." National Observer, 5 September, p. 19.
        It is an interesting coincidence that the publication of Maurice Samuel's Blood Accusation and Bernard Malamud's The Fixer should have occurred within the same year. Malamud takes the historically unheroic Mendel Beiliss and transforms him into an existential hero: "a Jew without a world, without a God, with only his inner resources to nourish him." Malamud's digressions into historical and philosophical discussion do not really contribute to an otherwise successful novel.

40   LIPTZIN, SOLOMON. The Jew in American Literature. New York: Block Publishing Co., pp. 226-28.
        While in the past Jews were urged to find the truth in Christianity, Malamud reverses history and allows Jews and non-Jews to discover the "deeper truth of Judaism." Such instances occur in The Assistant and "The Lady of the Lake."

41   LYNCH, WILLIAM. "Malamud's New Novel and . . . ." Providence Sunday Journal, 11 September, p. H-9
        The characters in Malamud's fiction are highly individualized and easily remembered. Yakov Bok in The Fixer is no exception. An ordinary but compelling character, Bok illustrates that even the most inconsequential of men are capable of heroic stature. As an ethically oriented writer, Malamud is joined by such contemporaries as Bellow, Roth, Mailer, and Gold. See also accompanying interview with Malamud (Meras, 1966.45).

1966

42   McCOLUM, PEARLMARIE. "The Revised New Syllabus and the
        Unrevised Old." University of Denver Quarterly 1, no. 3
        (Autumn):136-41 passim.
           While writers like Barth claim that the realistic novel is
        no longer possible, Malamud's The Fixer continues in that
        tradition. Although excellent in its own way, The Fixer does
        not inspire the reader as much as The Assistant. Morris Bober's
        capacity to relate to Frank Alpine and, by extension, to mankind
        makes Yakov Bok seem too inward and cerebral a character by
        comparison.

43   MADDOCKS, MELVIN. "Malamud's Heroic Handyman." Christian
        Science Monitor, 8 September, p. 13.
           Malamud is the only contemporary writer who had been able
        to prevent his victim from becoming an antihero, and in The
        Fixer Yakov Bok develops along the lines of the traditional
        hero. Because of its density of texture and Yiddish idiom, this
        "amazing novel" must be experienced as more than "a moral
        abstract."

44   MATHEWSON, JOSEPH. Review of The Fixer. Harper's Bazaar 99
        (November):116.
           The Fixer has as much depth as Kafka's The Trial. It
        differs from the latter, however, in emphasizing irrational
        cruelty that is directly physical rather than psychological and,
        as a result, it has more of an immediate impact on the reader.
        While Kafka's Joseph K. is a symbol of modern man, Malamud's
        Yakov Bok "is the eternal sufferer . . . at home in the first
        century as in the twentieth."

45   MERAS, PHYLLIS. ". . . An Interview with its Author."
        Providence Sunday Journal, 11 September, p. H-9.
           Malamud discussed with the interviewer the origins of The
        Fixer. After his short story, "The German Refugee," Malamud
        decided that he wanted to write about politics again but on a
        larger scale, with an emphasis on man's significance. Thus
        through his conception of Yakov Bok, Malamud was able to achieve
        an allusiveness that at once referred to the persecution of
        blacks in America and the destruction of the Jews by the Nazis.
        See also accompanying review (Lynch, 1966.41).

46   MUDRICK, MARVIN. "Who Killed Herzog? Or, Three American
        Novelists." University of Denver Quarterly 1, no. 1
        (Spring):61-96.
           Expresses skepticism over the value of the Jew as sufferer
        in contemporary American literature since anti-Semitism, its
        root cause, is presumably no longer an agency of his suffering.

Thus the heroes of Malamud, Bellow, and Roth--in their exaggerated unhappiness--seem anachronistic and unconvincing. When the Jew is presented as suffering victim in their novels, it is usually the result of his desire for a manipulative non-Jewish woman. Reprinted: 1970.18.

47   "The Outsider." Time 88 (9 September):106, 108.
        Because of its dialogue and wit, The Fixer "is a re-markable work," a humanistic tragedy; its only disappointment is that it fails to be anchored in a contemporary American society.

48   PETERSON, VIRGINIA. "Fact of the Matter." Reporter 35 (20 October):57-58.
        Bernard Malamud's The Fixer and Maurice Samuel's Blood Accusation are reviewed jointly. The Fixer, although a distinguished work of the imagination, does not satisfy the reader with sufficient attention to historical fact. "While Mr. Samuel, in his documented presentation . . . stands on the outside looking in, Mr. Malamud . . . stands on the inside looking out."

49   PETRARKIS, HARRY MARK. "One Man's Battle Against Injustice." Chicago Tribune: Books Today, 11 September, p. 1.
        Considers Yakov Bok's experiences in The Fixer similar to those of early Christians. In Malamud's novel, however, Bok takes on the lineaments of a tragic hero, but the book also evokes the tragic history of a people so often rendered in Yiddish literature. In his representation of injustice, Malamud takes his place with Sholom Aleichem, I.L. Peretz, and Isaac Bashevis Singer.

50   PHILLIPSON, JOHN S. Review of The Fixer. Best Sellers 26 (15 September):211.
        This novel makes a deeply religious statement about man's mysterious ability to cope with suffering in behalf of justice and mankind. The capacity of some Christians for great cruelty must be a numbing experience for other Christians.

51   PINSKER, SANFORD [SIGMUND]. "Salinger, Malamud and Wallant: The Jewish Novelist's Quest." Reconstructionist 32 (25 November):7-14 passim.
        These three Jewish novelists are involved in a quest for Christ, the outgrowth of the thin line separating Jewish and Christian ethics. In The Assistant, for example, Morris Bober is associated with two Christian motifs: redemptive suffering and the feeding of the poor. "Even Bober's sacred notion of the law is really more 'Christian' than Jewish."

1966

52   PRITCHETT, V.S.   "A Pariah."   New York Review of Books 7 (22
      September):8-10.
          Anchored in Jewish fable, the Russian novel, and Russian
      history, The Fixer achieves its own originality primarily
      through Yakov Bok: "the drama of the crisis of moral
      consciousness in a pariah who has been forced to think for
      himself." Capable of wit, and a kind of black comedy in the
      midst of his suffering, Bok remains recognizably human through
      the novel. Malamud's artistic deftness is also visible in his
      building of a tight, suspenseful plot.

53   Review of The Fixer. Choice 3, no. 9:771
          This novel is reminiscent of Singer's The Slave and
      Schwarz-Bart's The Last of the Just (1960), but Malamud's Yakov
      Bok seems to have greater substance than the characters of these
      other novels.

54   RIBALOW, HAROLD U.   "What's This Jewish Book Craze All
      About?" National Jewish Monthly 81, no. 3 (November):48-49.
          A number of significant Jewish novels, including Malamud's
      The Assistant, have had a delayed general reader acceptance.
      Early partisan critics of Malamud's The Assistant, recognizing
      it as a major work, did not dream that it would win The National
      Book Award. The Fixer "has attracted a degree of attention
      absent when The Assistant was published a short decade ago."
      Moris Bober and Yakov Bok have given added stature to Jews.

55   RICHMAN, SIDNEY. Bernard Malamud. New York: Twayne
      Publishers, 160 pp.
          Offers an analysis of specific novels and stories with
      chapter 1 supplying an exceptionally acute overview of Malamud's
      work. This chapter is subdivided into five special topics:
      "The 'Jewishness' of Malamud"; "The Self Alone"; "Struggle for
      Roots"; "Literary Tradition"; "Malamud's Comic Mode." Central
      to Richman's reading is the observation that Malamud's Jews are
      cut off from society and themselves while harboring an identity
      which they bear either consciously or unconsciously. "It is the
      struggle to establish unity with some unacknowledged center of
      one's personalty, a quest for lost roots, which directs
      Malamud's Jewish heroes." Chapter 2 is devoted to The Natural;
      chapter 3, The Assistant; chapter 4, A New Life; chapter 5, "The
      Stories." In chapter 6, "Conclusion," Malamud is perceived as
      "tending the resources of human personality which seem to be
      disappearing not just from literature but from life itself." A
      selected annotated bibliography concludes the book. Reprinted
      in part: 1970.5.

56   ROSENTHAL, RAYMOND. "A Christian Problem." New Leader 49
      (12 September):18-19.

Trying to render the rhythms of Yiddish speech spoken in Russia became a stylistic obstacle for Malamud in The Fixer as much as it was for Hemingway when he tried to convey the rhythms of Spanish in For Whom the Bells Tolls. When Yakov Bok moves into a general colloquial English, free of Yiddish inflection, he finds a new and convincing voice. Having meaning beyond the historical moment, the materials of his novel serve as a parable for contemporary anti-Semitism. "Anti-Semitism is not an occasion for a search for Jewish identity; it is a Christian problem."

57   S., P. "Malamud's 'The Fixer': Great Novel, Superb Condemnation of Czarist Cruelty." Detroit Jewish News, 9 September, p. 30.
      Both as a novel and as a social document, Malamud's book is the best of its kind in a decade, and Yakov Bok emerges as one of Malamud's greatest characters. Even though the author himself prefers to see the novel as a universal commentary on the suffering of all men, "Malamud has nevertheless exposed the crime of the Beiliss case and of the ritual murder charge."

58   SAMUELS, CHARLES THOMAS. "The Career of Bernard Malamud." New Republic 155 (10 September):19-21.
      Malamud's first novel, The Natural, was largely ignored; the second, The Assistant, established his reputation and was generally acknowledged to be an important work; the third, A New Life, was artistically uneven. His latest book, The Fixer, repels because of its essential violence and its unconvincing plot. Its contrived dramatic structure makes it a more suitable art form for the stage. Malamud is, nevertheless, a disciplined and skillful writer, an asset to contemporary American literature, but he has been unduly influenced by critics to become a writer of social consciousness. Abridged: 1972.38.

59   "Schlemiel Triumphant." Newsweek 68 (12 September)109-10.
      In The Fixer Malamud has departed from Maurice Samuel's Blood Accusation, with its emphasis on the public trial, in order to concentrate on the subjective responses of Yakov Bok to his entire ordeal. Thus the reader is in close touch with the transformation in personality Bok undergoes from schlemiel to hero. In an interview with Saul Maloff of Newsweek, Malamud appraised The Fixer as his best work, partially because it reflects his humanistic vision: "The defense of the human is the great thing. The great thing is to explicate life in order to defend it."

60   SCHOLES, ROBERT. Review of The Fixer. Northwest Review 8, no. 2 (Fall-Winter):106-8.

1966

Although Malamud's individual style and tone are still recognizable in The Fixer, this work does not possess the artistic finish of his three earlier novels. The major deficiency of The Fixer is its limited development of Yakov Bok's character. The use of dream materials or opposing characters in conjunction with Bok are inadequate agents for his development. In short, Malamud's attempt to blend history with imagination does not work. Enlarged: 1979.54.

61   SCHOTT, WEBSTER. "A Small Man Uncrushed by Brutal Power."
      Life 61 (16 September):14.
      Malamud's The Fixer is another successful example of the author's thematic affirmation of life against death. Yakov Bok's Job-like sufferings are convincingly dramatized as Bok, through "speech, gesture, [and] motive," reveals his fundamental humanity. Emotionally, the reader is compelled to experience Malamud's vision.

62   SCHROTH, RAYMOND A. Review of The Fixer. America 115 (17
      September):284.
      Malamud's novel takes the theme of suffering found in his earlier fiction to a new plateau of meaning. Although Malamud claims that suffering is, in essence, a Jewish experience, Christians will find universal meaning in it. Possibly, the American reader will not feel the sickness of czarist Russia with the immediacy that he would feel if Malamud had probed the sickness of American society.

63   SHEAR, WALTER. "Culture and Conflict in 'The Assistant.'"
      Midwest Quarterly 7, no. 4 (Summer):367-80.
      The Assistant dramatizes the conflicting cultural forces at work through Malamud's fiction. Jewish tradition collides with American cultural values, the American success story with the reality of poverty, producing anguish and despair in the characters. Ultimately, it is Morris Bober's Jewish experience that sustains the ethical vision of the novel. Reprinted: 1970.5

64   SHULMAN, ROBERT. "Myth, Mr. Eliot, and the Comic Novel."
      Modern Fiction Studies 12, no. 4 (Winter 1966-67):395-403.
      Considers Malamud's The Natural a significant advance over the novels of F. Scott Fitzgerald and Nathaniel West in its comic and surrealistic adaptation of T.S. Eliot's The Waste Land. Through idiomatic usage, absurdity, fantasy, and jokes Malamud's use of Eliot's techniques and motifs gains freshness.

65   SPIEGEL, MOISHE. Review of The Fixer. Chicago Jewish Forum
      25 (Winter):152-54.
          Unlike Maurice Samuel's Blood Accusation, Malamud's The
      Fixer uses fact as an imaginative departure for the purposes of
      his novel. In keeping with his thematic intentions, Malamud
      elaborates the suffering of Yakov Bok at the expense of his-
      torical accuracy. The most annoying flaw in the novel, however,
      is the excessive detail used at the beginning which proves to be
      an obstacle to reader interest. At times the novel stirs that
      interest by reading like a detective story inviting the reader
      to ponder the outcome of Bok's trial. Unfortunately, the trial
      is never dramatized, and the novel never reaches a point of
      emotional and intellectual climax.

66   STELLA, CHARLES. "Malamud Adds to Literary Stature."
      Cleveland Press, 9 September, p. 16.
          The strength of The Fixer likes in its hero, Yakov Bok,
      who is a vehicle of humor, wisdom, and gentleness. Bok is an
      imaginative triumph who has helped to increase the already high
      stature of Malamud's art.

67   STERN, DANIEL. "Novel on Blood Libel Is Malamud's Best."
      Hadassah 48, no. 1 (September):15.
          Regards this novel as Malamud's greatest achievement thus
      far. It is especially successful in its ability to unite the
      world of nineteenth-century Russia with a twentieth-century
      vision and technique. The characterization of Yakov Bok as an
      ordinary man without any special resources at the outset of his
      ordeal makes him all the more compelling a hero. In his
      excursion into political philosophy, however, Malamud begins to
      sound formulaic. At its best, the book "is a rich compound of
      irony, folk humor and sophisticated imagery."

68   THORP, DAY. "Malamud's Powerful Novel about Justice."
      Washington Sunday Star, 11 September, p. G2.
          The Fixer is ultimately about man's quest for justice; the
      issues of anti-Semitism and the Jewish condition in czarist
      Russia must be considered secondary subjects.

69   TUCKER, MARTIN. Review of The Fixer. Commonweal 85 (2
      December):272.
          Without resorting to irony and stylistic experiments,
      Malamud presents simply and directly a harrowing but
      nevertheless beautiful narrative, gradually allowing the hero,
      Yakov Bok, to grow through experiencing the pain of human
      indignity.

70   WEISS, SAMUEL. "Passion and Purgation in Bernard Malamud."
      University of Windsor Review 2, no. 1 (Fall):93-99.

1966

The highest priority of Malamud's art is to deepen the humanity of the reader. In this connection suffering becomes an educative experience for both the Malamud hero and the reader. In A New Life S. Levin's willingness to suffer in behalf of others is clear, but his motivations remain elusive. (The article does not cite secondary sources.)

71   WOHLGELERNTER, MAURICE. "Blood Libel--Fact and Fiction." Tradition 8, no. 3 (Fall):62-72.
        Maurice Samuel's historical account, Blood Accusation, possesses the imaginative impact of fiction, while Bernard Malamud's The Fixer is a magnificent imaginative rendering of fact. Both writers concern themselves with the use of the big lie, the tactic by which modern governments undermine rational thought. For Malamud the dramatization of Yakov Bok's suffering takes precedence over Samuel's presentation of the legal process. Malamud's use of the Beiliss case may have been stimulated by his personal discovery in the fifties of a de-pleted European Jewry. In The Fixer, Malamud turns militant and insists that the Jews in taking direct action on their own behalf also act for humanity.

72   "Yakov, Fixer of Everything." St. Louis Globe Democrat, 17-18 September, p. 4F.
        The Fixer does not provide us with the kind of hero we have in Hemingway's fiction, the man who is courageous in a particular moment of time. Rather, Malamud's hero, Yakov Bok, is an embodiment of the collective heroism of ordinary people through the centuries.

73   YEVISH, IRVING. "Letter to the Editors." New York Times Book Review 71 (2 October):46.
        Dissents from Elliot's view (1966.17) that Malamud's metaphorical equation of Jewishness with suffering is potentially offensive to non-Jews and goes on to reject Elliot's assertion that Russia under the czar, despite its many perversions, "was still a recognizably civilized state." See also Elliot (1966.16).

1967

1   BAKER, WILLIAM. Review of The Fixer. World Jewry 10 (May-June):25.
        This novel is characterized as much by its American idiom as by its Russian names and settings. The orientation that Malamud would like the reader to receive remains unclear. His materials do not have an authentic ring, and the novel seems to be orchestrated for the sake of its best-seller potential.

2   BLUMBERG, ARNOLD. "Two Boards, One Pawn." Jewish Life
       (March-April):73-79.
       Although Maurice Samuel and Bernard Malamud are highly
talented in their own genres, neither Blood Accusation nor The
Fixer are wholly successful. Samuel's book is occasionally
marred by his departure from a chronological order which
includes comments on Mendel Beiliss's trial before Beiliss is
ever indicted; and Malamud's Yakov Bok possesses a courage that
is unrelated either to the love of God or the love of himself.
Rather, it seems to emerge from "a perverse stubbornness."
Blumberg denies Bok the role of the existential hero who
struggles against a capricious fate for the sake of humanity.

3   BOOKMAN, PETER. "Poet of the Ordinary." Books and Bookmen
       12, no. 7 (April):68, 73.
       Malamud has demonstrated a unique grasp of his characters
in previous fiction, and The Fixer is no exception. His
continued insight into human nature is revealed through Yakov
Bok's gradual maturation in consciousness and conscience. Not
exclusively a Jewish book, The Fixer makes human catastrophe its
central theme, and through its artistic control, dramatic
impact, and intense reader involvement, the novel has all the
earmarks of a masterpiece.

4   BRADBURY, MALCOLM. "Far Beyond the Pale." Manchester
       Guardian Weekly 96 (13 April):13.
       Although The Fixer is undoubtedly an important novel, it
is not Malamud at his best. Yakov Bok's characterization
becomes thin as the novel, losing "density and texture," moves
in the direction of parable.

5   BURGESS, ANTHONY. "Blood on the Matzos." Spectator 218 (14
       April):424-25.
       Discusses The Fixer in relation to Maurice Samuel's Blood
Accusation. Malamud's alteration of Samuel's materials are for
the sake of unity and immediacy. In The Fixer Yakov Bok's
consciousness becomes the exclusive point of view, and Malamud's
sustained use of the jail as setting evokes in the receptive
reader a sense of the inescapable human condition.

6   _____. The Novel Now: A Student Guide to Contemporary
       Fiction. London: Faber & Faber, pp. 197-98. Reprint. New
       York: Norton, 1967.
       Malamud's novels have greater kinship with the values of
Yiddish literature than with the fiction of Herbert Gold or Saul
Bellow. The relationship between spirit and flesh, between the
natural and the supernatural in Malamud's books, recalls the
quality of mind of his Yiddish predecessors. At the same time,
"Malamud is devoid either of conventional piety or sentimentality."

1967

7   CHARLES, GERDA. Review of The Fixer. Conservative Judaism
        21, no. 3 (Spring):80-81.
            Praises this novel for its ability to render the horror
        and the poignancy of Yakov Bok's role as victim. Malamud
        creates out of the raw materials of Bok's misfortunes, failures,
        and character an authentic embodiment of Jewishness. "Mr.
        Malamud's imagination is a strange, brilliant and terrifying
        garden."

8   CORKE, HILLARY. "New Novels." Listener 77 (13 April):501.
            In this review of The Fixer, Corke finds the novel lacking
        in major flaws or abounding in artistic virtues. Its
        deficiencies, however, preempt the commentary. The novel
        suffers from a too easy manipulation of the reader's emotions, a
        lack of depth, and the dullness of the hero.

9   "Dr. Rahv Evaluates Noted Author's Jewishness in 'Malamud
        Reader.'" Jewish News (Detroit), 10 September, p. 10.
            The introduction to this collection discusses the key
        elements of Malamud's Jewishness--his special sensibility,
        compassion, and concern with suffering--as well as the
        Jewishness of some of his contemporaries.

10   ELKIN, STANLEY. "The Fixer." Massachusetts Review 8, no. 2
        (Spring):388-92.
            The immediate appeal of The Fixer is in its ability to
        move the reader. But this very quality is really an expression
        of its unfortunate melodramatic tactics: the novel is tuned to
        a high pitch of almost unrelieved physical and psychological
        aggression. Intellectually, the novel lacks depth since there
        is no intelligent devil's advocate to challenge Yakov Bok's
        moral position.

11   FEATHERSTONE, JOSEPH. "Bernard Malamud." Atlantic Monthly
        219 (March):95-98.
            An appreciation of Malamud and a recapitulation of some
        critical judgments on his fiction. Malamud celebrates the
        individual life rather than a community or people. Stylisti-
        cally, he is noted for mixing the commonplace and the
        grotesque. Although Yakov Bok of The Fixer is a memorable
        figure, Malamud has inflated his stature beyond the credible.
        Finally, the author's own ambivalence toward his Jewishness is
        reflected in his work.

12   FINEMAN, IRVING. "The Image of the Jew in Fiction of the
        Future." National Jewish Monthly 83, no. 4 (December):48-51.
            Considers Malamud's Jews the idealized products of the
        author's imagination. Such figures as Morris Bober of The
        Assistant and S. Levin of A New Life lack credibility.

56

Successful future novelists who attempt to portray Jews authentically will have to fortify them with a knowledge of their Jewish inheritance.

13   FLEISCHMANN, WOLFGANG BERNARD. "The Contemporary 'Jewish Novel.'" Jahrbuch für Amerikastudien 12:159-66 passim.
      Denies that there is an identifiable genre as the so-called "Jewish Novel." The qualities which Malamud invests in his characters in The Assistant--"suffering, charity, and hope"--belong to Christians as well as Jews. "As Malamud's Gentile Frank Alpine commits himself to Judaism, his Jewish Helen Bober goes off to college and, by implication, to the great American world."

14   GRABER, RALPH. "Baseball in American Fiction." English Journal 56, no. 8 (November):1107-14.
      This survey of baseball fiction is directed to secondary school English teachers, and notes that Malamud's The Natural offers insights into human behavior and the tragicomedy of modern existence. "Malamud has shown how difficult is to be a hero . . .[and] resist the forbidden fruits which the masses of weaker flesh enjoy."

15   GREIFF, LOUIS K. "Quest and Defeat in The Natural." Thoth 8 (Winter):23-34.
      Discusses the geometry of baseball--the straight line and the circle, expressed in the home run and circling the base paths. As a diagrammatic metaphor for unity and wholeness, it expresses the healthy balance between life and death which Roy Hobbs fails to grasp. The eternal child, Malamud's hero yearns for connection only with the vital energies of life. Thus he compulsively courts Memo Paris who supplies him with a vision of sustained erotic bliss, and he rejects Iris Lemon, despite her own erotic powers, because they are limited by her associations with time and death. His failure to choose wisely in women reflects his errors of judgment at the plate.

16   HANDY, WILLIAM J. "Malamud's The Fixer: Another Look." Northwest Review 8, no. 3 (Spring):74-82.
      Dissents from Robert Scholes's (1966.60) evaluation of The Fixer as a poor historical novel which fails to portray external events. The heart of the book really lies in Yakov Bok's subjective response to events around him. Appropriately, the question of Bok's literal freedom in the final section is never introduced: "it is not the thematic problem of the novel."

1967

17   HUTCHINSON, J.D. "Jewish Heritage Enhances Malamud's Work."
Sunday Denver Post, 3 December, p. 19.
    Reviews A Malamud Reader and concurs with its editor,
Philip Rahv, that Malamud is distinguished from other
contemporary Jewish writers in his conscious attempt to confront
Jewish sensibility and experience and to affirm humanistic
themes. His most notable success in these areas is "The Magic
Barrel." The other stories in this collection serve as a useful
index to the themes and techniques of Malamud's other work.

18   INGLIS, RUTH. "The Book-Makers." Nova, 17 August, p. 16.
    An interview with Bernard Malamud in London. Malamud,
appearing serious throughout the meeting, entertained questions
on the autobiographical element in his fiction, on The Fixer,
and on his character, Arthur Fidelman. Malamud minimized the
autobiographical part of his work asserting that his fiction
involved "acts of the imagination," and that as a writer, he had
many voices. "After we parted it struck me that this great
comic writer had not laughed once in the entire hour."

19   JACOBSON, DAN. "The Old Country." Partisan Review 34, no. 2
(Spring):307-8.
    This review of The Fixer expresses ambivalence. The book
is awkward in its handling of historical setting and character.
The Russia of the novel is placed in conversation rather than
actually dramatized, and the characters serve as "represen-
tatives and explainers" rather than being individualized. The
novel, nevertheless, has the unforgettable Malamud style and is
often highly dramatic.

20   KEMPTON, KENNETH PAYSON, ed. "For Plot Read Idea." In Short
Stories for Study. Cambridge, Mass.: Harvard University
Press, pp. 316-21.
    Speculates on Malamud's creative process and its relation
to his artistic execution in "The Prison." The germ for
Malamud's story begins with a man whose mind is as confining as
any actual prison. Within the plot, the protagonist's sense of
entrapment is externalized through the unwanted wife, Rosa, and
the ungrateful girl, his symbolic double. Both figures are
effectively used as obstacles to his real and imagined freedom.

21   KILLINGER, JOHN. "Is Anybody There?" Christian Herald 90,
      no. 3 (March):49, 56-57.
          Responds to The Fixer from a Christian perspective. The
      novel is another example of the death-of-God theology which,
      understandably, seems more prevalent among Jewish writers than
      Christian. Malamud avoids a final resolution, and this
      inconclusiveness seems appropriate because Yakov Bok's situation
      is ongoing and universal. Malamud, however, does not recognize
      "the true significance of the suffering of Christ, which is
      fully understood only in the light of the resurrection." While
      Malamud's Bok concludes that suffering is pointless, Dostoevski
      perceives suffering as the only vehicle through which God is
      known.

22   KING, FRANCIS. "Wrenched from Obscurity." Sunday Telegraph,
      9 April, p. 9.
          While The Fixer is a good novel, it is nevertheless
      depressing. In addition to creating an unusual hero, Malamud
      has managed to achieve the richness of detail, dramatic
      structure, and sharply defined characterization reminiscent of
      Dostoevski. The major flaw of the book is Malamud's occasional
      tendency to moralize rather than dramatize.

23   KRAMER, MAURICE. "The Secular Mode of Jewishness." Works 1,
      no. 1 (Autumn):99-116 passim.
          The Assistant does not celebrate traditional ritualistic
      Judaism. For Morris Bober, minding the store is, in itself, an
      act of faith and a symbol of his ethical existence, as it later
      becomes for Frank Alpine, his assistant. "Frank most unexis-
      tentially accepts a body of truth, a ritual, a way of life
      serving a purpose." To the extent that such behavior, with its
      attendant suffering, keeps human feeling alive, it serves a
      meaningful purpose.

24   KUEHL, JOHN. "Characterization & Structure" Bernard
      Malamud." In Creative Writing & Rewriting: Contemporary
      American Novelists at Work. New York: Meredith Publishing
      Co., Appleton-Century-Crofts, pp. 69-96. Reprint in: Write
      and Rewrite: A Study of the Creative Process (1967).
          Discusses the changes Malamud made in the story, "A Long
      Ticket for Isaac," until its final draft as "Idiots First." The
      essential alterations in the latter are in character and
      structure. While Mendel is referred to early in "A Long Ticket
      for Isaac" as a dying man, his true condition is not immediately
      recognized in "Idiots First" until the scenes in the cafeteria
      and the rabbi's house. The structure of the first draft is
      anticlimactic since the Ginzburg-Mendel confrontation occurs
      well before the story ends. In "Idiots First" Malamud included
      fresh material at the end of the story which adds to the
      strength of both characterization and structure.

1967

25   LANDIS, JOSEPH C. "Reflections on Jewish American Writers."
      In Jewish Book Annual, vol. 25. New York: Jewish Book Council
      of America, 140-47 passim.
          If one were to accept the premise that a homogeneous
      school of Jewish writing exists, it would have to be based on
      the ethical vision of Judaism of such writers as Saul Bellow and
      Bernard Malamud who share the ideal of Mentshlekhkayt. This
      ideal is especially relevant to Malamud who conceives of Jewish
      experience as a metaphor for man's moral growth.

26   LEECH, ANASTASIA. Review of The Fixer. Tablet 221 (15
      April):416.
          Unlike Kafka's surrealistic rendering of suffering,
      Malamud's presentation of it in this novel is realistic in its
      detail. Given Malamud's humane vision, and absence of
      stylization, these two works are largely dissimilar. "The Fixer
      is about the Jew in history . . . and though in no way unique it
      makes its contribution to the pool of such records in the fiction
      of this century."

27   LEHAN, RICHARD. "The American Novel--A Survey of 1966."
      Wisconsin Studies in Contemporary Literature 8, no. 3
      (Summer):437-49 passim.
          The power of The Fixer comes from Malamud's ability to
      impose on Yakov Bok a timeless state of suffering in which his
      psychological and intellectual processes are gradually
      revealed. For Yakov Bok the conditions of czarist Russia are
      hellish, and "for Malamud, Hell really exists--not in some
      distant underworld--but in the world that men create and allow
      to exist."

28   LEVIANT, CURT. "'The Fixer' Fixation." Jewish Frontier 34,
      no. 1 (January):24-25.
          Argues that Malamud's novels grow progressively worse, and
      The Fixer is no exception. The novel is essentially melodra-
      matic, and it contains the artistic principles on which melo-
      drama operates: for example, hurried exposition, animated
      conversation at the beginning, stock characters, and dialogue
      unrelated to personality. Maurice Samuel's Blood Accusation,
      published in the same year as The Fixer, is a more satisfactory
      treatment of the same subject.

29   LEWIN, LOIS SYMONS. "The Theme of Suffering in the Work of
      Bernard Malamud and Saul Bellow." Ph.D. dissertation,
      University of Pittsburgh, 209 pp.
          Compares and contrasts the nature and significance of
      suffering in the fiction of these writers. Malamud's novels and
      stories suggest that suffering is "a precondition of existence,
      the one possible mode of goodness and engagement in the world,"

serving as a badge of one's human identity. Eventually, it leads to affirmation and a kind of religious ecstasy. In Bellow's work suffering has no significance unless it offers the hero an insight into life, and it is often abruptly terminated through some mysterious but nevertheless cathartic experience: "communicating with a lion, weeping at a stranger's funeral, or lying in a hammock watching the stars." See Dissertation Abstracts International 38 (1968):5021A-22A.

30   LOCKERBIE, D. BRUCE. "Some Things Can't Be Fixed." Eternity 18, no. 2 (February):56.
        Asserts that Yakov Bok of The Fixer fulfills the criteria for the Aristotelian tragic hero. Bok is neither unusual for his goodness nor his vice, but he is nevertheless flawed by some error. "Bok's error is . . . his being a Jew in Csarist Russia." The Christians in The Fixer who persecute Jews have as much reality as contemporary Christians.

31   MALAMUD, BERNARD. "'Living Is Guessing What Reality Is.'" U.S. News and World Report 87 (8 October):57.
        Comments on mass culture, artistic creativity, and the illusion in reality: Malamud feels that he is given a great deal of freedom by his publisher at a time when publishers have become purely profit making conglomerates; that students currently have become more concerned than in previous years about writing well; that writing is largely hard work rather than a continual flow of inspiration; and, finally, that reality is ultimately unknowable. "The more I experience life," Malamud observed, "the more I become aware of illusion as primary experience."

32   _____. "Theme, Content and the 'New Novel.'" New York Times Book Review 72 (26 March):2, 29.
        The observations in this essay are part of Malamud's acceptance speech for the National Book Award given for The Fixer. Malamud considers the writer's conscious use of a major theme meaningful if it causes him to make an artistically meaningful response to it. An opposing view, the Robbe-Grillet theory of the novel, does not concern itself with theme or the writer's response to his materials. Surely, after the catastrophes of the twentieth century, the artist must try to understand the meaning of human experience. "Art must interpret, or it is mindless."

33   MARCUS, MORDECAI. "The Unsuccessful Malamud." Prairie Schooner 41, no. 1 (Spring):88-89.
        The limitations of The Fixer are detailed in this review. The novel is simplistic in conception, melodramatic in plot, and lacking in humor. "The result is an essentially static picture pretending to be dynamic."

1967

34 MELLARD, JAMES M. "Malamud's Novels: Four Versions of
    Pastoral." Critique 9, no. 2:5-19.
        Malamud's use of the pastoral mode supplies him with an
    extremely effective set of received conventions in narrative
    structure, characterization, imagery and symbolism, and
    rhetorical strategy. The controlling archetype in each of his
    novels involves a son replacing a father or a young hero
    replacing the old. In The Natural other mystic associations are
    present and include vegetation rites, the Fisher King motif, and
    the Grail quest. In novels such as The Assistant and The Fixer,
    these elements undergo special adaptation. Finally, at the
    center of Malamud's pastoral mode is the Jew as mythical man,
    embodying all the possibilities of the human condition. Thus,
    "to be anti-Semitic is to be against the human being."
    Reprinted: 1970.5.

35 MELLARD, JAMES, [M.]. "Malamud's The Assistant: The City
    Novel as Pastoral." Studies in Short Fiction 5, no. 1
    (Fall):1-11.
        Asserts that Malamud's lower-class and proletarian
    characters, his use of nature imagery, and his themes of death
    and rebirth are, in effect, adaptations of pastoral conventions.

36 PINSKER, SANFORD SIGMUND. "The Schlemiel as Metaphor:
    Studies in the Yiddish and American Jewish Novel." Ph.D.
    dissertation, University of Washington, 278 pp.
        Defines the schlemiel as a character prone to misfortune
    but who is nevertheless sustained by an ironic vision of himself
    and the world. Pinsker traces the schlemiel's origins to the
    biblical story of Shelumiel ben Zurishadda (Num. 1:6) as well as
    the Talmudic commentaries. This study closely examines the work
    of Mendele Mocher Seforum, Sholom Aleichem, Isaac Bashevis
    Singer, Bernard Malamud, and Saul Bellow. In the work of the
    last two writers, the psychological difficulties of the
    schlemiel are addressed. See Dissertation Abstracts
    International 28 (1968):3679A-80A. Revised for publication:
    1971.35.

37 PRICE, R.G.G. "New Novels." Punch 252 (March):319.
        The Fixer is a backward glance at the plight of Jews prior
    to their experiences in America. Malamud's narrative skill is a
    major accomplishment in "making boredom and dread and timeless-
    ness continually gripping." Unfortunately, Malamud does not say
    anything new about them.

38 RAHV, PHILIP, ed. Introduction to A Malamud Reader. New
    York: Farrar, Straus & Giroux, pp. vii-xiv.

Malamud's preoccupation with Jewishness is a source of his major themes and also is the basis for his style and language. He is more successful in his short stories than in his novels, and perhaps The Magic Barrel is the best example of his mastery of technique in this genre. Reprinted: 1969.37.

39   RATNER, MARC. "The Humanism of Malamud's The Fixer." Critique 9, no. 2:81-84.
The Fixer represents a new departure in Malamud's fiction in his creation of a truly heroic character actively engaged in confronting evil. Moving beyond Spinoza's concept that freedom exists within the mind, Yakov Bok recognizes the necessity of participating in and changing history. "Malamud's hero moves from being 'fixed' by circumstances and events to being the 'fixer.'"

40   RIBALOW, HAROLD U. "Bernard Malamud: 'The Suffering of the Jews. . . .'" Reconstructionist 33 (23 June):12-16.
Malamud has asserted that the Holocaust has not as yet taken hold of the literary imagination, and in The Fixer he uses Yakov Bok as the symbol for the destruction of six million Jews. The novel conveys with brilliant irony and economy the nature of Jewish suffering.

41   RICHLER, MORDECAI. "Write, Boychick, Write." New Statesman 73 (7 April):473-74.
The Jewish-American writer has been accepted, yet there is a lingering ghetto sensibility in his fiction. Malamud's The Fixer, for example, literally addresses itself to the ghetto experience, but despite the virtues of the novel, the problems of the shtetl seem forced, especially because Malamud's preoccupation with its grimness is too slickly rendered. "In The Fixer, as in so many middlebrow novels and films, there is hardly an effect without an exact cause. . . ." Our expectations of what is to come are too easily cued.

42   ROSE, WILLIAM. "America Mazel Tov." Shenandoah 18, no. 4 (Summer):74-77.
Briefly compares Malamud's The Fixer to Philip Roth's When She Was Good, novels which deal with victims, isolation, heroism, and the value of life. Malamud has been particularly daring in locating the story of his hero, Yakov Bok, in a remote time and place. While The Fixer is unavoidably depressing, Bok's courage enhances the novel to the extent of making it "a real triumph for American fiction."

43   SNOWDEN, RICHARD L. Review of The Fixer. Chicago Maroon: Literary Review 4, no. 5 (May):6, 12.

1967

Despite the generally acknowledged excellence of this
novel, a number of reviews were narrowly conceived if not
petty. Perhaps some readers were put off by its historical
subject, as well as its graphic account of anti-Semitism and
brutality. The novel, however, moves well beyond those
materials as it represents the spiritual odyssey of its hero,
Yakov Bok. The Fixer may not possess the depth nor the scale of
The Brothers Karamozov, but it does eloquently dramatize the
growth of an ordinary man to a man of spiritual stature.

44   "Sons of Perdition." Times Literary Supplement, no. 3397 (6
        April):286.
        Malamud's The Fixer, unlike Maurice Samuel's Blood
Accusation, concentrates on the character of its hero-victim
rather than on the historical trial. But Malamud's Yakov Bok
develops in his story as "no more than the sum of his suffering"
and fails to possess dramatic vitality. Bok's prose has a
simplicity new to Malamud which recalls Bellow's Henderson in
Henderson the Rain King. The Fixer lacks the substance of
Malamud's earlier works and their interesting experiments with
fantasy.

45   TAJUDDIN, MOHAMMAD. "The Tragicomic Novels of Camus,
        Malamud, Hawkes, Bellow." Ph.D. dissertation, Indiana
        University, 188 pp.
        Defines tragicomedy as "an ordering of fictive material
which is mainly tragic, but which is placed in the wider context
of the nontragic, the antitragic, and the comic." The writers
under discussion share a number of points of contact in
rendering their novels tragicomic: humor, irony, the grotesque.
Such qualities deny to their heroes the stature of tragedy, but
the heroes are, at the same time, nobler than their counterparts
in comedy and are possessed of a poise and philosophical bent
missing in the heroes of "pure" comedy or "pure" tragedy. See
Dissertation Abstracts International 28 (1968):2698A-99A.

46   TRILLING, LIONEL, ed. The Experience in Fiction: A Reader
        with Commentaries. New York: Holt, Rinehart & Winston, pp.
        385-87.
        The last scene of Malamud's "The Magic Barrel" is
pictorially the most intense and most meaningful in the entire
story, and it is prepared for by the earlier episodes. Leo
Finkle's search for a wife is climaxed by his meeting with
Stella and represents a quest for experience in the Blakean
sense--an attempt to know the human condition in its passion and
in its pain. Reprinted: 1979.62.

47   WINEGARTEN, RENEE. "Malamud's Tightrope." Jewish Observer
        and Middle East Review 16 (7 April):17-18.

The Fixer is not anchored in an authentic
prerevolutionary Russia; rather, that Russia is a product of
Malamud's literary imagination. In keeping with its
subjective rendering of the facts, the novel uses the Mendel
Beiliss case as an occasion for imaginatively embellishing
it. As a consequence, the characters in the novel lack
credibility, detached as they are from carefully observed
models. Finally, in its application to American life, the
novel seems remote. "One should add that an 'artistic
failure' by Malamud is more stimulating than many other
modish successes."

1968

1   ALLEY, ALVIN D., and AGEE, HUGH. "Existential Heroes: Frank
     Alpine and Rabbit Angstrom." Ball State University Forum 9,
     no. 1 (Winter):3-5.
         Although Frank Alpine and Robert Angstrom share a similar
     existential characterization, they are developed along slightly
     different lines. Hell for Malamud's hero is of his own making,
     and it is only through his participating in a communal and
     ritual suffering that he is able to achieve self-acceptance.
     Updike's hero is trapped by his own environment and identity,
     but he endures, however, only by looking to himself for
     guidance.

2   ANGOFF, CHARLES. "Jewish-American Imaginative Writing in the
     Last Twenty-Five Years." Jewish Book Annual. Vol. 25. New
     York: Jewish Book Council of America, pp. 129-39 passim.
         Malamud's intellectual Jewishness is his greatest fault.
     Such novels as The Assistant, A New Life, and The Fixer lack the
     ethnic authenticity of The Magic Barrel whose characters seem
     identifiably Jewish in their ethos.

3   DRAKE, ROBERT. "Signs of the Times, or Signs for All
     Times?" Christian Century 95 (25 September):1204, 1206.
         Jointly discusses William Styron's The Confessions of Nat
     Turner and Bernard Malamud's The Fixer. Unlike Styron's topical
     book on racial persecution, Malamud's book rises above the tired
     theme of anti-Semitism in czarist Russia and raises lasting
     human issues. "The real theme of The Fixer is not anti-Semitism
     but man's inhumanity to man." Unfortunately, Styron's novel is
     too deeply preoccupied with contemporary racial issues to
     achieve the ring of universal truth. Although The Fixer ends
     inconclusively, its central intention, Yakov Bok's refusal to be
     dehumanized, is convincingly realized.

4   EIGNER, EDWIN M. "Malamud's Use of the Quest Romance." Genre
     1, no. 1 (January):55-74.

1968

In The Natural, The Assistant, A New Life, and The Fixer, the hero is forced to confront a quasi-supernatural woman, a kind of Lady of the Lake or Loathly Lady, and must overcome her negative temptation in order for his quest to succeed. In each instance the Lady becomes an index to the hero's level of maturity. In the first two novels, the shallowness and immaturity of the hero's aspirations inevitably lead to failure. In A New Life, S. Levin emerges as a positive Malamudian hero in his moral and emotional commitment to Pauline Gilley. The Fixer is highly ironic in its use of the Loathly Lady, for Yakov Bok is himself responsible for his wife Raisl's loathliness. Her unfaithfulness is the result of his attempts to kill her traditional beliefs. But Bok's ultimate acceptance of Raisl is tantamount to his renewed relationship to other Jews and his own Jewish identity, indeed a condition of his spiritual growth. Reprinted: 1970.5.

5   FINK, GUIDO. "Styron, Malamud: Le nuove vie del best seller umanitario." Paragone, n.s. 38, no. 218 (April):130-36.
In reviewing Bernard Malamud's The Fixer and William Styron's The Confessions of Nat Turner, Fink observes that American novels with liberal, humanitarian themes have had a long history of commercial success. Malamud and Styron have added another ingredient to these novels--the elements of violence and revolution. In France, The Fixer was regarded as a rejection of the Schwarz-Bart conception of Jewish experience. (Malamud's Yakov Bok achieves a heroic stature in modern Jewish literature that is new, while Schwarz-Bart's Ernie Levy, in The Last of the Just, continues in the path of dehumanization and debasement that Jews have historically endured.)

6   FREESE, PETER. "Parzival als Baseballstar: Bernard Malamuds The Natural." Jahrbuch für Amerikastudien 13:143-57.
The medieval legend of Parzival gives form and meaning to the contemporary reality of Malamud's novel. Through the webb of symbolic references, Roy Hobbs enacts a modern-day Grail quest. Although he fails in his attempt to purify himself, he reaches a new phase of his development and offers insights into his unrealized new life.

7   FRIEDMAN, ALAN WARREN. "Bernard Malamud: The Hero as Schnook." Southern Review, n.s. 4, no. 4 (October):927-44.
In his connection to the contemporary novel, Malamud is important for two reasons: the first is that his figures are naturalistically rendered to an unusual degree; the second is that Malamud attaches to that naturalistic conception an enduring Jewish spirit in which comedy and despair are grafted to each other. In The Fixer "Yakov [Bok's] situation becomes ludicrous, for against this poor schnook . . . are arrayed all the forces of organized despotic society. . . . " Yet Malamud's

strength as a writer comes from his ability to wrestle meaning
out of negation and despair. Reprinted: 1970.5.

8   GLICKSBURG, CHARLES I. "A Jewish American Literature?"
     Southwest Review 53, no. 2 (Spring):196-205 passim.
        Concludes that there is no single vision of the Jew on
     which all contemporary Jewish American writers can agree. The
     Jewish writer in America is a part of the American writing
     establishment rather than an exponent of an exclusively Jewish
     vision of life. While Malamud's fiction may reveal the Jew as a
     suffering and compassionate human being, the fiction of such
     writers as Salinger, Mailer, and Fiedler crystallizes altogether
     different Jewish images.

9   GREENE, A.C. Review of The Fixer. Dallas Times Herald, 4
     September, p. E-7.
        This is a novel about self-importance and human dignity.
     Malamud is one of the few contemporary writers still concerned
     with questions of good and evil and is capable of giving them
     compelling presentation.

10   GUERIN, ANN. "The Tormented Tale of an Innocent." Life 64
     (16 February):88-92.
        Discusses the M-G-M filming of Malamud's The Fixer di-
     rected by John Frankenheimer. Made entirely in Budapest, The
     Fixer was the first American film to be shot in its entirety be-
     hind the Iron Curtain. The Eastern European rural setting con-
     veys the Chagallike quality of Malamud's novel. This article in-
     cludes photographs and anecdotes related to the production.

11   GUNN, GILES B. "Bernard Malamud and the High Cost of
     Living." In Adversity and Grace: Studies in Recent American
     Literature. Edited by Nathan A. Scott, Jr. Chicago:
     University of Chicago Press, pp. 59-85.
        To find the equivalent for the kind of affirmative love
     registered throughout Malamud's fiction one must return to
     Whitman's "Song of Myself." Moreover, Malamud's thematic
     concerns--the sympathies of the heart, his distrust of
     intellect, and the celebration of innocence--unite him with such
     writers as Hawthorne, Melville, Twain, Eliot, and Fitzgerald.

12   HARTUNG, PHILIP T. "The Screen." Commonweal 89 (27
     December):441-42.
        In the film of The Fixer, Alan Bates' interpretation of
     Yakov Bok is perceptive, and the screen image of Malamud's hero
     highly believable. The major weakness of the film is Dalton
     Trumbo's thin script which undermines the richness of the

1968

novel. The visual experience of brutality is excessive, but
this medium does capture the essential quality of the prose
narrative. "As hymn celebrating the survival of the human
spirit, 'The Fixer' is in a class by itself."

*13   [Interview with Bernard Malamud.] Jerusalem Post Weekly.
        Overseas Edition, 1 April, p. 13.
            Source: Field and Field, p. 7, 1975.5; unverified.

14   JOSIPOVICI, GABRIEL, "Freedom and Wit, the Jewish Writer and
        Modern Art." European Judaism 3, no. 1 (Summer):51-50
        passim.
            Yakov Bok in The Fixer survives existentially through the
        use of his wit, the hallmark of his distinctive voice, as well
        as a weapon against his oppressors. This voice, moreover, is a
        feature of Malamud's style and is recognizably Jewish and modern
        in its protest "against the dangers and excesses of Romanti-
        cism." A long section of this essay deals with the romantic
        imagination and its propensity to explain man in nonrational
        terms as an insidious tendency that nurtured anti-Semitism.

15   KATTAN, NAIM. "A propos de Bernard Malamud: Le roman juif
        américain." Les Langues Modernes 62, no. 2 (March-April):
        158-69.
            Explores Malamud's connection to American Jewish writers
        and the defining traits of his fiction. Like other Jewish
        American writers, Malamud examines Jewishness within the
        framework of American culture. The amalgamation of a Yiddish
        ethos with American urban civilization serves as the basis for
        his major theme: the discovery of what it is to be human. For
        Malamud, Judaism, with its regard for the sanctity it attaches
        to human life, inevitably leads to this knowledge. Accordingly,
        Malamud rejects tragic resignation in favor of acts of will,
        patience, hope, and compassion, qualities which are the very
        essence of Judaism. Artistically, his work is characterized by
        the playful tension between realism and fantasy. Kattan
        comments on The Natural, The Assistant, A New Life, and The
        Magic Barrel.

16   KERMODE, FRANK. "Bernard Malamud." In Continuities.
        London: Routledge & Kegan Paul, pp. 216-22.
            Reprint of 1962.11

17   MEETER, GLEN. Bernard Malamud and Philip Roth: A Critical
        Essay. Contemporary Writers in Christian Perspective.
        Edited by Roderick Jellema. Grand Rapids, Mich: William B.
        Eerdmans Publishing Co., 48 pp.
            This essay is divided into six titled parts. Part 1
        examines Malamud and Roth's use of Jewish-Christian encounters;

part 2 compares and contrasts Malamud's universalizing tendency
with Roth's sense of the immediate; part 3 discusses the
similarity of intention and accomplishment in their short
stories; part 4 considers each writer's handling of the quest
pattern; part 5 explores how Malamud and Roth treat conversion;
part 6, the conclusion, asserts that both writers have
reintroduced "religious awareness and religious feeling" into
American fiction.

18   PEARSON, GABRIEL. "Bellow, Malamud, and Jewish Arrival." In
      Explorations: An Annual on Jewish Themes. Edited by Murray
      Mindlin with Chaim Bermant. Chicago: Quadrangle Books, pp.
      18-37.
          Bellow and Malamud furnish contrasting responses to Jewish
      identity. Being Jewish in Bellow is merely one part of an indi-
      vidual's experience. For Malamud Jewishness becomes symbol and
      myth and is rendered through characters who are burdens to them-
      selves and others. Through their Yiddish inflections, Malamud
      is ably to convey the "lost language of the heart." His por-
      trayal of Jewish failure and pathos seems anachronistic at the
      very moment in history when Jews have arrived. Malamud's art,
      however, may be regarded as a moral preserve for those essential
      human qualities embodied in a disappearing Jewish ethos.

19   SCHLESINGER, ARTHUR, Jr. "The Fixer, 'Prurient Relish in
      Violence.'" Vogue 152, no. 10 (December):180.
          Unlike Malamud's novel, the film version of The Fixer is
      an artistic confusion--the inappropriate color, the variety of
      accents, the inexplicable mood shifts are examples of the way in
      which the author's original vision has been violated. "The
      screenplay, by that old Popular Front Hack Dalton Trumbo,
      mingles sentimental cliché, sententious nonprofundities, fake
      social concern, and a prurient relish in violence."

20   STAMPFER, JUDAH. "Outer World, Inner Truth." Congress
      Bi-Weekly: A Journal of Opinion and Jewish Affairs 35 (8
      April):20-21.
          "The First Seven Years," originally published in Partisan
      Review, offers an excellent example of the quality to be found
      in A Malamud Reader. Recalling Jacob's seven years of labor in
      the Old Testament, the story carries mythic resonances while
      thematically it stresses inherent human worth over acquired
      social status. Throughout the stories in this reader, Malamud
      portrays his hero as demonically obsessed.

21   TANNER, TONY. "Bernard Malamud and the New Life." Critical
      Quarterly 10, nos. 1-2 (Spring-Summer):151-68.
          Throughout Malamud's fiction there is a unified vision
      that addresses itself to the hero's need for psychological and

1968

spiritual growth. Despite its strained realism, A New Life
sustains this fundamental theme, but Malamud's most successful
fable, involving the process of maturation, is The Fixer, a work
in which didacticism is charged with emotional relevance.
Although writing fables is always artistically a gamble,
Malamud's willingness to accept the risks places him squarely in
an American tradition.

22   TELLER, JUDD L. "From Yiddish to Neo-Brahmin." In Strangers
        and Natives: The Evolution of the American Jew from 1921 to
        the Present. New York: Delacorte Press, pp. 251-72 passim.
            Malamud rejects the Robbe-Grillet theory that fiction
        should record but not interpret experience. Along with other
        contemporary Jewish writers, Malamud seeks to find meaning in
        existence. A sense of Jewishness rather than Jewish doctrine
        motivates behavior in his fiction.

23   STAMERRA, SILVANA. "Il protagonista nella narrativa di
        Bernard Malamud." Zagaglia 10, no. 39:333-43.
            All of Malamud's characters attempt to detach themselves
        from an obscure but painful past, and their moral code is the
        fruition of the problems they have struggled with in their
        previous history. Even if they become worldly failures in the
        present, they nevertheless leave a legacy of idealism in their
        midst. From this perspective Malamud's characters are studied
        in their relations to themselves and to others.

24   TURNER, FREDERICK W., III. "Myth Inside and Out: Malamud's
        The Natural." Novel 1, no. 2 (Winter):133-39.
            The theme that has occupied Malamud from the beginning of
        his career and sustained throughout is the conflict between myth
        and the outer world. In The Natural Roy Hobbs's inability to
        exist outside of the myth of baseball is tragic rather than
        comic. Having given his life exclusively to this myth, he
        becomes vulnerable to the encroachments of reality embodied in
        such figures as Judge Goodwill Banner, the Knights' owner; Gus
        Sands, the Bookie; and Memo Paris, his love obsession. Too
        limited in his vision, Roy Hobbs can neither recognize nor cope
        with truth existing in the actual world. Reprinted: 1970.5

1969

1   ADELMAN, GEORGE. "Pictures of Fidelman." Library Journal 94
        (1 May):1899.
            This review commends Malamud's book for its "wild,
        funny-poignant set of pictures."

1969

2   ALTER, ROBERT. "Bernard Malamud: Jewishness as Metaphor."
     In After the Tradition: Essays on Modern Jewish Writing.
     New York: E.P. Dutton & Co., pp. 116-30.
         Malamud's immigrant milieu has given his artistic
     imagination its special character, as well as influencing his
     fictional technique. His central figure, the schlemiel, is a
     comic victim, struggling against his own weakness and the world
     and appropriately serves as Malamud's symbolic Jew. The
     schlemiel is given his most powerful rendering in The Fixer:
     here, literally and metaphorically, he is in a prison, the
     epitome of the Jewish experience. Calling on all of his
     resources in his attempt to survive, Bok mirrors Jewish
     existence in its anguish and heroism. Reprinted: 1970.5

3   AXTHELM, PETER. "Holes in the Ground." Newsweek (5
     May):112-13.
         Considers Pictures of Fidelman artistically uneven, but
     nonetheless moving and humorous in its characterization of
     Arthur Fidelman as a "slapstick Underground Man."

4   BARSNESS, JOHN A. "A New Life: The Frontier Myth in
     Perspective." Western American Literature 3, no. 4
     (Winter):297-302.
         S. Levin is convinced that a new life will come about as a
     result of his immersion in an Emersonian landscape, but his
     adventure is tragicomic because unknowingly he carries the
     encumbrances of his old life into the new.

5   BRONNER, LEAH. "The Jewish Vogue in Modern American
     Writings." In Gateways to Jewish Life. Johannesburg: B'nai
     B'rith, pp. 223-27 passim.
         Tries to account for the significant interest in contem-
     porary Jewish writers such as Malamud, Bellow, Friedman, Roth,
     Gold, and Potak. One explanation, suggested by Malamud, lies in
     the symbolic stance of the Jew as existential man illustrated,
     for example, by Malamud's own Yakov Bok.

6   BROYARD, ANATOLE. Review of Pictures of Fidelman. New York
     Times Book Review, 4 May, pp. 5, 45.
         In other works, Malamud has been able to convert suffering
     into artistic success, as well as a meaningful learning exper-
     ience for his hero. The Assistant is illustrative on both
     counts. In this collection Arthur Fidelman does not undergo any
     enlargement in wisdom in his Italian experience, nor does his
     Italian milieu emerge with any immediacy. The occasional charm
     of Malamud's writing does not compensate for his obscure thema-
     tic intentions. "Why, for example, does Fidelman paint

1969

'Prostitute and Procurer' instead of 'Mother and Son'?" The
writer rather than the reader must assume responsibility for
this mystery.

7   BURROWS, DAVID. "The American Past in Malamud's A New Life.
     In Private Dealings: Eight American Writers. Stockholm:
     Almqvist & Wiksell, pp. 86-94.
          Through a variety of historical, literary, and mythical
     allusions, S. Levin of A New Life expresses the vitality of
     American tradition, Malamud's irony notwithstanding. Beginning
     life in his own new world, Levin recapitulates in his actions
     the Emersonian pronouncements relating to self-reliance and the
     moral visions of Thoreau and James's Christopher Newman. In
     orchestrating such parallels and connections Malamud creates a
     contemporary version of the American Adam.

8   DAVENPORT, GUY. "Elegant Botches." National Review 21 (3
     June):549-59 passim.
          Pictures of Fidelman is flawed in two ways: in the
     flatness of its hero's characterization and in the insubstan-
     tiality of the ending.

9   DONOGHUE, DENIS. "Both." Listener 82 (30 October):607-8.
          The Jamesian theme of art and its relation to life is
     prominent in Pictures of Fidelman. Acknowledging Malamud's
     ability to comment simultaneously on both, Donoghue observes
     that Malamud wittily uses art as a metaphor for life and life as
     a metaphor for art.

10   ELLMANN, MARY. "Recent Novels: The Languages of Art." Yale
     Review 59, no. 1 (October):111-21 passim.
          Arthur Fidelman in Pictures of Fidelman is unconvincing
     as an artist and pompous in his pronouncement on art. Moreover,
     Malamud's unflattering images of Italy seem to express the
     author's unconscious American chauvinism. If Fidelman's com-
     panions are more talented and successful than he, Malamud compen-
     sates for his protagonist's deficiencies by making him morally
     superior. Malamud's most successful story in the group is
     "Pictures of the Artist," a triumph of farce and verbal comedy.

11   FARBER, STEVEN. "The Fixer." Hudson Review 22, no. 1
     (Spring):134-38.
          Malamud's Russians are portrayed as either sadists or
     bigots, and the movie version of The Fixer seems to perpetuate
     these stereotypes. Although the portrayal of Yakov Bok by Alan
     Bates is especially convincing in the opening scenes, the
     suffering depicted appears gratuitous, dissociated from the
     vision of the author, the writer of the screenplay, or the
     director.

12   FENTON, JAMES. "Simple and Classic." New Statesman 78 (17
        October):542.
        Pictures of Fidelman is faulted for the dullness of its
picaresque hero, the casualness of its style, and its failure to
be truly experimental.

13   FLEISCHER, LEONARD. "Fidelman's Follies." Congress
        Bi-Weekly: A Journal of Opinion and Jewish Affairs 36 (26
        May):20-22.
        Pictures of Fidelman is artistically uneven. The ending
of each section in this loose novel is always metaphoric, a
tactic which is facile and evasive. Malamud, however, does
capture effectively the heaven and hell of artistic creation,
and it is through Arthur Fidelman's assuming various roles--
refugee, pimp, thief, and homosexual--that his artistic and
human understanding grows. The book is superior to The Fixer.

14   FLINT, JOYCE MARLENE. "In Search of Meaning: Bernard
        Malamud, Norman Mailer, John Updike." Ph.D. dissertation,
        Washington State University, 162 pp.
        All three writers attack the goals of the liberal-humanist
dream: that man should become free of pain and strive to become
well adjusted; that happiness can be achieved through raising
the standard of living; and that sexual adjustment can
contribute to personal happiness. For Malamud the significance
of life is revealed through man's capacity for goodness, and
goodness can be practiced in any society. Updike and Mailer
arrive at altogether different conclusions: the former sees God
as the only way for man to satisfy his deepest need, a faith in
immortality; the latter sees man's salvation in the practice of
a romantic individualism and a reliance on instinct. See
Dissertation Abstracts International 30 (1970):3006A

15   FOREMAN, JOHN D. Review of Pictures of Fidelman. Best
        Sellers 29 (15 May):67.
        These stories are intended to serve as a collage in which
"the whole is different from the sum of the parts" rather than
being singled out individually. While Malamud's characters seem
to be conceived as symbols, their actual portraiture is
arresting enough to fix them in the reader's imagination.

16   "Goodbye, Old Paint." Time 93 (9 May):108.
        Arthur Fidelman in Pictures of Fidelman is a
"schlemiel-saint," a man with holy convictions but sadly inept
in their execution. Fidelman is partially redeemed from being
merely another stereotype of this commonplace figure by the
intensity of Malamud's prose whose power hints at "projections
of an interior morality play, more interesting possibly than
what gets staged."

1969

17   GREENFELD, JOSH. Review of Pictures of Fidelman.
      Commonweal 91 (5 December):314-15 passim.
           Considers this book one of the most underrated novels of
      the year. If Malamud's strengths as a writer lie in the short
      story, these short, unified narratives remind the reader of
      Malamud's best work in that genre. Unlike his other work,
      Pictures of Fidelman does not strain for mythic or symbolic
      profundity, and in its humor it offers more satisfaction to the
      reader than his earlier novels.

18   GROSS, JOHN. "Lieutenants and Luftmenschen." New York
      Review of Books 12 (24 April):40-43 passim.
           The elaborate fantasy in Pictures of Fidelman is the
      essence of its charm. Rich in themes and symbols, the stories
      invite the kind of close analysis they will undoubtedly receive
      in graduate seminars. Fidelman himself is archetypal, fitting
      into several categories: "the universal misfit, the American in
      Europe, the Jew in a predominantly Christian culture."

19   HAYS, PETER L. "The Complex Pattern of Redemption in the
      Assistant." Centennial Review, no. 2 (Spring):200-214.
           The Assistant is remarkable in its knitting together a
      narrative realism with myth, symbol, and a philosophy akin to
      that of Martin Buber. These elements work together toward a
      story of redemption in which Morris Bober functions not only as
      employer but as moral and spiritual teacher to Frank Alpine.
      Gradually, Frank's involvement with Morris becomes a form of
      religious experience and dramatically renders the Martin Buber
      I-Thou philosophy, which leads to his final conversion to
      Judaism. Reprinted: 1970.5.

20   HICKS, GRANVILLE. Review of Pictures of Fidelman. Literary
      Guild Review, (June), pp. 7-9.
           Regards this book as another example of Malamud's powerful
      imagination. At times insightful, at other times a schlemiel,
      the character of Fidelman is developed within the environment of
      a new Malamud style: "Joycean, full of allusions to the great
      artists, occasionally echoing Jewish fables and legends." Like
      other Malamud fiction, this work is also a blend of the serious
      and the humorous. Reprinted: 1970.9.

21   HILL, JOHN S. "Malamud's 'The Lady of the Lake': A Lesson
      in Rejection." University Review 36, no. 2 (December):
      149-50.
           In this story Malamud reveals the literal and psycho-
      logical consequences of rejecting one's past while such contem-
      poraries as Bellow dramatize the hero's continued involvement
      with it.

22   HORNE, LEWIS B. "Yakov Agonistes." Research Studies 37, no.
        4 (December):321-26.
            The triumph of perseverance is the theme of both Malamud's
        The Fixer and Milton's Samson Agonistes, and a comparison of
        these two works illuminate the mutual growth of their heroes.
        Shut out from God, Yakov Bok and Samson must live through
        suffering unaided. Through patience each man achieves a new
        vision of life leading to his salvation.

23   "I Paint with my Paint." Times Literary Supplement, no. 3529
        (16 October):1177.
            Pictures of Fidelman explores the painter's relationship
        to his art, a subject that is usually lacking in substance in
        most novels. In Malamud's episodic work, there is a kind of
        "whimsical complacency" which is often amusing, but the novel is
        also undermined by an excess of ingenuity.

24   JACKSON, KATHERINE GAUS. Review of Pictures of Fidelman.
        Harper's 238, no. 1428 (June):92-93.
            The abuse which Arthur Fidelman suffers is much less
        credible than the sufferings inflicted on Yakov Bok in The
        Fixer. Fidelman's predicaments are thematically interesting up
        to a point, but their endlessness becomes tedious to the
        reader. In creating a character similar to Arthur Fidelman,
        Joyce Cary does a better job with his Gully Jimson in The
        Horse's Mouth.

25   KAPP, ISA. "A Therapeutic Plainness." New Leader 52 (26
        May):7-9.
            Despite the literary pretentiousness of many contemporary
        writers, "there is a therapeutic plainness about the fiction of
        Bernard Malamud." Thematically, Pictures of Fidelman is
        concerned with failed artists and the problems of art, and
        perhaps no writer, other than Henry James, has as much to say
        about these matters. In his double role as artist and lover,
        Arthur Fidelman moves mercurially from dejection and despair to
        elation and ecstasy. Through him Malamud captures the magic and
        unpredictability of life.

26   KENNEDY, WILLIAM. "Malamud Finds Renewal in a Fidelman
        Collage." National Observer, 12 May, p. 23.
            Pictures of Fidelman extends Malamud's interest in the
        inevitable afflictions that life hands out to his sensitive
        heroes, but in this instance, Malamud's picaresque hero, Arthur
        Fidelman, is also a figure of some humor as he contends with
        life and art for the elusive perfection of both. "Pictures of
        the Artist," the last section of this novel, is an imaginative

1969

tour de force. Malamud "has made a collage out of artistic
lore, artistic parody, parable, surrealistic story."

27   KOSOFSKY, RITA NATHALIE. Bernard Malamud: An Annotated
      Checklist. The Serif Series, Bibliographies and Checklists,
      edited by William White, no. 7. Kent, Ohio: Kent State
      University Press, 63 pp.
            This annotated checklist on Malamud covers criticism in
      books and journals, and book reviews in newspapers and journals,
      through 1967. Of special interest is a section on Malamud's own
      writings which identifies individual stories in collections and
      anthologies and cites their original place of publication. The
      bibliography only includes criticism in English.

28   KOTLOWITZ, ROBERT. "The Making of 'The Angel Levine.'"
      Harper's 239, no. 1430 (July):98-99.
            Discusses the adaptation of Malamud's short story, "Angel
      Levine," into the movie version directed by Jan Kadar.
      Manischevitz, the tailor, renamed Mishkin in the movie, is
      played by Zero Mostel; his wife Fanny, by Ida Kaminska. The
      black angel, Harry Belafonte, "has become a tough minded
      militant given to attacks of sentimentality." As a director,
      Kadar was a major force in determining the vision of the film,
      especially in muting Belafonte's otherwise angry and aggressive
      performance.

29   LASK, THOMAS. "The Creative Itch." New York Times, 3 May,
      p. 33.
            The stories in Pictures of Fidelman lend themselves to
      various thematic speculations: art as ruthless obsession, the
      artist as amoralist, the importance of illusions. On a less
      sophisticated level these stories are amusing and well written,
      but they do not seem to be Malamud at his best.

30   LASSON, ROBERT. "The Story of a Professional Giver."
      Chicago Tribune Book World 3 (4 May):4.
            Although Pictures of Fidelman is essentially comic,
      Malamud's characters are never deprived of their dignity. The
      poignant and moving quality of his stories is sustained by the
      author's ability to maintain a direct relationship between his
      reader and his characters. "Malamud . . . is one of America's
      most precious natural resources."

31   MURRAY, MICHELE. "Further Adventures of Fidelman. National
      Catholic Reporter 5 (21 May):11.
            Expresses mixed feelings about Pictures of Fidelman. In
      using his hero from one story to another, Malamud fails to
      account for the various changes occurring in his character.
      While "The Last Mohican" is just about flawless in every

respect, Fidelman's psychological disintegration in "Still Life" seems excessive and unexplained. This is a book whose achievement is undermined by "an excess of masochism and sentimentality."

32   NADON, ROBERT JOSEPH. "Urban Values in Recent American
      Fiction: A Study of the Fiction of Saul Bellow, John Updike,
      Philip Roth, Bernard Malamud, and Norman Mailer." Ph.D.
      dissertation, University of Minnesota, 450 pp.
         Studies the impact of the large city on these writers and
      concludes that only Bellow and Mailer use the social dynamics of
      the city as a force affecting the lives of their characters.
      Despite the fact that much of Malamud's fiction is set in New
      York City, the city never emerges as subject, theme, or symbol in
      his work; rather, one experiences only a timeless and indefinite
      Lower East Side, registered through the Jewish sensibility of
      his characters. Such abstractness of setting seems related to
      Malamud's thematics, the quest of his characters for communion
      rather than community. See <u>Dissertation Abstracts International</u>
      30 (1969):2543A.

33   OLENDER, TERRYS T. "The Jewish Film Image--Good and Bad."
      <u>American Zionist</u> 59:27-28.
         The Dalton Trumbo screen version of the John Franken-
      heimer-Edward Lewis production of <u>The Fixer</u> captured Malamud's
      portrayal of man under adversity. Alan Bates, a non-Jew, acted
      the role of Yakov Bok with great sensitivity.

34   Øverland, Orm. "Fengsel og frihet: Noen kommentarer til
      Bernard Malamuds diktning" [Prison and freedom: Some
      comments on Bernard Malamud's writing]. <u>Minerva's</u>
      <u>Kvartalsskrift</u> 13:113-25.
         In Norwegian. Briefly discusses two stories from <u>The</u>
      <u>Magic Barrel</u>, <u>The Assistant</u>, and <u>The Fixer</u>. "Angel Levine" and
      "The Lady of the Lake" both concern themselves with liberation
      but in different ways. In the former, Manischevitz, the tailor,
      is liberated from his imprisoning skepticism by a new and more
      humane faith in mankind; in the latter, Henry Levin is damned to
      his own private hell because he has denied his Jewishness,
      self-acceptance existing as his only true passport to freedom.
      In <u>The Assistant</u> the bird symbolism associated with Frank Alpine
      ironically suggests the continuation of his entrapment. Through
      its political and social message at the end, <u>The Fixer</u> suggests
      the possibility of man's eventual freedom, but it is too early
      to say whether Malamud will follow this line in his future
      writing.

1969

35   PINSKER, SANFORD [SIGMUND]. "A Note on Malamud's 'Take
      Pity.'" Studies in Short Fiction 6, no. 2 (Winter):212-13.
           Suggests that Lawrence Perrine (1964.25) has failed to
      recognize striking points of contact between Malamud's story and
      Sartre's No Exit. Eva's continual rejection of Rosen's pity
      becomes for the coffee salesman an increasing source of
      anguish. Like Sartre, Malamud uses his plot to suggest that
      hell is other people, but this theme nourishes another that is
      exclusive to the story, the giving and taking of pity. For Eva,
      Rosen's obsessive pity becomes for her degrading, and for Rosen,
      Eva's continual rejection of his aid ultimately elicits from him
      hate. A true spiritual partnership between the sufferer and the
      giver is lacking.

36   _____. "The Achievement of Bernard Malamud." Midwest
      Quarterly 10, no. 4 (July):379-89.
           Because of the Nazi Holocaust, the Jew became the symbolic
      focus of human suffering in the fifties. More than any of his
      contemporaries, Malamud has been trying to use that suffering,
      and the possibility of transcendence, in order to create a
      tragic novel. These concerns are effectively registered in The
      Fixer.

37   RAHV, PHILIP. "A Note on Bernard Malamud." In Literature
      and the Sixth Sense. Boston: Houghton Mifflin Co., pp.
      280-88.
           Reprint of 1967.38.

38   ROSENFELD, ALVIN H. "Fidelman's Complaint." Judaism 18, no.
      4 (Fall):504-8.
           In his first four novels Malamud wrote compassionately
      about suffering and defeat, but this subject was wearying for
      both the reader and the author. Pictures of Fidelman seems to
      be Malamud's attempt to escape from an exclusively somber vision
      of life. Despite the new levity of this work, the hero, Arthur
      Fidelman, experiences the kind of futility and defeat found in
      Malamud's earlier fiction. Although Fidelman attempts to make a
      new life for himself in Rome as an artist, he remains an out-
      sider, venting his frustrations through his use of an abrasive
      wit. His participation in homosexual activity seems gratuitous
      and represents a wide departure from Malamud's moral serious-
      ness.

39   ROTH, PHILIP. "Writing American Fiction." In The American
      Novel Since World War II. Edited by Marcus Klein.
      Greenwich, Conn: Fawcett, pp. 142-58.
           Reprint of 1961.20.

1969

40   SCHOLES, ROBERT. "Portrait of Artist as 'Escape-Goat.'"
        Saturday Review 52 (10 May):32-34.
          Pictures of Fidelman is Malamud's most successful work and
an important publication event. The stories present Arthur
Fidelman, the unifying hero, in a series of Hogarthian
allegorical tableaux in which art and the moral life are
examined in relation to each other. "In the iconography of
these pictures, Fidelman's submission to Beppo symbolizes his
acceptance of imperfection in existence." Reprinted: 1979.55.

41   SCHULZ, MAX F. "Bernard Malamud's Mythic Proletarians." In
        Radical Sophistication: Studies in Contemporary Jewish-
        American Novelists. Athens: Ohio University Press, pp.
        56-68.
          Illustrates Malamud's fusion of Marxian assumptions with
mythic patterns. Thus the hero in his fiction exists on two
levels: in serving as the representative of the common man, he
is a proletarian hero; in bringing renewal to the wasteland he
is mythic. Because of the imperfections inherent in human
nature, however, neither the Marxian nor the mythic levels
offers a clear, unambiguous resolution. While earlier American
proletarian writers brought slogans to their endings instead of
a realized social utopia, Malamud's solution to the problem of
the ending was symbolism, the use of the Grail and vegetation
myths under which the Marxian vision is subsumed. Reprinted:
1970.5.

42   . "Malamud's A New Life: The New Wasteland of the
        Fifties." Western Review 6, no. 1 (Spring):37-44.
          Observes that A New Life embodies the wasteland symbolism
of Eliot's poem in order to reflect the America of the fifties;
but Malamud's suggestion of rebirth is more hesitant than
Eliot's and undercut by irony.

43   SHEED, WILFRED. "A Portrait of the Artist as Schlemiel."
        Life 66 (9 May):12.
          The humor of Pictures of Fidelman derives from Arthur
Fidelman's obsession and unsuccessful pursuit of art and love,
but these stories also carry an intent beyond the exaggerated
humor of their plots. Malamud uses the perspective of visual
art as a way of looking at the problems of the writer.
Abridged: 1972.40.

44   SKAGGS, MERRIL MAGUIRE. "A Complex Black-and-White Matter."
        In The Process of Fiction: Contemporary Stories and
        Criticism. Edited by Barbara McKenzie. New York: Harcourt,
        Brace & World, pp. 384-93.
          "Black Is My Favorite Color" is a satire, in part, on the
white liberal's relations with blacks. As an unreliable

1969

narrator, Nat Lime reveals a disparity between his proclaimed
love of blacks and a failure of sensitivity to them. Malamud
undermines the reader's confidence in Lime by having him speak
in cliches or contradict himself. "At its most complex level .
. . [the story] treats a subject more universal than the
relationship between New York Jews and Negroes, the ingratitude
with which charitable acts are sometimes met, or the unconscious
prejudices that direct human behavior."

45   STANTON, ROBERT. "Outrageous Fiction: <u>Crime and Punishment,</u>
        <u>The Assistant</u>, and <u>Native Son</u>." <u>Pacific Coast Philology</u> 4
        (April):52-58.
        These three novels present crime as an instrument of
growth and moral redemption in a world where God seems remote,
but Malamud consciously brings Dostoevski's ideas to a different
conclusion. Like Roskolnikov, Frank Alpine is a character of
extremes, gravitating either toward purity or corruption, and
his Manichean nature is reflected in such contradictory
activities as cleaning the store or robbing it. Unlike
Dostoevski who offers a vision of religious hope at the end of
<u>Crime and Punishment</u>, Malamud's conclusion offers none. "The
novel demonstrates that Morris's ineffectual virtue and Frank's
beneficient unscrupulousness are both disastrous in their
effect." Morris achieves only death and Frank a perpetual
imprisonment in the grocery.

46   STEGNER, PAGE. "Stone, Berry, Oates--and Other Grist from
        the Mill." <u>Southern Review</u>, n.s. 5, no. 1 (January):273-83.
        <u>A Malamud Reader</u> is the last book reviewed in this
article, and it contains the following previously published
material: excerpts from <u>The Fixer</u>, <u>A New Life</u>, and <u>The Natural</u>,
the complete text of <u>The Assistant</u>, ten stories taken from <u>The</u>
<u>Magic Barrel</u> and <u>Idiots First</u>. "This anthology is a fine
exhibition of . . . range and depth."

47   TUCKER, MARTIN. Review of <u>Pictures of Fidelman</u>. <u>Commonweal</u>
        90 (27 June):420-21.
        Losing one thing to gain another is the controlling idea
in <u>Pictures of Fidelman</u>. If Malamud is an authority on failure
and loss, that expertise seems to have become a fictional ploy
rather than an authentic condition of his character in this
recent work. Given Malamud's past accomplishments, we can only
speculate that <u>Pictures of Fidelman</u> is an interlude in an
otherwise successful career.

48   WOHL, AMIEL. "On Seeing <u>The Fixer</u>--Some Reflections. . . ."
        <u>American Zionist</u> 58, no. 7 (March):44-45.
        The film version of Malamud's novel dramatically under-
scores certain truths about the Jewish experience. As a re-

minder of both the historical and the contemporary conditions of
anti-Semitism in Russia, the film relives the suffering of all
the Jews through history. Through this medium we understand
with renewed clarity the meaning of the Jewish immigration to
America and the necessity for a Jewish state.

49   WOHLGELERNTER, MAURICE. "Pictures at an Exhibition."
      American Zionist 60, no. 2 (October):42-43.
          The tales in Pictures of Fidelman: An Exhibition do not
      represent Malamud's best work, largely because their Italian
      setting is not as deeply understood and felt as Malamud's world
      of the Brooklyn ghetto. The genuine Malamud envisions the theme
      of moral responsibility, but that theme is not present in this
      literary exhibition. "A Pimp's Revenge" may reflect metaphor-
      ically Malamud's own uncertainty in handling the materials of
      these stories: "Trying unsuccessfully to complete a portrait of
      himself and his mother that has obsessed him for years . . .
      [Fidelman] asks Esmerelda to model for his mother. . . . But
      instead of painting 'Mother and Son' . . .[he paints]
      'Prostitute and Procurer.'"

1970

1   BRYANT, JERRY H. "Novels of Ambiguity and Affirmation: The
      Moral Outlook." In The Open Decision: The Contemporary
      American Novel and its Intellectual Background. New York:
      Free Press; London: Collier-Macmillan, pp. 283-394, passim.
          Discusses Barth, Vonnegut, Malamud, Bellow, and Mailer as
      novelists who dramatize the pain of possessing consciousness.
      The more a Malamud hero becomes conscious of himself, the more
      he becomes aware of all human beings. Suffering is an
      especially important part of his education, and this theme is
      advanced through an incremental repetition in The Natural, The
      Assistant, A New Life, and The Fixer.

2   DUCHARME, ROBERT E. "Art and Idea in the Novels of Bernard
      Malamud." Ph.D. dissertation, Notre Dame University, 258 pp.
          Comprises five chapters and an appendix. The first
      chapter examines the controlling archetypes in Malamud's mythic
      system; the second deals with his ironic perspective in relation
      to his use of myth; the third concerns the father-son motif and
      its connection to the themes of suffering and responsibility;
      the fourth and fifth explore, respectively, the two concerns of
      the previous chapter. The appendix concludes this study with a
      discussion of the form and content of Pictures of Fidelman, a
      sequence of short stories. See Dissertation Abstracts
      International 31 (1971):4765A-66A. Revised for publication:
      1974.4.

1970

3   EDELMAN, LILY. Review of <u>Pictures of Fidelman</u>. <u>National</u>
     <u>Jewish Monthly</u> 84, no. 5 (January):48-49.
         While Chaim Potok often falters in demonstrating literary
     skill, Malamud maintains a high level of achievement. <u>Pictures</u>
     <u>of Fidelman</u>, an allegory about art and life, is once again
     testimony to this author's impressive talent. "Malamud proves
     once again that he is without equal in the art of transforming
     one Jew's pilgrimage into a compassionate tale of man's unending
     struggle to become and to remain a <u>mensh</u>."

4   FEINSTEIN, ELAINE. "Guilt." <u>London Magazine</u>, 23, ser. 12,
     no. 2 (June-July):166-68.
         Malamud's <u>The Tenants</u> is a fascinating novel which
     surrealistically dramatizes Jewish-black antagonism detached
     from any sense of guilt.

5   FIELD, LESLIE [A.], and FIELD, JOYCE [W.], eds. <u>Bernard</u>
     <u>Malamud and the Critics</u>. New York: New York University
     Press; London: University of London Press, 373 pp.
         The collection brings together the widest spectrum of
     criticism available on Malamud in the 1960s. The introduction
     offers a concise assessment of the following essays located in
     the four sections of the book: "The Jewish Literary Tradition"
     by Earl H. Rovit (1960.7); "Women, Children, and Idiots First:
     Transformation Psychology" by Samuel Irving Bellman (1964.2);
     "Jewishness as Metaphor" by Robert Alter (1969.2); "<u>The</u>
     <u>Natural</u>: World Ceres" by Earl R. Wasserman (1965.9); "Four
     Versions of Pastoral" by James M. Mellard (1967.34); "The
     Loathly Ladies" by Edwin M. Eigner (1968.4); "Myth Inside and
     Out: <u>The Natural</u>" by Frederick W. Turner, III (1968.24);
     "Victims in Motion: The Sad and Bitter Clowns" by Ben Siegel
     (1962.22); "The Scope of Caricature" by Sam Bluefarb (1964.5);
     "Comic Vision and the Theme of Identity" by Mark Goldman
     (1964.11); "The New Romanticism" by Charles Alva Hoyt (1964.13);
     "Mythic Proletarians" by Max F. Schulz (1969.41); "The Qualified
     Encounter" by Ihab Hassan (1961.11); "Culture Conflict" by
     Walter Shear (1966.63); "The Complex Pattern of Redemption" by
     Peter L. Hays (1969.19); "The Old Life and the New" by Theodore
     Solotaroff (1962.23); "The Sadness of Goodness" by Marcus Klein
     (1965.5); "Ironic Affirmation" by Ruth B. Mandel (1964.21);
     "History and Imagination: Two Views of the Beiliss Case" by
     Maurice Friedberg (1966.24); "The Hero as Schnook" by Alan
     Warren Friedman (1968.7); "The Stories" by Sidney Richman
     (1966.55).

6   FREEDMAN, WILLIAM. "From Bernard Malamud, with Discipline
     and with Love." In <u>The Fifties: Fiction, Poetry, Drama</u>.
     Edited by Warren French. Deland, Fla: Everett/Edwards, pp.
     133-43.

82

Cognizant of the Jewish history of discipline and
self-control, Malamud employs these values as themes in The
Natural and The Assistant. The former is a novel about Roy
Hobbs's failure to achieve control in the course of his life; the
latter dramatizes the commitment of Frank Alpine and Helen Bober
to such self-discipline as the means to their eventual personal
salvation. Reprinted: 1975.6

7   GOODMAN, OSCAR B. "There are Jews Everywhere." Judaism 19,
      no. 3 (Summer):283-94.
      Malamud continually explores the question of Jewish
identity. Depending upon the particular work, Jewish identity
may be comprehended in the symbiotic relationship of the giver
and the receiver, in the experience of frustrated sexuality, in
a metamorphosis from animality to humanity, and in all men who
suffer in themselves or for others.

8   GOSS, JAMES. "The Assembling of the meaning of God in the
      Short Stories of Flannery O'Connor, Bernard Malamud and John
      Updike." Ph.D. dissertation, Claremont Graduate School and
      University Center, 264 pp.
      Concerned with the question of whether the authors
discussed demonstrate a grasp of God in their fiction. The
meaning of God in their stories is contingent on what the
characters understand about themselves and the world they
inhabit. These writers hold, as it were, a dialogue with
theologians in which both literature and theology are examined
within the framework of existential categories and the results
compared. "Those critics who fail to appreciate our authors'
religious heritages inadequately interpret the literature." See
Dissertation Abstracts International 31 (1971):6700A.

9   HICKS, GRANVILLE. "Bernard Malamud." In Literary Horizons:
      A Quarter Century of American Fiction. New York: New York
      University Press, pp. 66-83.
      This chapter contains five reprinted reviews of Malamud's
fiction which include The Assistant (1957.8), The Magic Barrel
(1958.5), A New Life (1961.12), The Fixer (1966.32), and
Pictures of Fidelman (1969.20).

10   HOAG, GERALD. "Malamud's Trial: The Fixer and the
      Critics." Western Humanities Review 24, no. 1 (Winter):1-12.
      Despite Malamud's claim that The Fixer is not intended to
be a triumphant book, some critics insist that its triumph is
not carried with sufficient clarity or freshness; others feel
that Yakov Bok is not successfully conceived as the hero. Hoag
feels that these critics have failed to understand the movement
of the book and Malamud's characterization of Bok. Indeed, the

1970

scenic repetitiveness in the novel, along with its recurring instances of brutality, contribute to making Bok a convincing character whose growth is credible. Both Malamud's politics and Bok's suffering have an immediacy for the twentieth-century reader. Reprinted: 1975.6.

11 KAHN, SHOLOM K. "Will and Power in American Literature." Studi Americani (Rome) 16:429-51 passim.
      Examines the "problem of the will" through the perspective offered by American writers of poetry and fiction. In section 6 of this essay, Kahn attempts to isolate "a peculiarly Jewish attitude towards will and power," as it is reflected in the fiction of Bernard Malamud, particularly in The Fixer. In Yakov Bok's willingness to adopt another man's child, the result of his wife's infidelity, Bok reveals "the primacy of heart and will" that characterizes the essence of Jewish behavior.

12 KLEIN, MARCUS. "Bernard Malamud: The Sadness of Goodness." In After Alienation: American Novels in Mid-Century. Essay Index Reprint Series. Freeport, N.Y.: Books for Libraries Press, pp. 247-93.
      Reprint of 1965.5

13 LAMDIN, LOIS S. "Malamud's Schlemiels." In Modern Miscellany. Carnegie Series in English, no. 11 Pittsburgh: Carnegie-Mellon University, pp. 30-42.
      Two types of schlemiels are present in Malamud's fiction: those who lack insight into themselves and the world around them, and those who, despite intelligence and sensitivity, are forced by fate into the role of schlemiels. In the case of the latter figure, suffering is more intense because of his greater level of awareness. Lamdin compares and contrasts such schlemiels as Roy Hobbs, Arthur Fidelman, S. Levin, and Yakov Bok.

14 LEFCOWITZ, BARBARA F. "The Hybris of Neurosis: Malamud's Pictures of Fidelman." Literature and Psychology 20, no. 3:115-20.
      Malamud continually juxtaposes Arthur Fidelman's private neurosis, concerning his failure as artist, to his moral failure in the public world. Fidelman's narcissistic fantasies continually undermine his capacity for responsible action. His return to America to become a craftsman in glass and a lover of men and women is an ambitious if not an ironic resolution.

15 MALAMUD, BERNARD. Letter to Whit Burnett. In This Is My Best: In the Third Quarter of the Century. Edited by Whit Burnett. Garden City, N.Y: Doubleday & Co., p. 505.

Explains that his stimulus in writing "The Jewbird" came from reading Howard Nemerov's "Digressions Around a Crow" in the Spring 1962 Carleton Miscellany. "It was about a talking bird, and I said to myself, thinking of a Jewfish, suppose the bird had been Jewish. At that point the story came to life."

16   MAY, CHARLES E. "The Bread of Tears: Malamud's 'The Loan.'" Studies in Short Fiction 7, no. 4 (Fall):652-54.
      Malamud adapts the scriptural phrase, the "bread of tears," to fit the thematic intent of his story. The tears of Bessie are, in reality, a reflection of her own tough-mindedness rather than a sign of her weakness and misery, as traditionally tears have been for Jews. In refusing to lend Kobotsky money for a memorial stone to his dead wife, she affirms, in essence, the needs of the living wife. Her mock tears, like the tears Lieb sheds into his own bread, are in their own way miraculous.

17   MONTAGUE, GENE; HENSHAW, MARJORIE; and SALERNO, NICHOLAS A., eds. "[Analysis of] 'The Bill.'" In The Experience of Literature, 2d ed. Englewood Cliffs, N.J.: Prentice-Hall, pp. 12-22.
      Discusses Malamud's story from various angles: its modified use of omniscient point of view; the shape of its dramatic structure; the appearance of major and minor characters; the vagueness of its setting; and the symbolic significance of its recurring motif, the bill.

18   MUDRICK, MARVIN. "Malamud, Bellow, and Roth." In On Culture and Literature. New York: Horizon Press, pp. 200-230.
      Reprint of 1966.46.

19   PINSKER, SANFORD [SIGMUND]. "The 'Hasid' in American Literature." Reconstructionist 36 (6 March):7-15.
      Until very recently American Jews rejected the image of Hasid as Jew, but a current wave of nostalgia for this ultimate Jew now exists. In Malamud's The Assistant, the nonobservant Morris Bober is nonetheless reminiscent of the traditional Hasidic Jew in his ethical stance rather than in conscious ethical preoccupations.

20   RAFFEL, BURTON. "Bernard Malamud." Literary Review 13, no. 2 (Winter):149-55.
      Malamud's prose style is varied rather than distinctively Yiddish in its rhythms. It has as much in common with James T. Farrell's Studs Lonigan or the flatness of American urban speech. At times Malamud's prose can be semipoetic, as in The Natural. Such variety in prose is rather a symptom of an indecisiveness rather than a reflection of his ingenuity. In relation to humanity Malamud is not as emotionally committed as

1970

we have come to believe: "[he] does not like people any more
than he likes the world."

21   ROTHSTEIN, R. "Sight and Sound." <u>Hadassah</u> 57, no. 2
      (October):34.
          Judges the film adaptation of "Angel Levine" unfortunate
      because of its sentimentalism. Jan Kadar has attempted to
      emphasize the ambiguity of human relationships, but we are never
      sure of what the black angel (played by Harry Belafonte) and the
      Jewish tailor (played by Zero Mostel) are intended to represent.
      The actual condition of black-Jewish relationships in New York
      City never impinges on the film, and this omission deprives it
      of a needed substance.

22   RUPP, RICHARD H. "Bernard Malamud: A Party of One." In
      <u>Celebration in Postwar American Fiction</u>. Coral Gables:
      University of Miami Press, pp. 165-88 passim.
          Identity for Malamud's protagonists is established through
      reinvolvement with the past and the acceptance of guilt. These
      twin themes are addressed in <u>The Natural</u>, <u>The Assistant</u>, <u>A New
      Life</u>, <u>The Fixer</u>, <u>The Magic Barrel</u>, and <u>Idiots First</u>. One of the
      recurring motifs which tie these works to each other is the
      ritual lament: "It may be joint weeping over lost youth in a
      bakery, a confession of a misspent life after love-making, or a
      chant of the psalms of lamentation in prison." In each case,
      the lament issues from the most authentic part of the
      protagonist's self.

23   SHER, MORRIS. <u>Bernard Malamud: A Partially Annotated
      Bibliography</u>. Johannesburg: University of Witwatersrand, 24
      pp.
          Sher provides a concise but useful biographical
      introduction to Malamud prior to the bibliographical portion of
      his book. This section includes novels and stories published by
      Malamud and books, articles, and reviews about Malamud's work
      between 1952 and 1969. Part 1 summarizes novels, lists
      publishers, collections of stories, and the first appearance of
      stories. Part 2 supplies biographical comments and critical
      annotations of books, articles, and reviews.

24   SIEGEL, BEN. "Victims in Motion: Bernard Malamud's Sad and
      Bitter Clowns." In <u>Bernard Malamud and the Critics</u>. Edited
      by Leslie A. Field and Joyce A. Field. New York: New York
      University Press; London: University of London Press, pp.
      126-36.
          Reprint of 1962.22.

25   SOLOTAROFF, THEODORE. "Bernard Malamud's Fiction: The Old
      Life and the New." In The Red Hot Vacuum and Other Pieces on
      the Writing of the Sixties. New York: Atheneum, pp. 71-86.
         Reprint of 1962.23.

26   SULLIVAN, WALTER. "'Where Have All the Flowers Gone?' Part
      II: The Novel in Gnostic Twilight." Sewanee Review 78, no.
      4 (October-December):654-64 passim.
         Although Pictures of Fidelman has moments of good prose,
      Malamud seems to have an obsessive interest in the gross and the
      vulgar. These qualities seem to be displayed gratuitously
      rather than having an aesthetic rationale in any of the
      narratives.

27   SWEET, CHARLES A. "Bernard Malamud and the use of Myth."
      Ph.D. dissertation, Florida State University, 160 pp.
         Malamud's theme of the "Brudermensch ideal," that all men
      are responsible for each other, is carried by a mythic sub-
      structure originating in The Natural and developing through
      subsequent novels. In The Natural Roy Hobbs as hero quester
      strives to obtain his Grail (the National League Pennant) in
      order to restore the dying Fisher King (Pop Fisher), but he
      fails because he is incapable of accepting responsibility for
      the Fertility Queen (Iris Lemon). In The Assistant, the hero,
      Frank Alpine, undergoes a deepening of maturity, learning that
      suffering and the assumption of responsibility--for the Bober
      family--are inextricably linked. In A New Life, S. Levin,
      through his commitment to Pauline Gilley, succeeds on a personal
      level, but he fails in his public role as teacher and humanist.
      In The Fixer, Yakov Bok extends Malamud's theme of human
      responsibility to include an entire people, the Jews, and comes
      closest to any of Malamud's figures in fulfilling the role of
      mythic hero. See Dissertation Abstracts International 31
      (1971):4797A.

28   TRACY, ROBERT. "A Sharing of Obsessions." Southern Review,
      n.s. 6, no. 3(July):890-904 passim.
         Malamud's The Fixer invites comparison with Dostoevski's
      The Devils because of name similarities--Lebedev in the former
      and Captin Lebyadkin in the latter--and their atmosphere of
      conspiracy. In The Fixer, the monstrous and the malevolent are
      only partially seen by the reader, leaving him to guess at what
      is left unseen.

29   WECHSLER, DIANE. "An Analysis of 'The Prison' by Bernard
      Malamud." English Journal 59, no. 6 (September):782-84.
         When teaching this story to secondary students, the focus
      should be placed on the character and circumstances surrounding
      the protagonist, Tommy Castelli. Whether Tommy is responsible

1970

for the course of his life or merely a victim of fate should
invite discussion. The extent to which Tommy's point of view is
used as opposed to that of an impartial observer is a matter
also at issue.

30   WEINBERG, HELEN. The New Novel in America: The Kafkan Mode
      in American Fiction. Ithaca, N.Y.: Cornell University Press,
      pp. 168-78.
          Discusses Malamud's fiction in relation to other Kafkan
      novelists in the "activist mode." Kafka's influence on Malamud
      is represented by The Trial and The Castle, novels which reflect
      both the passive and the active hero, respectively. Roy Hobbs
      in The Natural shares the plight of Karl Rossman in Amerika
      through his victimization, wandering, and quest for identity.
      Malamud's S. Levin in A New Life resembles the hero of Kafka's
      The Castle in his insistence on freedom, his embracing of life's
      possibilities, and his arrival at a new sense of self. Both
      writers mix irony with affirmation, and worldly defeat with
      spiritual hope for the self.

31   WISSE, RUTH ROSKIES. "The Schlemiel as Hero in Yiddish and
      American Fiction." Ph.D. dissertation, McGill University
      (pages not given).
          Although an import from eastern European literature, the
      figure of the schlemiel in the works of such American writers as
      Saul Bellow and Bernard Malamud reflects the mood of America in
      the sixties. Through this figure, these writers explore "the
      paradox of failure as success within a secular humanist
      culture." See Dissertation Abstracts International 30
      (1970):293A. Revised for publication: 1971.55

1971

1   ALLEN, JOHN A[LEXANDER]. "The Promised End: Bernard
      Malamud's The Tenants." Hollins Critic 8, no. 5
      (December):1-15.
          The Tenants carries three closely connected themes:
      racial hostility versus brotherhood, art and its relation to
      life, and the victim as victimizer. The darkest of all
      Malamud's novels, this work offers only a remote suggestion of
      hope as Harry Lesser and Willie Spearmint feel the pain of the
      other during their murderous confrontation. The presiding
      vision is that of man's potential for destruction, symbolized in
      the tenement by the ubiquitous odor of decay. The loveless
      condition of Harry Lesser is foreshadowed by Arthur Fidelman in
      Pictures of Fidelman. Reprinted: 1975.6

2   BELL, PEARL K. "Morality Tale without Mercy." New Leader 54
(18 October):17-18.
     The Tenants is a parable about dehumanization. In Harry
Lesser's obsessive commitment to art, he loses a sense of what
it means to be human. Bell considers the novel Malamud's finest
work.

3   BROYARD, ANATOLE. "The View from the Tenement: I." New York
Times, 20 September, p. 23.
     Malamud's The Tenants is a risky, controversial, and
radical book about race relations. The tenement, as a setting,
is no longer the home for East Side Jews struggling to survive
but rather a contemporary symbol of civilization in the midst of
conflict and decay, involving the haves and have-nots. Harry
Lesser, "the landlord of literature," regards the black writer,
Willie Spearmint, in his repudiation of form, as an unwelcome
intruder on his metaphorical literary premises.

4   BROYARD, ANATOLE. "The View from the Tenement: II." New
York Times, 21 September, p. 35.
     Continues his review of The Tenants from the previous day.
Willie Spearmint, a black writer, regards the sympathetic Jewish
writer, Harry Lesser, as attempting to subvert the communication
of his revolutionary rage. Although the conclusion of the book
falls apart literally and symbolically, Malamud writes out of
the depth of his concern for humanity and can be forgiven his
artistic lapses.

5   CANTINELLA, JOSEPH. Review of The Tenants. Saturday Review
of Literature 54 (25 September):36.
     Initially, this novel is similar to Mann's Tonio Kröger or
James's The Middle Years in its concern with the artist's
struggle to create art out of life, but The Tenants develops
into a despairing statement about man's inherent egotism and
selfishness. In its management of its formal elements, Malamud
has been highly successful.

6   CRAIB, RODERICK. Review of The Tenants. Commonweal 95 (24
December):309, 311.
     In addition to its narrowly focused Jewish-black
confrontation, The Tenants offers an insight into American
culture of the seventies, and the pessimism of Malamud's vision
is mitigated by the dynamic quality of his art.

7   DICKSTEIN, MORRIS. Review of The Tenants. New York Times
Book Review 76 (3 October):1, 4, 16, 18, 20.
     Malamud has the most authentic Jewish imagination in
American literature, but he has not been successful in rendering
the aims of contemporary black militant writers. As their

representative, Willie Spearmint in The Tenants seems no more, at times, than a stereotype or a parody of their movement. Yet while Bellow's Mr. Sammler's Planet can only use a black as a negative cultural symbol, Malamud has successfully caught the personal rage of black toward white and the range of their conflicts.

8   DOLLARD, PETER. "A Clash between Two Writers, a Jew and a Black." Library Journal 96 (15 October):3346.
     Praises the ending of The Tenants for its unusual revelation in which Harry Lesser's own heart of darkness is revealed. He is more like Willie Spearmint than he realizes.

9   DUCHARME, ROBERT [E.]. "Structure and Content in Malamud's Pictures of Fidelman." Connecticut Review 5 (October):26-36.
     Pictures of Fidelman is a picaresque chronicle, episodic in structure and various in its narrative styles. Subsequent to the earlier Fidelman pieces, Malamud began thinking of publishing additional stories that would establish a single work, a novel of episodes. The controlling ideas of suffering and responsibility, as they relate to Fidelman, are the basis of a loose novelistic unity.

10   FISCH, HAROLD. "The American Jewish Renaissance." In The Dual Image: The Figure of the Jew in English and American Literature. [New York]: Ktav Publishing House, pp. 111-30 passim.
     Non-Jews venturing into "the spiritual zone of Jewish suffering" share a fate similar to that of Jews, and both The Assistant and The Fixer offer examples of the suffering of these Gentiles.

11   FREEDMAN, RICHARD. Review of The Tenants. Book World 7 (19 September):4.
     The Tenants furnishes a nightmare inversion of Leslie Fiedler's thesis that white and colored characters in American fiction have homoerotic feelings toward each other. The intensity of the Harry Lesser-Willie Spearmint relationship has the tautness and economy of a Beckett play.

12   GIDDEN, NANCY ANN. "Fictional Techniques in the Work of Bernard Malamud." Ph.D. dissertation, Florida State University, 310 pp.
     Explores the variety of Malamud's fictional techniques in four novels--The Natural, The Assistant, A New Life, and The Fixer--and three collections of stories--The Magic Barrel, Idiots First, and Pictures of Fidelman. Malamud's technical virtuosity in his use of point of view, plot, setting, and style is as impressive as his expression of humanist themes. See Dissertation Abstracts International 34 (1973):3392A-93A.

13   GLASSGOLD, PETER. "Malamud's Literary Ethic." <u>Nation</u> 213
      (15 November):504-5.
          Reduced to its essence, <u>The Tenants</u> uses the act of
      writing as a metaphor for selfhood. Thus the written work of
      Harry Lesser and Willie Spearmint, Jew and black, becomes both a
      battle of books and a battle between men.

14   GOENS, MARY BOTSFORD. "Process and Vision in Malamud's
      Novels." Ph.D. dissertation, University of California,
      Irvine, 172 pp.
          Malamud's style is studied in relation to his themes.
      Chapter 1 examines language and point of view in <u>The Natural</u>;
      chapter 2, language and character in <u>The Assistant</u>; chapter 3,
      lyric structure in <u>The Fixer</u>; chapter 4, the function of irony
      in <u>A New Life</u>; chapter 5, the use of parody, stream of
      consciousness, and cinematic techniques in <u>Pictures of
      Fidelman</u>. One sees finally a dynamic tension between Malamud's
      fictional diversity and his thematic consistency. See
      <u>Dissertation Abstracts International</u> 32 (1971):3303A.

15   GUTTMAN, ALLEN. <u>The Jewish Writer in America: Assimilation
      and the Crisis of Identity</u>. New York: Oxford University
      Press, pp. 112-20 passim.
          Malamud's vision of the Jew is often difficult to
      classify. In his irony he resembles Philip Roth, and in his
      belief in peoplehood he is reminiscent of Ludwig Lewisohn.

16   HALIO, JAY L. "Fantasy and Fiction." <u>Southern Review</u>, n.s.
      7, no. 2 (April):635-47 passim.
          Fantasy is the vehicle for developing Malamud's central
      theme in <u>Pictures of Fidelman</u>--the liberating force of love
      through which Arthur Fidelman is released from the prison of his
      art and egotism. In their own employment of fantasy, Leonard
      Michaels and Isaac Bashevis Singer resemble Malamud.

17   HANDY, WILLIAM J. "Malamud's <u>The Fixer</u>. In <u>Modern Fiction:
      A Formalist Approach</u>. Crosscurrents/Modern Critiques, edited
      by Harry T. Moore. Carbondale: Southern Illinois University
      Press; London: Feffer & Simmons, pp. 131-58 passim.
          <u>The Fixer</u> addresses itself to the existential problem of
      being, and this theme is dramatized through the psychological
      and moral dynamics of Yakov Bok's point of view. Bok's literal
      quest for freedom sustains the plot of the novel and is counter-
      pointed by shifting images of incarceration and liberation.
      Bok's freedom remains problematic even at the conclusion, but
      Malamud's hero does finally achieve an inner poise and a
      "whimsical detachment."

1971

18   HARPER, HOWARD M., Jr. "Trends in Recent American Fiction."
        Contemporary Literature 12, no. 2 (Spring):204-29 passim.
            Pictures of Fidelman (1969) possesses more unity as a
        collection of short narratives than either The Magic Barrel
        (1958) or Idiots First (1963). As Fidelman's consciousness
        grows, the stories become successively "more complex and
        beautiful." Through the crude sexual incidents of the plot,
        Malamud creates metaphors of artistic and spiritual stress.
        Harper judges the book to be brilliant, inventive, and
        insightful, "Malamud's finest achievement."

19   HILL, WILLIAM B., S.J. Review of The Tenants. Best Sellers
        31 (15 October):316.
            Despite the difficulties of plot, this novel contains a
        dynamic prose style, interesting characters, and significant
        reflections on the problems of the writer. Malamud does not
        resolve the issues that he introduces, but the work is
        "beautifully written, solid, substantial."

20   HIRSCH, DAVID H. "Jewish Identity and Jewish Suffering in
        Bellow, Malamud, and Philip Roth." In Jewish Book Annual,
        vol. 25. Edited by A. Alan Steinbach. New York: Jewish
        Book Council of America, pp. 12-22 passim.
            Malamud has introduced into English prose the rhythms of
        Yiddish: through misplaced adverbs, inverted syntax, eliminated
        prepositions, or the vague use of the relative pronoun, "this."
        The suffering of Malamud's characters, rather than their habits
        of speech, is the essence of their Jewishness. Although many
        critics regard The Fixer as the fullest expression of Jewish
        suffering, Hirsch dissents from their view, finding Malamud's
        language inadequate to the task of representing Jewish suffering
        in Russia.

21   KNOKE, PAUL D. "The Allegorical Mode in the Contemporary
        American Novel of Romance." Ph.D. dissertation, Ohio
        University, 160 pp.
            Bernard Malamud's The Natural is studied as an allegorical
        narrative embracing the Grail legend, baseball lore, and Jungian
        psychology, material which may be regarded as twice-told tales.
        Special attention is directed to parts 1 and 2 of the novel with
        regard to their analogical relationships to each other. Other
        allegorical narratives in this study displaying the same kind of
        narrative flexibilty as The Natural include John Knowles's A
        Separate Peace, John Updike's The Centaur, and Saul Bellow's
        Henderson the Rain King. See Dissertation Abstracts
        International 32 (1971):2695A.

22   LEER, NORMAN. "The Double Theme in Malamud's Assistant:
      Dostoevsky with Irony." Mosaic 4 (Spring):89-102.
         Demonstrates that in Crime and Punishment and The
      Assistant, both main characters are possessed of a pronounced
      dualism. Their ambivalence leads to a pattern of inner conflict
      and expiation. With Malamud's hero, the expiation is more
      direct, but the end result is more ironic since Frank Alpine has
      no social context of his own in which to receive redemption.
      Where in Dostoevski the double theme arouses and often fulfills
      expectations that a resolution of inner conflict will occur, in
      Malamud only some of these expectations are fulfilled, the
      disparity between expectation and reality creating irony.

23   LEFF, LEONARD J. "Malamud's Ferris Wheel." Notes on
      Contemporary Literature 1, no. 1 (January):14-15.
         Considers the silent fixture of the ferris wheel in The
      Natural and The Assistant a mythic symbol for the experiences
      which Roy Hobbs and Helen Bober undergo--journey, separation,
      initiation, and return--in their respective narratives.

24   _____. "Utopia Reconsidered: Alientation in Vonnegut's God
      Bless You, Mr. Rosewater." Critique: Studies in Modern
      Fiction 12, no. 3: 25-53 passim.
         Suggests that in The Assistant Frank Alpine's alientation
      is so complete that his conversion to Judaism can offer him only
      a token identity. (The article is primarily concerned with
      Vonnnegut's novel.)

25   LEVY, ERIC PETER. "Metaphysical Shock: A Study of the
      Novels of Bernard Malamud." Ph.D. dissertation, Stanford
      University, 186 pp.
         The experience that leads the Malamud hero to understand
      that suffering is a natural condition of humanity comes as a
      metaphysical shock, its impact forcing him to view that
      suffering from a completely new vantage point. Since it is so
      pervasive, the hero begins to embrace suffering beyond his own
      as a commitment to humanity. See Dissertation Abstracts
      International 32 (1971):5796A.

26   LINDROTH, JAMES. Review of The Tenants. America 125 (25
      December):561.
         The Tenants is a marriage of tragedy and social comedy
      which turns into "apocalyptic nightmare." In this novel Malamud
      brings the Victorian debate of art versus social responsibility
      up to date.

27   McPHERSON, WILLIAM. "Learning to Love, Hate." Washington
      Post, 29 September, pp. D1, D6.

1971

> The Tenants is sporadically excellent--an ironic, witty,
> and fantastic novel--but ultimately it fails to satisfy.
> Possibly the reason is that Malamud's message is as difficult to
> take for the reader as Willie Spearmint's is for Harry Lesser.

28   MADDOCKS, MELVIN. "Life is Suffering but. . . ." Atlantic
      228, no. 5 (November):132, 134, 136.
         In The Tenants Malamud's theme of suffering is no longer
      balanced by the existence of positive humanistic values or, for
      that matter, the attractions of his wit, characters, or plot.
      Rather than being about black anti-Semitism, the novel is really
      centered in Malamud's growing doubts about redeeming life.
      "Willie [Spearmint] stands for all in life that can't be charmed
      by Malamud--all that can't be made to yield to his admirable
      moral earnestness and literary tact."

29   MALIN, IRVING. "Lines between Life and Art." Congress
      Bi-Weekly: Journal of Opinion and Jewish Affairs 38 (10
      December):20.
         The Tenants uses characters and events primarily to
      reflect upon the conflict between art and life. Through
      Levenspiel's plea for mercy, Malamud seems to endorse the
      traditional Jewish value placed on life, but "when all is said
      and done art alone is the landlord . . .[and] people merely the
      tenants of style."

30   MANO, D. KEITH. "A Balanced Ticket." National Review 23 (3
      December):1358-59.
         The Tenants is Malamud's best book to date, and it has
      that distinctive informal speech which flavors Malamud's style.
      If the book offends some, it is a result of its unflinching
      honesty on the subject of black-white confrontation.

31   MARKOVIC, VIDA E. "S Bernardom Malamudom" [An Interview].
      Savremenik (Belgrade): 17, no. 33:282-86.
         In Serbo-Croation. Observes Malamud's controlled
      intellectual excitement and his capacity for maintaining his own
      sense of identity in the midst of his audience at Corvallis,
      Oregon. Malamud considered that for himself experiments in
      genre were not as important as the presentation of meaningful
      content. James Joyce, for example, somewhere between Ulysses
      and Finnegans Wake, became overly concerned with linguistic
      technique at the expense of substance. Concerning his
      character, Arthur Fidelman, Malamud noted his tendency to
      self-indulgence and self-contempt. On the other hand, Yakov Bok
      became for him a symbol of the unconquerable human spirit.
      Malamud continues in his concern for humane interaction between
      people and the growth of man's soul.

1971

32   MURRAY, MICHELE. "Unarguably, Malamud at His Best."
     National Catholic Reporter 7 (22 October):12.
        Praises The Tenants for its handling of language and for
its effective presentation of a clash between two opposing
sensibilities. The work is marred by Malamud's capitulation to
violence and sentimentality, but it nevertheless remains "a sad
and beautiful story of the artist's desires and failures and the
way commitment to art can dry up the springs of life--the aging
artist's nightmare."

33   PEROSA, SERGIO. "Incontri americani: 4. Bernard Malamud."
     Studi Americani 17:402-11.
        The center of Malamud's inspiration is the individual's
desire to achieve freedom and moral affirmation. These themes
are developed in The Fixer within the framework of history and
have application for the present. The torment in the novel
arises from historical issues, not from an irrational or random
caprice of an absurd universe. For Malamud it is through
history that a new ideology can be created offering hope for the
future.

34   PINSKER, SANFORD [SIGMUND]. "Christ as Revolutionary/
     Revolutionary as Christ: The Hero in Bernard Malamud's The
     Fixer and William Styron's The Confessions of Nat Turner."
     Barat Review 7, no. 1 (Spring-Summer):29-37.
        Compares Malamud and Styron's use of historical sources
for novelistic purposes. For Malamud, the trial of Mendel
Beiliss held mythic possibilities. From the bland and
uninspiring figure of Beiliss, Malamud's Bok emerges as a
militant Christ figure, embracing both politics and revolution.
Styron's Nat Turner is historically a more controversial figure
than Malamud's Bok; and for some black writers Styron's
characterization of Turner--as man and revolutionary--is
unflattering to black sensibilities.

35   _____. "The Schlemiel as Moral Bungler: Bernard Malamud's
     Ironic Heroes." In The Schlemiel as Metaphor: Studies in
     the Yiddish and American Jewish Novel. Carbondale: Southern
     Illinois University Press, pp. 87-124.
        Revision of 1967.36. The characters of Bernard Malamud's
fiction involve themselves in moral actions, the end result of
which is failure. In their characterization as schlemiels,
individuals who are inept, despite the worthiest of motives,
they invariably suffer as a result of their good intentions.
This study examines the patterns of bungling that occur in The
Magic Barrel, The Assistant, A New Life, and The Fixer. For-
saking the concentrated irony and ambiguity surrounding the
schlemiel in the first three works, Malamud establishes Yakov
Bok of The Fixer as a hero possessed of tragic dignity.
Reprinted 1975.6.

1971

36   PRESCOTT, PETER S. "Ying, Yang, and Schlemiel." <u>Newsweek</u> 78
      (27 September):110, 112.
          Despite its violence <u>The Tenants</u> is essentially a
      well-constructed comic parable. The polarity between life and
      art is engagingly dramatized but remains for Malamud and the
      reader incapable of resolution.

37   Review of <u>The Tenants</u>. <u>Antioch Review</u> 31, no. 3 (Fall):438.
          This tautly written novel brings hostility and suffering
      to a new plateau in Malamud's fiction. In a world that seems no
      longer habitable, the reader is likely to hope that Levenspiel's
      cry for mercy becomes more than a lamenting wail.

38   Review of <u>The Tenants</u>. <u>Publisher's Weekly</u> 200 (23 August):
      74.
          A bitter comedy, this novel may be shocking and troubling
      for many. While we never discover what Harry Lesser's work is
      about, Malamud provides samples of the "black writer's work that
      steer a very daring line between parody and truth."

39   RICHLER, MORDECAI. "Malamud's Race War." <u>Life</u> 67 (22
      October):10.
          Malamud, like Melville, has attempted to produce a mighty
      theme in <u>The Tenants</u>, but the reader will find the novel
      frustrating and, like Levenspiel, the landlord, ask for mercy.
      The book is "muddled, slipshod, and even inchoate in places."

40   RIDLEY, CLIFFORD A. "Malamud Weaves a Fable in Black."
      <u>National Observer</u> 10 (30 October):21.
          <u>The Tenants</u> establishes two kinds of men as well as two
      styles of art. Harry Lesser appears pompous, incapable of love,
      and spiritually dead. Despite his many faults, Willie Spearmint
      is redeemed by his vitality and by an art that seems more
      directly concerned with life than Lesser's.

41   SALE, ROGER. "What Went Wrong?" <u>New York Review of Books</u>
      17, no. 6 (21 October):3-6.
          Praises Malamud's conscious and measured intentions in <u>The
      Tenants</u>, but finds the plot strategy unclear and the motivations
      of Harry Lesser in falling in love with Irene, Willie Spear-
      mint's girl, equally obscure. These problems may reflect
      Malamud's inability to work through the racial issue within the
      scope of a novel. His material might have fared better in the
      form of a short fable.

42   SCHLUETER, PAUL. "Seeds of Destruction." <u>Christian Century</u>
      88 (8 December):1448.

Malamud's The Tenants portrays two writers--one Jewish, the other black--who are destroyed by their particular obsessions. The hatred of these characters for each other is not well motivated, and the ending of the novel unsatisfying. Despite these flaws, the novel must be ranked among Malamud's best.

43   SHENKER, ISRAEL. "For Malamud It's Story." New York Times
        Book Review 76 (3 October):20.
            Relates an interview with Malamud concerning his
        philosophy of composition in which these ideas feature:
        Malamud's stress on revision, his insistence on the importance
        of story, and his willingness to take chances with and surprise
        the reader. With regard to character, a typical Malamud
        character "fears his fate, is caught up in it, yet manages to
        outrun it." Such a figure is usually the source of pity as well
        as humor. Reprinted: 1972.41

44   SHEPPARD, RONALD Z. "Condemnation Proceedings." Time 98 (27
        September):96-97.
            Malamud seems to have had trouble in resolving the ending
        of The Tenants. As a parable that ends on a note of compassion
        rather than in Solomon-like wisdom, the book reveals the
        author's humanity and fundamental honesty.

45   SKOLNIK, NORMA. "Novels--Major and Minor." Jewish Spectator
        36, no. 10 (December):30-31.
            The Tenants is characterized by comedy as well as by its
        tragic intensity. The structure of the novel is achieved
        through the play of realism and fantasy. "This is a bold and
        gripping novel, born of the anguish of our time and situation."

46   SPIVAK, MARK. "7 x Malamud at the Library." Washington
        Post, 9 November, p. B2.
            Seven Malamud stories were given a dramatic reading on 8
        November as part of the Library Congress Whittall Poetry and
        Literature Series. Arnold Moss and four other Broadway actors
        performed. All of these stories embody a fundamental charac-
        teristic of Jewish experience, the presence of humor in the
        midst of suffering. Given the responsive laughter of the
        audience, one evening devoted to Malamud seemed insufficient.

47   STANDLEY, FRED L. "Bernard Malamud: The Novel of
        Redemption." Southern Humanities Review 5, no. 4
        (Fall):309-18.
            Observes that The Natural, The Assistant, A New Life, and
        The Fixer offer a new affirmative mood in modern fiction,
        departing from all the modern themes associated with man's
        insignificance and the absurdity of human life. All four novels

1971

explore "the melancholic suffering state of the human
condition," but thematically they also suggest that man's
redemption is possible within the actual world despite the
annihilating forces that often brutalize the human spirit.
Malamud's celebration of human life seems anachronistic at this
moment in time.

48   STETLER, CHARLES. Review of <u>Pictures of Fidelman</u>. <u>Studies
      in Short Fiction</u> 8, no. 2 (Spring):341-43.
          <u>Pictures of Fidelman</u> invites comparisons with <u>Winesburg
      Ohio</u> and <u>Dubliners</u>. The unifying elements binding the separate
      Fidelman stories to each other come from the metaphoric use of
      art, sex, and Jewishness. Stetler concludes that Malamud "has
      successfully united all the American traditions--Twain and
      James, realism and naturalism--with his Jewish heritage. . . ."

49   STONE, RICHARD. "Malamud: Exposing Racial Fraud?" <u>Wall
      Street Journal</u>, 12 October, p. 20.
          In the last few years the topic of race has been a special
      source of controversy among intellectuals and writers, and now
      Bernard Malamud has added his voice to it in <u>The Tenants</u>. In
      his sometimes humorous version of the white man's burden,
      Malamud has been adept at achieving moments of "brilliant
      satire," but without contributing any new insights to the
      problem of racism in America. "At times when journalists are
      turning their work into novels, Mr. Malamud has unfortunately
      turned his into journalism."

50   STRASSBERG, MILDRED P. "Religious Commitment in Recent
      American Fiction: Flannery O'Connor, Bernard Malamud, John
      Updike." Ph.D. dissertation, State University of New York at
      Stonybrook, 149 pp.
          Malamud, along with O'Connor and Updike, emerges as an
      integrating figure on the contemporary American scene through
      his attempt to establish a bridge between Christian and Jew. In
      their own way, these three writers attempt to unite "body and
      soul, thought and act, religion and morality." Without
      flinching, they face the various contradictions of life and
      remain affirmative. See <u>Dissertation Abstracts International</u> 32
      (1972):6457A.

51   SYRKIN, MARIE. "From Frank Alpine to Willie Spearmint. . . ."
      <u>Midstream</u> 17, no. 9 (November):64-68.
          The contemporary toughness of Malamud's style in <u>The
      Tenants</u> undermines the effectiveness of the novel in addition to
      its other problems: its rigid allegory, a thesis existing at
      the expense of character, and an unconvincing plot. In contrast
      to the unrealized characters of <u>The Tenants</u>, Frank Alpine and
      Morris Bober of <u>The Assistant</u> are more human and individualized.

The characters and situation used to explore the black-Jewish conflict in The Tenants have less substance than the problem itself.

52   TANNER, TONY. "A New Life." In City of Words: American Fiction 1950-1970. New York: Harper & Row, pp. 322-43.
        Observes that Malamud's novels are parables of initiation involving the hero's movement from immaturity to maturity, but in attitudes rather than years. Time itself often becomes for his hero an obsession or a source of anguish. Although these parables are sustained throughout the fiction, Malamud maintains their vitality by experimenting with different fictional modes. The variety of artists alluded to in Pictures of Fidelman reminds us of Malamud's own diversity of narrative representation.

53   WARBURTON, ROBERT W. "Fantasy and the Fiction of Bernard Malamud." In Imagination and the Spirit: Essays in Literature and the Christian Faith Presented to Clyde S. Kilby. Edited by Charles A. Huttar. Grand Rapids, Mich.: William B. Eerdmans Publishing Co., pp. 387-416.
        Explores the lexical and psychological definitions of fantasy as a prelude to an examination of Malamud's fiction. This study locates three distinct categories of fantasy running through his work: "objective or traditional fantasy, subjective fantasy, and reciprocal fantasy." Objective fantasy involves place, time, or characters foreign to our notions of the real and is illustrated by "Take Pity" and "The Jewbird." Subjective fantasy arises through the manifestation of some form of spiritual truth within the context of ordinary life, as in The Assistant or The Fixer. In reciprocal fantasy, the fantastic and the ordinary influence each other so that neither dimension remains the same. "The Magic Barrel," "Idiots First," and "Angel Levine" are representative of this third kind.

54   WEALES, GERALD. "Fictional Chronicle." Hudson Review 24, no. 4 (Winter):716-30.
        Finds the subject matter of The Tenants too reminiscent of The Assistant and "Angel Levine," and the racial confrontation rather tired "black" comedy. "The difficulty with The Tenants . . . is that the book itself is never as interesting as the aesthetic, psychological and social assumptions that give it an open-ended form."

55   WISSE, RUTH R[OSKIES]. The Schlemiel as Modern Hero. Chicago: University of Chicago Press, pp. 39, 82-32, 110-18.
        Revision of 1970.31. Among contemporary Jewish writers only in Malamud is the condition of the schlemiel positively presented. In "The Last Mohican," for example, Shimon Susskind forces Arthur Fidelman to confront and accept his true identity

1971

as a schlemiel. Later stories in the same series involving
Fidelman characterize him as an unredeemed schlemiel whose
failures are now deprived of meaning.

56   YARDLEY, JONATHAN. "The Obscure Sufferers." New Republic
      165 (16 October):24, 26.
          Asserts that The Tenants is an improvement over The Fixer,
      largely because Malamud is in his element when he depicts the
      brutal atmosphere of the urban scene. The suffering that
      Malamud represents is a phenomenon of the human condition rather
      than the result of topical racial issues.

1972

1   ALTER, ROBERT. "Updike, Malamud, and the Fire This Time."
      Commentary 54, no. 4 (October):68-74.
          Compares Malamud's The Tenants to Updike's Rabbit, Run and
      Rabbit Redux in their handling of racial conflict and perceives
      that both novelists convey the sense of an eroding white
      identity in the face of black self-assertion. The apocalyptic
      vision of each writer originates, however, from a differing
      conception of the protagonist. For Malamud, Harry Lesser's
      battle with the black writer, Willie Spearmint, is presented as
      an individual nightmare; Updike's Harry Angstrom's fear is
      anchored to both a private and a collective sense of complicity
      and guilt for the black man's condition.

2   BARON, ALEXANDER. "Malamud's Design." Jewish Quarterly 20,
      no. 1 (Spring):44-45.
          Experiences a qualified pleasure in reading The Tenants, a
      book flawed in comparison to Malamud's previous novels and short
      stories. The debate between Lesser and Levenspiel establishes
      one structural element in the novel, the movement between past
      and present tense, but it is Levenspiel's repeated cry for mercy
      that gives it its central structure. The intentions of
      Malamud's art are possibly too visible and may be symptomatic of
      the basic weakness in this novel.

3   BEN-ASHER, NAOMI. "Jewish Identity and Christological
      Symbolism in the Work of Three Writers." Jewish Frontier 39,
      no. 9 (November):9-15.
          Treats Boris Pasternak's Doctor Zhivago, Andre Schwarz-
      Bart's The Last of the Just, and Bernard Malamud's The Assistant
      as works that touch on the relation of suffering to Jewish
      identity. The informing idea of each novel is that an
      individual's life may serve a sacrificial and redemptive purpose
      for mankind.

100

4   CHARLES, GERDA. "Flaws in a Marvellous Writer." Jewish
        Observer and Middle East Review 21 (19 May):17.
             Apart from its technical ingenuity and penetrating
        insights, the Tenants is a disappointing novel. It is too
        modish in its use of violence and sex, unconvincing in its
        characterization of the sensitive but morally debauched Harry
        Lesser, and somewhat precious in its elaboration of Lesser's
        view that art is more important than life.

5   COHEN, SANDY. "The Theme of Self-Transcendence in the
        Fiction of Bernard Malamud." Ph.D. dissertation, Auburn
        University, 180 pp.
             Through a painful process of self-scrutiny, Malamud's
        heroes move from eros to caritas, transcending the narrow limits
        of their own egotism, and their character development is traced
        through six novels. See Dissertation Abstracts International 33
        (1972):1163A. Revised for publication: 1974.2.

6   CUDDIHY, JOHN MURRAY. "Jews, Blacks and the Cold War at the
        Top." Worldview 15, no. 2 (February):30-40.
             Bernard Malamud's The Tenants is an allegory reflecting
        the cold war in the early sixties between Jews and blacks for
        the cultural status of being designated the true victims of
        society. Malamud's novel reproduces symbolically the various
        intellectual debates between blacks and Jews over this issue
        that appeared in such journals as Midstream. Ironically, Harry
        Lesser's attempt to tutor Willie Spearmint in the importance of
        form over feeling is similar to the instruction Jewish
        contemporary writers gleaned--Saul Bellow, in particular--in
        subduing emotion, that is, Yiddishkeit materials, from their
        Gentile American masters. "That Malamud chose the top story of
        an old tenement as his scene for the cultural clash between
        black and Jewish literary intellectuals demonstrates his gift
        for inspired metaphor."

7   FAULKNER, HOWARD JOHN. "Bernard Malamud: The Promise of a
        New Life." Ph.D. dissertation, University of Oklahoma, 167
        pp.
             The thematic movement in Malamud's fiction is from an old
        life to a new one, that point at which the Malamud hero
        discovers the redemptive value of suffering. After A New Life,
        however, renunciation receives less emphasis in his work while
        experiments in form and technique begin to feature. See
        Dissertation Abstracts International 33 (1973):5720A.

8   FEINSTEIN, ELAINE. "Guilt," London Magazine, n.s. 12, no. 2
        (June-July):166-68.
             Feelings of guilt associated with Jews and blacks in their
        relations with each other in New York City are translated into a
        complex but effective fictional expression in The Tenants.

1972

9   FINKELSTEIN, SIDNEY. "The Anti-Hero of Updike, Bellow, and
     Malamud." American Dialog 7, no. 2 (Spring):12-14, 30.
         Asserts that these writers create an unattractive image of
     the black man that subverts the movement for black liberation.
     Moreover, the pitting of a white man against a black in
     Malamud's The Tenants is myopic and fails to take into account
     the guilt of capitalist imperialism for the condition of both
     men.

10   FREESE, PETER. "Bernard Malamud's 'The Assistant.'"
     Literatur in Wissenschaft und Unterricht 5 (October):247-60.
         Finds the criticism of The Assistant between 1961 and 1971
     almost unified in its high appraisal of the novel and in general
     agreement over its mythic, symbolic, and thematic elements.
     Critics need to be reminded of two sources for the novel,
     Malamud's "The First Seven Years" and "The Apology," beyond the
     biographical source of Malamud's own family life in Brooklyn.
     Three main areas of investigation still need to be pursued:
     language, style, and narrative technique.

11   FRIEDMAN, ALLEN WARREN. "The Jews Complaint in Recent
     American Fiction: Beyond Exodus and Still in the
     Wilderness." Southern Review, n.s. 8, no. 1 (January):41-59
     passim.
         Malamud's novels, along with those of other Jewish
     American writers, reveal a continuing anxiety over the problem
     of rootlessness and belonging. The Assistant and The Fixer,
     while reflecting these concerns, express an underlying
     agnosticism and secular humanism that have always been a source
     of strength in Judaism.

12   GREENBERG, ALVIN. "A Sense of Place in Modern Fiction: The
     Novelist's World and the Allegorist's Heaven." Genre 5, no.
     4 (December):353-66 passim.
         Malamud's The Natural is ultimately anti-allegorical since
     it loses the ingredient essential to allegories: the power to
     suggest redemption through ritual experience. The return of the
     baseball season subsequent to Roy Hobbs's defeat as a baseball
     hero during the previous year fails to carry with it a sense of
     renewal.

13   GREENFIELD, JEROME. "Without Hope." American Zionist 62,
     no. 5 (January):41-42.
         Despite the subtlety and passion of The Tenants, the moral
     legitimacy of Malamud's treatment of the racial problem is
     doubtful. Black anti-Semitism is represented symbolically as an
     aspect of the "tragic human condition," rather than as "a
     concrete and urgent social issue."

14   GRIFFITH, JOHN. "Malamud's The Assistant." Explicator 31
no. 1 (September): Item 1.
    Documents the detailed allusions in the novel between
Frank Alpine and St. Francis of Assisi and finds them partially
ironic.

15   HANSEN, ERIK ARNE. "I: Bernard Malamud: II: A New Life."
In Six American Novels: From New Deal to New Frontiers.
Edited by Jens Bøgh and Steffen Skovmand. Aarhus: Akademisk
Boghandel, pp. 237-85.
    Suggests that Malamud's fiction is variously mythic,
sociological, and, with The Tenants, apocalyptic, but regardless
of the mode it is always anchored in a particular time and
place. Throughout his work Malamud's vision is Emersonian in
its conception of the self as a potentially redemptive force,
capable of reviving what is truly human in all men. S. Levin,
in A New Life, for example, moves beyond his own egotism in
order to commit himself to the hapless human condition,
symbolized by Pauline Gilley and her children.

16   HARPER, PRESTON FRANK. "Love and Alienation in the Novels of
Bernard Malamud." Ph.D. dissertation, Texas Christian
University, 143 pp.
    The typical Malamud hero initially makes his appearance
psychically fragmented and socially isolated. Only when he
becomes capable of unselfish love does he achieve wholeness and
relationship. Malamud, however, considers the ramifications of
different kinds of love, in addition to love of others: (1)
love of self; (2) transcendent love; (3) love of nature. See
Dissertation Abstracts International 33 (1973):4414A.

17   HIRSCH, FOSTER. "How Do Men Live Together?" Judaism 21, no.
2 (Spring):247-49.
    The Tenants is uniquely Malamud, bearing the technique,
conventions, and atmosphere associated with his earlier
fiction. Although the black and Jewish writers of the novel are
skillfully depicted up to a point, Malamud does not go far
enough in developing their characterization. The novel remains
largely at the level of clever racial stereotypes, but it fails
to explore with any depth the racial issues. At best The
Tenants is gratifying as a stylistic experiment in which ornate
imagery and other forms of verbal ingenuity impress the reader
with the author's skill.

18   HOWES, VICTOR. "I Dig a Different Drum." Christian Science
Monitor, 20 January, p. 6.
    The Tenants is a fable of apocalypse and does not
represent the actual racial situation of blacks and Jews in
Manhattan.

1972

19   IWAMOTO, IWAO. "Judea-Kei Sakka no Miryoku--Bellow to
      Malamud" [The charm of Jewish writers]. Eigo Seinen (Tokyo)
      118, no. 5: 13-15.
          In Japanese. The most engaging contemporary novels now
      written are by such Jewish writers as Malamud, Bellow, Salinger,
      and Mailer. The charm of reading Malamud, for example, comes
      from his ability to unite uniquely Jewish traits with those of
      general humanity. Malamud's special vogue seems to be
      tragicomedy in the manner of Singer's Gimpel The Fool, yet
      Malamud's saints (and Bellow's antiheroes) transcends a narrowly
      circumscribed Jewish identity in their universal appeal.

20   KELLER, MARCIA. Review of The Tenants. Library Journal 97
      (15 February):83.
          Grim and despairing, this novel suggests that no salvation
      is obtainable through either art or life. The Tenants will
      provoke discussion among young adults but at the same time
      destroy any possibility for optimism about man.

21   KORG, JACOB. "Ishmael and Israel." Commentary 53, no. 5
      (May):82, 84.
          The Tenants is a risky novel because of its difficult
      racial subject matter and its problematic ending. In his desire
      to acknowledge an essential brotherhood between Harry Lesser and
      Willie Spearmint, Malamud has Lesser fantasize a double marriage
      involving members of the opposite races. Malamud's experiments
      with form resemble those of Gide, Kafka, and Joyce whose formal
      techniques reflect their attempts to deal with the riddle of
      existence. The reiteration of "mercy" at the very end of The
      Tenants invokes a higher power to resolve the human problems
      incapable of resolution through art.

22   KORT, WESLEY A. "The Fixer and the Death of God." In
      Shriven Selves: Religious Problems in Recent American
      Fiction. Philadelphia: Fortress Press, pp. 90-115.
          Part 1 offers an interpretative summary of the novel,
      focusing on Yakov Bok's gratuitous suffering and his
      preoccupation with God's absence. Part 2 relates Malamud's
      other fiction to the spiritual vacuum of a world deprived of
      God. Part 3 concludes that God's disappearance from human
      affairs is a mystery which cannot be solved but only
      contemplated. The continual assertion of God's absence or the
      proclamation of his continual presence are both extreme
      positions which engender a "loss of feeling and depth . . . that
      threaten both the theological and literary worlds."

23   LIPSIUS, FRANK. Review of The Tenants. Books and Bookmen 17
      (May):65-66.

The racial conflict between Jew and black in Malamud's The Tenants is too blatant and fosters a shallowness in characterization. "But still, Malamud is one of America's finest writers, and his successes and failures are interesting and important."

24   LODGE, DAVID. "The Lost American Dream." Tablet 226 (15 April):349-50.
Reminiscent of Updike's Rabbit Redux, Malamud's The Tenants is nonetheless a very different kind of book. Essentially a fable about art, Malamud's novel expresses the conflict between form and substance, as represented by two writers, one a Jew and the other black, each standing for an opposing obsession within the literary psyche.

25   LUDWIG, JACK. "The Dispossessed." Partisan Review 39, no. 4 (Fall):596-602.
Part of this essay is in the form of a parodic treatment of Malamud's The Tenants. Ludwig concludes that the traditional Malamudian themes of suffering and compassion seem pointless and futile.

26   MARCUS, MORDECAI. "The Tenants." Prairie Schooner 46, no. 3 (Fall):275.
Although beautifully written, the novel relies too heavily on parable, at the expense of density of character and plot.

27   MAY, CHARLES E. "Bernard Malamud's 'A Summer's Reading.'" Notes on Contemporary Literature 2, no. 4 (September):11-13.
Suggests that the story is a parable on the role of imagination in one's life. When George Stagonovich lies about completing a hundred books for his summer reading schedule, Mr. Cattanzara supports that lie in the neighborhood. Ultimately George converts that lie into truth by actually doing the reading.

28   MILLER, THEODORE C. "The Minister and the Whore: An Examination of Bernard Malamud's 'The Magic Barrel.'" Studies in the Humanities 3, no. 1 (October):43-44.
Malamud shares a closer relationship with Nathaniel Hawthorne and Blaise Pascal than he does with Sholom Aleichem. Reversing the Hester Prynne-Arthur Dimmesdale relationship, Malamud uses Stella Salzman to redeem Leo Finkle. Finkle falls in love with Stella for the very existential absurdity of her inappropriateness, and she becomes the occasion for his attempt to invest life with meaning through love.

1972

29   OPPEL, HORST. "Die Suche nach dem Menschen." In <u>Die Suche</u>
      <u>nach Gott in der amerikanischen Literatur der Gegenwart</u>.
      Abhandlungen der Geistes- und Sozialwissenschaftlichen
      Klasse, no. 8. Mainz: Verlag der Akademie der
      Wissenschaften der Literatur, pp. 368-82.
          In furnishing experiences of self-revelation, Malamud's
      fiction is notably superior to that of most of his contem-
      poraries. The values in his work are also those of Saul
      Bellow's character, Herzog, a man searching for the human
      qualities in life. Although the reality of Malamud's fiction is
      undistinctive at first glance, it is, in fact, complex and
      contradictory. Nobility and baseness are usually intertwined,
      and tragedy is always mingled with the comic and the grotesque.
      Collectively, his characters comprise a society of holy fools
      involved in a search for God.

30   OZICK, CYNTHIA. "Literary Blacks and Jews." <u>Midstream</u> 18,
      no. 2 (June-July):10-24.
          From "Angel Levine" in <u>The Magic Barrel</u> to <u>The Tenants</u> the
      Jewish-black relationship undergoes a radical shift in Malamud's
      fiction, reflecting the changes of these groups to each other in
      American society during the sixties. In "Angel Levine" Malamud
      can entertain at the level of fantasy the possibility of a black
      man alleviating Jewish suffering through an act of supernatural
      mercy, but in <u>The Tenants</u> a Jew and a black man can only
      encounter each other as murderous enemies. Reprinted: 1975.6;
      1983.17.

31   PENDELTON, ELSA. "Fantasy in Fiction." <u>Progressive</u> 36, no.
      2 (February):49-50.
          In <u>The Tenants</u> Malamud tries to invest a black man with
      almost exclusive symbolic significance, and unlike Twain's Jim,
      Malamud's Willie Spearmint lacks human authenticity. The novel
      takes on greater meaning if Harry Lesser and Willie Spearmint
      are regarded as two sides of the same personality in a war for
      total supremacy. The movement between fantasy and reality
      invites a metaphorical reading of the novel.

32   PORTER, PETER. "Really Black." <u>New Statesman</u> 84 (24
      March):397-98.
          Through his allegorical representation of black hostility
      in <u>The Tenants</u>, Malamud reveals that he is a novelist "of rare
      skill and imagination." Through the effective use of novelistic
      detail, Malamud's allegory is given dramatic immediacy.

33   PRADHAN, S.V. "The Nature and Interpretation of Symbolism in
      Malamud's <u>The Assistant</u>." <u>Centennial Review</u> 16, no. 4
      (Fall):394-407.

1972

As a post-World War II novelist, Malamud's interests dwell
on the marginal man and his immediate problems in society rather
than on the cosmic issues of Joyce or Faulkner. Thus Malamud
uses setting and characters as social symbols that suggest the
plight of Jews in recent history.

34   Review of The Tenants. Choice 9, no. 3:369.
        Claims that Malamud's Harry Lesser fails to achieve any
measure of redemption. For both Lesser and Willie Spearmint,
there is an inability to unite form and substance, a symptom of
their failure as men and artists.

35   Review of The Tenants. Economist 243 (13 May):73-75.
        If any writer other than Malamud had written a novel about
the writing of a novel, his reader might well be let down, but
Malamud is an exceptionally talented writer. The struggles of
Harry Lesser, Jewish writer, and Willie Spearmint, black writer,
raise many challenging questions on the relation of art to
life. This novel "is a paradigmatic discussion of a particular
society in a particular phase and of the importance of the
liberal ethic in that place and time."

36   Review of The Tenants. Virginia Quarterly Review 48, no. 1
        (Winter):xix.
        In comparison to most contemporary writers who explore
socially relevant problems, Malamud's talent seems much richer.
It is, therefore, unfortunate that in this novel "Malamud tries
too hard, . . . is too comfortable, too remote, too old to
understand what is going on in a world remote from his own."

37   RIEMER, JACK. Review of The Tenants. Commonweal 95 (25
        February):502.
        This novel is "the most memorable work of the year." The
compassion of The Assistant is missing in The Tenants, perhaps a
reflection of the decade in which the later novel was written.

38   SAMUELS, CHARLES THOMAS. "The Fixer." In The Critic as
        Artist: Essays on Books 1920-1970. Edited by Gilbert A.
        Harrison. New York: Liveright, pp. 291-98.
        An abridged text of 1966.58.

39   SHARFMAN, WILLIAM. "Inside and Outside Malamud."
        Rendezvous: Journal of Arts and Letters 7, no. 1
        (Spring):25-38.
        Psychologically speaking, Malamud's stories deal with
people who are emotionally akin to adolescents--they suffer from
a sense of being trapped in the world or excluded from it.
Eventually, these figures progress from preoccupation with self
to commitment to others, a change that is tantamount to arriving
at adulthood, as exemplified by Frank Alpine and Yakov Bok.

1972

40   SHEED, WILFRED. "Bernard Malamud: <u>Pictures of Fidelman</u>."
In <u>The Morning After: Essays and Reviews</u>. New York:
Warner, pp. 78-80.
     An abridged text of 1969.43

41   SHENKER, ISRAEL. "Bernard Malamud on Writing Fiction."
<u>Writer's Digest</u> 52, no. 7 (July):22-23.
     Reprint of 1971.43

42   "Tenements for Two." <u>Times Literary Supplement</u>, no. 3656 (24
March):325.
     <u>The Tenants</u> does not represent Malamud's very best work,
but it does offer a serious examination of black-white culture
conflict, symbolized in the physical combat of Willie Spearmint
and Harry Lesser. In addition, Malamud's shrewd insights, along
with his use of black slang, keeps the reader's interest.

43   WAUGH, AUBERON. "<u>The Tenants</u>." <u>Spectator</u> 228 (8 April):
549-50.
     Finds <u>The Tenants</u> not worth reading, largely due to its
distorted liberal response to black militancy.

44   WYNDHAM, FRANCIS. "Putting it Down in Black and White."
<u>Listener</u> 87 (23 March):390.
     Malamud is at his best in <u>The Tenants</u>, distilling a grim
poetry alternating with comedy out of the banality of urban
experience. He manages, moreover, to weave together two
disparate themes: the artist's uncertainty about the nature of
art and the antagonisms between black and white in America.

45   ZUCKER, DAVID H. "Secret Sharers." <u>Shenandoah</u> 23, no. 2
(Winter):84-87.
     The dynamics of <u>The Tenants</u> is a result of Malamud's
ability to unite the separate but related elements of the
novel: "the subtle tie between the two writers; the
Lesser-Levenspiel comic conflict; the love triangle; the
psychology of obsession; the presence of the tenement-like
<u>momento mori</u>."

1973

1   BRESLIN, JOHN B. Review of <u>Rembrandt's Hat</u>. <u>America</u> 129 (7
July):15.
     Alienation is a constant motif in this collection of short
stories, but Malamud has been able to make this literary
catchword a felt as well as an illuminating experience.

1973

2   BROYARD, ANATOLE. "If the Hat Doesn't Fit. . . ." New York
Times 17 May, p. 41.
     This review of Rembrandt's Hat faults Malamud for becoming
too avante-garde: of using "glib ellipsis, of awkward hamish
surrealism." Another blemish in his work is in his use of a
"homely" language that seems intended to convince the reader of
his sincerity and seriousness.

3   COOPERMAN, STANLEY. "Philip Roth: 'Old Jacob's Eye' with a
Squint." Twentieth Century Literature 19, no. 3
(July):203-16.
     Bernard Malamud's aesthetic and human concerns are
crystallized in this discussion as a basis for distinguishing
Philip Roth's orientation to the writing of fiction from that of
Malamud. In his 1963 speech at Princeton University, Malamud
stated that the visible world could not have value unless it was
transformed by the imagination into a moral dimension. This
position is amplified by his well-known dictum that "all men are
Jews." For Roth "all Jews are men," and their imperfect lives
should be the stuff of fiction. Malamud's conception of mankind
leads to abstraction.

4   CUNNINGHAM, VALENTINE. "Old Hats." Listener 90 (11
October):491-92.
     Characteristic of his other fiction, Malamud's Jewishness
is again visible in Rembrandt's Hat, and his concern with
communication failure, whether oral or written, is also evident
in this collection and effectively handled.

5   DAICHES, DAVID. "Some Aspects of Anglo-American Fiction."
Jewish Quarterly 21, nos. 1-2, (Spring-Summer):88-93.
     Submits that Anglo-American Jewish fiction features three
major stands: (1) the older literature of the shtetl (e.g.,
Aleichem, Sforim, and Peretz); (2) the documentation of Jewish
immigrant life (e.g., Zanguill's The Children of the Ghetto);
(3) the symbolic use of the Jew, as featured in such a
consciously Jewish writer as Bernard Malamud in The Assistant.
The quintessence of the Jewish experience, Malamud's fiction
"brings echoes of the older Yiddish tragicomic mode of writing
into his novels and stories, and [Malamud] is a master of wry
self-mockery as a form simultaneously of self-exploration and
moral criticism."

6   DEEMER, CHARLES. "Old Masters' New Stories." New Leader 56
(17 September):19-20.
     The collection of stories in Rembrandt's Hat is considered
to be the best in this review in relation to other collections
by Cheever, E.M. Forster, and Nabokov. Malamud's fiction is

1973

distinguished by its power to transform the attitude of the
reader to his characters by the time his stories end.

7   DUCHARME, ROBERT [E.]. "Myth and Irony in The Fixer."
        Interdisciplinary Essays (Mount St. Mary's College) 3, no. 1
        (December):31-36.
            Asserts that Malamud's use of mythic structure in The
        Fixer serves a twofold purpose: the first is to recall a stable
        order of reality; the second is to extract new meaning from the
        original mythical structure. Much of Yakov Bok's suffering
        parallels the suffering of Christ as represented in the Gospels,
        but Yakov Bok eventually resists his role as passive sufferer.
        If Bok allows himself to suffer, it is for the Jewish victims of
        persecution, "but he will not accept suffering as having some
        vicarious mystical value." Malamud's ironic treatment of
        traditional Christian suffering is directed to an improvement
        rather than an acceptance of the human condition.

8   EDELMAN, LILY. "Without Preachment: Another Magic Barrel of
        Malamud Stories." National Jewish Monthly 87, no. 10
        (June):54-56.
            Although Malamud has refrained from protracted discussions
        of Jewishness in his own writing, he uses Feliks Levitansky from
        "Man in the Drawer" (in Rembrandt's Hat) as the platform for
        asserting the universality rather than the particular Jewishness
        of his own work. Levitansky's observation that imagination
        rather than an intimacy with Jews is the source of his authority
        of his fictional portraits of Jews echoes the few remarks
        Malamud has made on this subject. Those critics who explicate
        Malamud for the Jewish elements in his work miss the larger
        human dimension to which those works are tied. "The Talking
        Horse" underscores Malamud's general concern with discovering
        what is truly human. As Abramowitz partially drags himself from
        out of a horse's body, "the reader is left to ponder what must
        be one of the most powerful metaphors ever created for mankind's
        painful liberating lurch from bestiality toward menschlichkeit."

9   FREESE, PETER. "Bernard Malamud." In Amerikanische
        Literatur der Gegenwart in Einzeldarstellungen. Edited by
        Martin Christadler. Kröners Taschenausgabe, vol. 412.
        Stuttgart: Alfred Kröner Verlag, pp. 105-28.
            Offers a general accounting of the thematic and structural
        elements in Malamud's fiction, including the Grail quest,
        initiation, the process of change, and the use of spatial
        movement. The Malamud hero, as represented by Morris Bober or
        Yakov Bok, is marked by his acceptance of spiritual paternity.
        The Yiddish influences on Malamud have yet to receive the
        attention they deserve.

10   GOLUB, ELLEN. "The Resurrection of the Heart." English
        Review of Salem State College 1, no. 2:63-78.
        Discusses S. Levin of A New Life in relation to the folk
character of the schlemiel, a man who is "a believer in
miracles, falsehoods, and promises." Typical of Malamud's other
heroes, S. Levin is a spiritual version of Horatio Alger.
Reminiscent of Leo Finkle of The Magic Barrel, Levin commits his
love to a "forbidden woman." Both for Levin and for Jewish
tradition love is to be equated with life.

11   GREBSTEIN, SHELDON NORMAN. "Bernard Malamud and the Jewish
        Movement." In Contemporary American-Jewish Literature:
        Critical Essays. Edited by Irving Malin. Bloomington:
        Indiana University Press, pp. 175-212.
        Despite the work of Jewish writers prior to Bellow,
Malamud, and Roth, a so-called Jewish literary movement was not
in evidence and did not come into being until after the Nazi
Holocaust. Subsequent to it the Jew in recent history and
literature took on a new and added significance to postwar
Jewish writers. Understandably, the pervasive theme of this
group is suffering, yet it sees that suffering as redemptive and
human life as significant. Malamud, more than any other writer
in the Jewish Movement, crystallizes its essential themes and
carries them, in part, through his use of Jewish humor. In
addition, Malamud's style and technique--his effective manipulation of diction and point of view--are intimately related to
these themes. Reprinted: 1975.6

12   GUTTMAN, ALLEN. "Jewish Humor." In The Comic Imagination in
        American Literature. Edited by Louis D. Rubin, Jr., New
        Brunswick, N.J.: Rutgers University Press, pp. 329-48.
        Malamud's fiction, especially Pictures of Fidelman, is
always touched by humor, and that humor can be bizarre and
obscene, as in the case or "Still Life."

13   HASSAN, IHAB. "Bernard Malamud." In Contemporary American
        Literature: 1945-1972. New York: Frederick Ungar Publishing
        Co., pp. 38-42.
        Briefly comments on Malamud's canon through The Tenants
(1971), offering the following observations: that Malamud's
Jews stand for humanity at large; that his novels are poised
between the actual and the mythic; and that his art, while not
particularly experimental, displays a high degree of crafts-
manship.

14   HOFFMAN, DORIS JUANITA. "The Novelist as Rhetorician:
        Characterization in the Short Fiction of Bernard Malamud."
        Ph.D. Dissertation, University of Washington, 207 pp.

1973

Explores two aspects of characterization in Malamud's
short fiction: (1) as an expressions of a character's actions
and attitudes; (2) as it is revealed in human relationships and
the author's response to his character. The dissertation
focuses on characterization within a dramatic framework and on
Malamud's rhetorical strategies. See Dissertation Abstracts
International 34 (1974):5364A.

15   JOHNSON, MARIGOLD. "Small Mercies." New Statesman 86 (28
      September):433.
         The success of Rembrandt's Hat is a result of Malamud's
      "stylistic wit," a feature of his Yiddish idiom. These stories
      may strike the reader as suffocating, spatially or psycholo-
      gically, but they are rescued by Malamud's brand of humor.

16   KAZIN, ALFRED. Bright Book of Life: American Novelists and
      Storytellers from Hemingway to Mailer. Boston: Little,
      Brown & Co., Atlantic Monthly Press Book, pp. 104, 127,
      139-44.
         Similar to nineteenth-century writers of Yiddish fiction,
      Malamud focuses on a people, and his concern with their
      Jewishness is reflected in his language and style. As a
      signature of their most authentic identity is their poverty
      which colors the totality of their existence. Their lives,
      however, are portrayed through Malamud's benevolent irony. "The
      Assistant, which in the thoroughness of its workmanship, its
      fidelity to the lived facts of experience, its lack of smartness
      and facile allegorizing, is . . . the most satisfying single
      Jewish novel of this period. . . ."

17   KIELY, ROBERT. Review of Rembrandt's Hat. New York Times
      Book Review 78 (3 June):7.
         Malamud's ability to use the genre of the short story to
      its greatest advantage is reflected in Rembrandt's Hat, a
      collection of stories drafted in the manner of Chekhov, Joyce,
      or Hemingway. His ability to mingle the ordinary with fantasy
      is central to his art, and "The Silver Crown" is an especially
      notable example of his success. Whether or not a given story
      fails or succeeds, Malamud's fiction is consistently "serious
      and intelligent."

18   KIRBY, DAVID K. "The Princess and the Frog: The Modern
      Short Story as Fairy Tale." Minnesota Review 4 (Spring):
      145-49.
         Malamud's "Angel Levine" is reminiscent of the
      princess-frog fairytale insofar as the frog equivalent, Angel
      Levine, is as much in need of redemption as the princess
      character, the tailor. Instructive comparisons can be made of
      Malamud's use of the fairytale formula with Hortense Calisher's
      adaptation of it in "Heartburn" and Truman Capote's in "Miriam."

19   KNOPP, JOSEPHINE Z.   "The Ways of Mentshlekhkayt: A Study of
        Morality in Some Fiction of Bernard Malamud and Philip
        Roth."   Tradition 13, no. 3 (Winter):67-84.
             The ethical concept of mentshlekhkayt is concerned with
        the improvement of the human condition through man's active
        involvement with his fellowman and community.   While Roth's work
        examines the corruption of this concept among American middle-
        class Jews, Malamud, in such stories as "The Mourners" or "Angel
        Levine," deals with man's alienation from but eventual
        rededication to its principles.

20   KOBASHI, MOTO.   "The Tenants [Short essays on The Tenants:
        Metaphors of human relationships]."   Waseda Shogaku
        239:91-110.
             In Japanese.   Part 1 reviews Malamud's fiction prior to
        The Tenants as it presents human relationships and concludes
        that such relationships are conveyed through the medium of
        realism or romanticism.   Part 2 discusses the discordant
        feelings of the characters in The Tenants as they reveal
        themselves through their individualized responses to art,
        politics, sex, and race.   Part 3 comments on two aspects of
        structure, Malamud's disordering and reordering of time, and his
        juxtaposition of abstract and sensuous language, the latter also
        serving as a vehicle for characterizing Harry Lesser and Willie
        Spearmint, respectively.   Part 4 concludes with a discussion of
        language in relation to theme, texture, and tone.

21   LEMON, LEE T.   "Working Quietly."   Prairie Schooner 47, no. 3
        (Fall):270.
             Malamud's low-keyed narrative style and his exploration of
        commonplace events are both reflected in Rembrandt's Hat.
        Although this collection displays much talent and possesses
        reader appeal, it does not have the impact of truly major
        fiction.   (This review notes points of contact between
        Rembrandt's Hat and John Cheever's collection, The World of
        Apples.)

22   LEONARD, JOHN.   "Cheever to Roth to Malamud."   Atlantic 231,
        no. 6 (June):112-16.
             Rembrandt's Hat offers messages "but not communication."
        Malamud's characters seem incomplete, and his attitude toward
        them is ambiguous.

23   LEWIS, STUART A.   "The Jewish Author Looks at the Black."
        Colorado Quarterly 21, no. 3 (Winter):317-30.
             In The Tenants Malamud's Willie Spearmint, a black writer,
        creates from impulse while Harry Lesser, white and Jewish, is
        guided primarily by principles of form.   In "Black is My

1973

Favorite Color," Nat Lime's "liberal" sentiments with regard to
blacks embraces a form of covert stereotyping. In both works
the black embodies an emotional vitality with which the Jew
needs to identify.

24   LUTTWAK, EDWARD N. "A Good Writer in Good Form." National
      Review 25 (26 October):1191-92.
          It is in the genre of the short story that Malamud
      unquestionably succeeds, and in Rembrandt's Hat we have a
      collection of short stories that rivals his best. "Man in the
      Drawer," although not up to the level of the others, absorbs the
      reader in its evocation of contemporary Moscow life.

25   MICHAELS, LEONARD. "Sliding into English." New York Review
      of Books 20 (20 September):37-40.
          The characters in Rembrandt's Hat resemble each other in
      their continual and ineradicable misery, but the stories differ
      in the way that Malamud manages his language, "modulating toward
      English or Yiddish" within or between stories. Through Yiddish
      inflection Malamud makes an appeal to the auditor for sympathy;
      in slipping into English, he intimates the receding emotional
      relationships of his characters. "Talking Horse" and "My Son
      the Murderer" illustrate the effectiveness of Malamud's Yiddish-
      English. This language registers the longing of his characters
      for emotional intimacy and the chill of their isolation and
      carries a sublime pathos.

26   MUDRICK, MARVIN. Old Pros with News from Nowhere." Hudson
      Review 26, no. 3 (Autumn):545-61.
          Observes of Rembrandt's Hat that each of the stories in
      the collection possesses a distinct structure which leaves its
      imprint on the reader's imagination, the most noteworthy being
      "The Letter" and "My Son the Murderer." Malamud has not
      perceptibly advanced beyond the techniques and themes of his
      earlier stories.

27   MUELLER, LAVONNE. "Malamud and West: Tyranny of the Dream
      Dump." In The Cheaters and the Cheated: A Collection of
      Critical Essays. Edited by David Madden. Deland, Fla:
      Everett/Edwards, pp. 221-47.
          Establishes points of contact between The Natural and The
      Day of the Locust. Both the world of baseball and the world of
      Hollywood are, figurately speaking, "dream dumps," imaginative
      structures that have been nurtured by the dream of American
      success. In their own ways, Roy Hobbs and Tod Hackett are
      artists caught between the integrity of their own vision and the
      corrupting demands of the masses. Each hero is eventually
      destroyed by a seductive woman whose "false and contrived"
      dreams embody the dreams of the American masses.

28   NOVAK, WILLIAM. Review of The Tenants. Response 7:147-51.
      The novel is a product of American racial history and, as
such, the bleakness of its subject leaves little room for
affirmation. Artistically, the narrative is flawed. Hovering
between realism and myth, its realistic dimension lacks
plausibility and its mythic dimension is diluted by the
complications of the plot. "The real problem with the novel
. . . is that it is not, in fact, a novel at all, but a long
story."

29   OATES, JOYCE CAROL. "The Finite and the Fabulous." Wash-
      ington Post Book World, 10 June, p. 3.
      The relationship between the ordinary and the
extraordinary, a technique Malamud had cultivated twenty years
earlier, is notable once again in his collection of stories,
Rembrandt's Hat. The best example of the interplay between
these two modes of reality is in "The Silver Crown." Here, as
well as in the other stories, "Malamud magically transposes
brief, finite units of experience into the most imaginative--and
readable--art."

30   PHILLIPS, ROBERT. Review of Rembrandt's Hat. Commonweal 99
      (30 November):245-46.
      In its development of the two central themes of this
collection, "The Silver Crown" stands out as especially
successful. Malamud's most original story in this group is
"Talking Horse," a probing allegory on the relations of God and
Man.

31   "Poor in Spirit." Times Literary Supplement, no. 3735, (5
      October):1158.
      In comparison to The Magic Barrel, Rembrandt's Hat
contains human relationships that "have become sharper and more
extraordinary," although in the latter, the texture of reality
may have thinned. Central to the stories in Rembrandt's Hat is
the heroic image of the artist who risks himself in the service
of his vision.

32   POSS, STANLEY. "Serial Form and Malamud's Schlemihls."
      Costerus 9:109-16
      The form of Malamud's tales, illustrated by two
collections, The Magic Barrel and Idiots First, seems entirely
appropriate to his tragicomic hero, the schlemiel. In his quest
for fulfillment, this character is involved in persistent and
continuous struggles, embodied in the cumulative and incremental
structure of the plot.

1973

33   PRESCOTT, PETER S.   "The Horse's Mouth."   Newsweek 81 (4
        June):101-2.
            The most impressive story in Malamud's collection,
        Rembrandt's Hat, is "The Talking Horse," an existential fantasy
        "which makes comedy of the narrator's desperate quest for
        freedom and his own identity." Malamud displays an
        unprecedented imagination among contemporary writers of the
        short story.

34   RABINOWITZ, DOROTHY.   Review of Rembrandt's Hat.   World 2 (5
        June):66.
            Rembrandt's Hat reveals Malamud at the top of his form,
        and this collection moves the reader more than any comparable
        collection of short fiction by one of his contemporaries. The
        most accomplished story in the group is "The Silver Crown" which
        suggests that "disjointedness . . . is more logical than logic."

35   RAO, A.V. KRISHNA.   "Bernard Malamud's The Assistant: The
        American Agonistes."   Triveni: Journal of Indian Renaissance
        42, no. 2 (July-September):28-34.
            Malamud's Jew is an Everyman with an unusual concern for
        right conduct and moral relationships. This novel expresses
        Malamud's major theme, moral victory despite worldly failure,
        and it exemplifies his ability to explore with insight Jewish
        experience in the context of contemporary American life.

36   Review of Rembrandt's Hat.   New Republic 168 (9 June):32.
            Malamud is our best contemporary spinner of tales as
        evidenced in this collection. Two unusually fine stories in it
        are "Man in the Drawer" and "Talking Horse." The well-executed
        dramatic structure of the former is a reflection of the author's
        moral and aesthetic integrity; the sense of the miraculous in
        the latter is made credible by his deftness and control.

37   REYNOLDS, RICHARD.   "'The Magic Barrel': Pinye Salzman's
        Kadish."   Studies in Short Fiction 10, no. 1 (Winter):101-2.
            Prior to becoming the special prayers for the dead, the
        kadish was associated in Talmudic and Rabbinic literature with a
        plea for the resurrection of the departed at the time of the
        Messiah. If Leo Finkle is aware of Salzman's recitation of the
        kadish, as a rabbinical student, he would understand that the
        prayer is directed to the resurrection of Stella through his
        love.

38   RICHEY, CLARENCE W.   "'The Woman in the Dunes': A Note on
        Bernard Malamud's The Tenants."   Notes on Contemporary
        Literature 3, no. 1 (January):4-5.

Asserts that as a movie goer, Harry Lesser of The Tenants must have seen Hiroishi Teshigahara's The Woman in the Dunes (1960), a film which contributes the raw materials for his Sisyphus-like obsession. Just as the protagonist of the film compulsively shovels sand, so Lesser can have no existence beyond the manipulation of words.

39 RIDLEY, CLIFFORD. "Short Stories Extinct? Don't Believe It." National Observer, 2 June, p. 21.
  Compares and contrasts John Cheever's The World of Apples with Malamud's Rembrandt's Hat and finds Malamud's collection less optimistic. While Malamud invites sympathy for his characters, as in "Talking Horse," Cheever delights in the humanity of his. Humiliation is often the lot of a Malamud character.

40 RIESE, UTZ. "Das 'neue Leben' ohne Neues: Zum Menschenbild in Bernard Malamuds Romanen The Natural and The Assistant." Zeitschrift für Anglistik und Amerikanistik 21:11-33.
  Takes a Marxian approach to Malamud's two novels. Roy Hobbs in The Natural is an embodiment of a perverted social system nourished by individual self-esteem, ignoring collective relationships either with his team or the public. Although he renounces his old values, he is incapable of formulating a new program of action for himself. Critics who approach the novel through myth ignore the forces of history that have shaped it. Like The Natural, The Assistant also dramatizes the destruction of the hero, Morris Bober, in an exploitive capitalist society. Although Malamud seems to protest his fate, he is too limited by his class perspective to be sufficiently vocal.

41 ROSENFELD, ALVIN H. "The Progress of the American Jewish Novel." Response 7, no. 1 (Spring):115-30.
  Considers The Fixer the most important historical Jewish novel written to date. In moving away from the abstractness of allegory and fable of his past work to the concreteness of history in his present work, Malamud's preoccupation with suffering takes on an added depth. Yakov Bok himself surely speaks to Malamud's fictional purposes when he says: "The world's bad memory needs the Jew, who carries a remembered pack on his back and serves as history's agent and its scribe."

42 RUOTOLO, LUCIO P. "Yakov Bok." Six Existential Heroes: The Politics of Faith. Cambridge, Mass.: Harvard University Press, pp. 121-39.
  The Fixer is discussed from an existential perspective, and it illustrates the growing tendency of the existential novel to take a political turn. Although Yakov Bok's suffering results in self-pity, displays of rhetoric, and a capitulation

1973

to fatalism, Bok eventually eschews such behavior in favor of struggle. During his imprisonment, he recognizes that fleeing from his past amounts to denial of his own identity and meaning: "It means to commit the self necessarily to an abstract system of value that is distinct from the existential dimension of human personality." For Bok self-acceptance becomes the first step to a new sense of social responsibility.

43 RUSSELL, MARIANN. "White Man's Black Man: Three Views." CLA Journal 17, no. 1 (September):93-100.
    The blacks portrayed by Updike in Rabbit Run and Rabbit Redux, Bellow's Mr. Sammler's Planet, and Malamud's The Tenants are destructive and threating, serving as a symbol of cultural dissolution. Unlike the other novelists, Malamud tries to move beyond stereotype in order to suggest that the contrasting qualities of the Jew and black are, in reality, complements to each other. However, apocalypse rather than epiphany prevails in Malamud's novel and in the work of all three novelists the black man remains a stranger.

44 SHERES, ITA G. "Prophetic and Mystical Manifestations of Exile and Redemption in the Novels of Henry Roth, Bernard Malamud, and Saul Bellow." Ph.D. dissertation, University of Wisconsin, 330 pp.
    The novels of these three writers share a common thematic movement, a shift from alienation to illumination and to corresponding states of exile and redemption. Such convergence may be explained by their indebtedness to the prophetic and mystical writings of Judaism. Malamud, in particular, seems to have come under the influence of Isaac Luria, a sixteenth-century Jewish philosopher, in working out in fictional terms the redemptive process which, according to Luria, begins in exile. See Dissertation Abstracts International 33 (1973): 6375A.

45 SKOW, JOHN. "Ending the Pane." Time 101 (28 May):99-100.
    Rembrandt's Hat once again explores the human condition with Malamud's usual lucidity. These stories are figurative confrontations between God and man. Job-like in their characterization, Malamud's heroes seem to be mysteriously chosen for affliction, and the two best representations of their plight can be seen in "Man in the Drawer" and "Talking Horse." "This is primal stuff, and Malamud's greatest talent is for melding it with the most mundane sort of everyday life."

46 SOLOTAROFF, THEODORE. "Philip Roth and the Jewish Moralists." In Contemporary American-Jewish Literature: Critical Essays. Edited by Irving Malin. Bloomington: Indiana University Press, pp. 13-29 passim.
    Reprint of 1959.3.

47   STERN, DANIEL. "Commonplace Things, and the Essence of
      Art." Nation 217 (3 September):181-82.
          Asserts that in Rembrandt's Hat, as well as in other
      fiction, Malamud fulfills the William Dean Howells conception of
      the novelist who is capable of profundity in his use of the
      commonplace. At the same time, Malamud's uniqueness lies in his
      ability to transform the commonplace into new and profound
      dimensions of meaning through the use of fantasy. The eight
      stories in this collection reflect this unique interplay, in
      particular, "Talking Horse." In this Beckett-like comedy,
      Malamud seems to ponder the nature of the God-man relationship.

48   VANDERBILT, KERMIT. "Writers of the Troubled Sixties."
      Nation 217 (17 December):661-64.
          Reviews eight works of fiction reflecting the sixties
      including The Tenants. Malamud's novel is "a fable of art and
      racism" in which black and white become involved in role
      changing because of their attraction to each other's charismatic
      identity. Willie Spearmint stimulates Harry Lesser's awakening
      to his own dormant instincts, while Lesser engenders in
      Spearmint a crippling obsession with form. The human
      affirmations of Malamud's earlier work is missing in The
      Tenants.

49   WEGELIN, CHRISTOF. "The American Schlemiel Abroad:
      Malamud's Italian Stories and the End of American
      Innocence." Twentieth Century Literature 19 (April):77-88.
          Contemporary American writers dealing with the
      international theme no longer portray American innocence; both
      Americans and Europeans are rendered darkly. Malamud's Arthur
      Fidelman is an interesting case in point. In contrast to his
      Jamesian counterparts, Fidelman does not remain innocent and
      detached; he meets his Europeans on their own level, often in
      situations involving kafkaesque distortion.

50   WHITTON, STEVEN JAY. "The Mad Crusader: The Quest as Motif
      in the Jewish Fiction of Philip Roth and Bernard Malamud."
      Ph.D. dissertation, University of South Carolina, 178 pp.
          In their modification of the traditional quest motif,
      Malamud and Roth establish both the hero and the enemy within
      the self. While the problems explored by Roth seem contempor-
      arily Jewish, those presented in Malamud are universal and
      suffered by Everyman, as well as by Jews. Another distinction
      separating Roth's heroes from Malamud's is the continued
      selfishness of the former and the emergence of selflessness in
      the latter. See Dissertation Abstracts International 34
      (1973):1943A.

1973

51   WINEGARTEN, RENEE. "Malamud's Head." <u>Midstream</u> 19, no. 8
       (October):76-79.
            Offers brief comment on selected stories in Malamud's
       collection, <u>Rembrandt's Hat</u>, occasionally connecting these
       stories to Malamud's other work. "The Silver Crown," for
       example, embodies two of his major themes, the conflict between
       art and life, and materialism versus spirituality. Winegarten
       finds that in his collection Malamud surpasses his earlier
       fiction in the control of his materials. Reprinted: 1975.5.

1974

1   CHARLES, GERDA. "The Smooth and the Rough." <u>Jewish Observer
       and Middle East Review</u> 23 (18 January):25.
            The title story of <u>Rembrandt's Hat</u>, despite its richness,
       reflects a curious feature of Malamud's fiction, the rudeness of
       his characters toward each other. "It is a strange and puzzling
       paradox that Malamud has both a great regard and a great
       disregard for human feeling running side by side through
       every one of his books."

2   COHEN, SANDY. <u>Bernard Malamud and the Trial by Love</u>.
       Melville Studies in American Culture, edited by Robert
       Brainard Pearsall. Amsterdam: Rodopi N.V., 132 pp.
            Revision of 1972.5. Although the theme of self-
       transcendence runs through all of Malamud's fiction, this study
       does not perceive a steadily evolving vision. Devoting chapters
       to the examination of this theme in individual works--<u>The
       Natural</u>, <u>The Assistant</u>, <u>A New Life</u>, <u>The Fixer</u>, <u>Pictures of
       Fidelman</u>, and <u>The Tenants</u>--Cohen discusses how Malamud's form
       and technique affect this theme in each book. The last chapter,
       "From Self to Society," offers a statement on Malamud's social
       consciousness, successes and failures, and takes special note of
       his poetic mixture of Yiddish and English.

3   DICKSTEIN, MORRIS. "Cold War Blues." <u>Partisan Review</u> 41,
       no. 1 (Winter):30-53.
            Speculates on Malamud's concern with suffering in his
       fiction of the 1950s and concludes that his work in its comic
       and Talmudic response to human misery was well suited to the
       fear-ridden political atmosphere of the McCarthy and Eisenhower
       years.

4   DUCHARME, ROBERT [E.]. <u>Art and Idea in the Novels of Bernard
       Malamud: Toward the Fixer</u>. The Hague: Mouton, 149 pp.
            Revision of 1970.2. Explores the consistent use of
       certain themes and techniques in <u>The Natural</u>, <u>The Assistant</u>, <u>A
       New Life</u>, and <u>The Fixer</u>, especially the father-son motif. From

120

The Natural through The Fixer a tension develops between two of Malamud's central themes--suffering and responsibility--and in The Fixer this tension is the source of the book's intellectual and dramatic substance. An appendix examines Pictures of Fidelman which recapitulates the father-son motif and the conflict between suffering and responsibility.

5   FEINSTEIN, ELAINE. "Unashamed Humanism." London Magazine, 2d ser. 13, no. 6 (February-March):137-40.
     Malamud is fortunate to have at his disposal the Yiddish literary tradition which gives form to the moral and psychological epiphanies found in Rembrandt's Hat.

6   FREESE, PETER. "Bernard Malamud." In Die amerikanische Kurzgeschichte nach 1945: Salinger, Malamud, Baldwin, Purdy, Barth. Schwerpunkte Anglistik, edited by Edward Standop, vol. 8. Frankfurt-am-Main: Athenäum Verlag, pp.180-245.
     Furnishes a chapter in eight parts with topics related to Malamud's stories and novels. In surveying his career, Freese identifies three pervasive themes: (1) the necessity of suffering; (2) sympathy for others; and (3) the significance of the past. Malamud has taken over the Joycean epiphany, the Doppelgänger from Dostoevski, and the shtetl Jew from the older Yiddish writers, giving him a new and timeless existence. Representative works discussed include "Take Pity," "The Magic Barrel," "Angel Levine," Pictures of Fidelman, and A New Life. Malamud is still a productive writer, and it is too early to make a definite judgment about his work.

7   GEBSATTEL, JEROME VON. "The Assistant." In Kindlers Literature Lexicon. Vol. 4. Munich: Deutscher Taschenbuch Verlag, p. 1221.
     Reprint of 1964.9.

8   GOLLIN, RITA K. "Understanding Fathers in American Jewish Fiction." Centennial Review 18, no. 3 (Summer):273-87 passim.
     Denies the assertion from some quarters that the mother has replaced the father as a contemporary force in American Jewish fiction. On the contrary, in this fiction the father becomes the route through which traditional moral values are learned, and the best example of such fathers is Morris Bober of The Assistant. Bober instructs through his "selfless humanity" both his daughter and his surrogate son, Frank Alpine.

9   INGE, THOMAS. "The Ethnic Experience in Literature: Malamud's The Assistant and Roth's Call it Sleep." Journal of Ethnic Studies 1, no. 4 (Winter):45-50.
     Argues that the Jewish-American experience represented by Malamud and Henry Roth also stands for the human condition. In The Assistant Morris Bober's Jewishness embodies the tragedy of

1974

Everyman. Call it Sleep also incorporates the universal in the particular. Although it is anchored in a Jewish urban ghetto in the early twentieth century, its accurate portrayal of Jews is a faithful rendering of mankind.

10   KAUFMAN, MICHAEL. "Moscow is Urged to Free Author." New York Times, 13 February, p. 12.
      Bernard Malamud, as one of the voices denouncing the arrests of Alexander I. Solzhenitsyn, offered a statement of protest for Radio Liberty which read: "Détente is a two way street. If the Soviet Government wants détente with the United States of America . . . they can begin by détenting with Alexander Solzhenitsyn. Détente ultimately means mutual respect."

11   KREITZER, NEIL DAVID. "The Quest for Identity in the Novels of Bernard Malamud." Ph.D. dissertation, University of California, Davis, 290 pp.
      Reminiscent of the initiation story, the pattern of quest in Malamud's fiction moves the hero from an old life to a new one in conjunction with a father figure who offers moral or aesthetic counseling. As a preparatory condition for achieving his quest, a new identity, the hero must first come to terms with his past. His success is marked by the practice of such Judaic-Christian virtues as charity and mercy. See Dissertation Abstracts International 35 (1974):2278A.

12   LEVIANT, CURT. "Bernard Malamud: My Characters are God Haunted." Hadassah Magazine 55, no. 10 (June):18.
      In an interview with Malamud, Leviant elicited these summarized remarks. Malamud did not receive a formal Jewish education. He was influenced by Yiddish, modern Israeli, and some of the classic American writers. His Jewish characters, although not religiously observant, are ethically motivated if not obsessed with God.

*13   MENASCE, ESTHER. "Umanesimo ebraico nell'opera di Bernard Malamud." Revista Mensile di Israel, April-June, pp. 3-6.
      Source: Grau, p. 102, 1981.6; unverified.

14   NYE, ROBERT. Review of Rembrandt's Hat. Books and Bookmen 19, no. 4 (January):71-72.
      Regards much of Malamud's fiction, the present collection included, an attempt to break through the language of conventional literature in order to say something fresh, but Malamud's thematic intentions never emerge with any real clarity. Rembrandt's Hat is characterized by occasional brilliance of phrasing, but it is a fragmentary brilliance which leaves the reader unsatisfied.

15   PETILLION, PIERRE-YVES. "Le manuscrit en cendres." Critique
      30, no. 326 (July):601-32.
         The imploring voice of Levenspiel is a resonating chord
      throughout Malamud's dark novel, The Tenants. Falling within
      the apocalyptic tradition of American literature, the novel most
      closely resembles in spirit Hawthorne's "Earth Holocaust."
      Through Harry Lesser, the symbolic lord of a decaying realm,
      Malamud's novel also has affinities with Eliot's The Waste Land,
      Shakespeare's Richard II, and The Tempest.

16   RAO, G. NAGESWARA. "Isolation and Reconciliation in
      Malamud's The Fixer." In Indian Studies in American
      Literature. Edited by M.K. Naik, S.K. Desai, and S.
      Makashi-Punekar. Dharwar: Karnatak University;
      Delhi:Macmillan India, pp. 255-62.
         Whatever critical perspective we may apply to Malamud's
      fiction, one fact remains constant, the struggle to affirm the
      significance of human life in the face of suffering. In this
      connection The Fixer emerges as Malamud's most compassionate and
      most accomplished work. It effectively fuses two patterns of
      archetypal suffering found in his earlier novels, the suffering
      of Sampson in The Natural and that of Job in The Assistant, with
      a third, the redemptive suffering of Christ found in The Fixer.
      In reenacting the alienation of his biblical predecessors from
      God, Yakov Bok also discovers the terms of reconciliation.

17   ROTH, PHILIP. "Imagining Jews." New York Review of Books 21
      (3 October):22-28 passim.
         Rejects the moral image of the Jew and the libidinous
      image of the Gentile that Malamud (and Bellow) projects in his
      fiction. In The Assistant, Morris Bober, the epitome of passive
      Jewish suffering and love, is countered by Frank Alpine, a
      "corrupt, violent, and lustful" Italian. In the hands of other
      Jewish writers, Morris Bober's relationship with Frank Alpine
      might have been conceived as vindictive rather than redemptive.
      For Malamud, however, ethical Jewishness is developed with a
      vengeance. Elsewhere in his fiction Jews (and Gentiles)
      continue to conform to his ethical conceptions. In The Fixer
      Yakov Bok's murder of the czar exists only in his imagaination,
      while Arthur Fidelman in Pictures of Fidelman moves from lust to
      love. Reprinted. 1975.23.

18   SHARMA, D.R. "Malamud's Jewishness: An Analysis of The
      Assistant." Literary Criterion 11 (Winter):29-37.
         Malamud's dedication to the preservation of mankind
      distinguishes his fiction from the more ethnically oriented
      concerns of Sholom Aleichem or Isaac Bashevis Singer. The
      Assistant is, perhaps, the best expression of Malamud's all
      embracing humanism, and his central characters, Morris Bober and

1974

Frank Alpine, because of the similarity of their ethos and experience, complement each other in carrying Malamud's themes of selflessness and sacrifice. Morris Bober, however, is not merely an unconscious suffering victim. Through his Yiddish irony, Bober reveals a grasp of the hopelessness of his situation that invests him with a tragic stature.

19   _____. "The Natural: A Nonmythical Approach." Panjab University Research Bulletin (Arts) 5, no. 2 (October):3-8.
Argues that there is a nonmythical dimension to The Natural which has been overlooked in its commentary: Roy Hobbs, like his Malamudian counterparts, is in quest of a new life. In purely human terms, he moves from intellectual dullness and immaturity to a developing self-consciousness in which suffering becomes a tutor in wisdom. Such growth relates this novel to Malamud's later work.

20   SUSMAN, MAXINE SYLVIA. "Interpretations of Jewish Character in Renaissance and Recent Literature." Ph.D. dissertation, Cornell University, 288 pp.
Studies Jewish characterization in Malamud's The Fixer, as well as in Marlowe's The Jew of Malta, Shakespeare's The Merchant of Venice, Eliot's Daniel Deronda, and Bellow's Mr. Sammler's Planet in the light of Renaissance stereotypes of Jews. In The Fixer, Yakov Bok's point of contact with the Renaissance stage Jew, who stands firm in the law and his bond, is in Bok's commitment to his own personal covenant and in the Jewish principles of law and justice. See Dissertation Abstracts International 35 (1974):1063A.

1975

1   ASTRO, RICHARD. "In the Heart of the Valley: Bernard Malamud's A New Life." In Bernard Malamud: A Collection of Critical Essays. Edited by Leslie A. Field and Joyce A. Field. Englewood Cliffs, N.J.: Prentice-Hall, pp. 143-55.
Observes that A New Life is characterized by a variety of generic elements: it is an allegory of personal growth, a love story, a western adventure, a comedy, and an academic novel. As a roman à clef, the novel, Astro asserts, is limited by Malamud's difficulty in working its underlying biographical and factual substance into a sufficiently effective novelistic medium.

2   BLUEFARB, SAM. "The Syncretism of Bernard Malamud." In Bernard Malamud: A Collection of Critical Essays. Edited by Leslie A. Field and Joyce W. Field. Englewood Cliffs, N.J.: Prentice-Hall, pp. 72-79.

1975

Among contemporary Jewish writers Malamud is unique in his
ability to synthesize Jewish themes and motifs with those
belonging to Western literature and, more particularly, American
literature. Elements of Hawthorne, James, and Dostoevski are
transformed by Malamud into a uniquely Jewish character.

3   BURGE, NORA E.   "Women in Bernard Malamud's Novels and Short
      Stories." M.A. thesis, University of Houston, 112 pp.
      Chapter 1 uses The Natural as a norm for examining women
in connection with a popular hero. In this context his women
are given mythic characterizations. Chapters 2, 3, and 4 discuss
women in the company of artists, intellectuals, and ordinary
men. Chapter 5 summarizes the findings of the study: that
Malamud uses women mythically and also develops them as
individuals. See Masters Abstracts 13 (1976):142-43.

4   DESMOND, JOHN.   "Malamud's Fixer--Jew, Christian, or
      Modern?" Renascence 27, no. 2 (Winter):101-10.
      Throughout Malamud's fiction there is a central
preoccupation--the threat of man's diminished humanity. This
theme is associated with Yakov Bok's quest to discover his own
identity and place in history, and it is given dramatic
immediacy through the richness of his characterization. Desmond
argues that Bok's fantasy of killing the czar limits his heroic
role to that of merely a humanist redeemer. Without a vision of
an eternal framework, Bok fails to transcend the barbarism of
men in history.

5   FIELD, LESLIE [A.].   "Portrait of the Artist as Schlemiel:
      Pictures of Fidelman." In Bernard Malamud: A Collection of
      Critical Essays. Edited by Leslie A. Field and Joyce A.
      Field. Englewood Cliffs, N.J.: Prentice-Hall, pp. 117-29.
      Considers Arthur Fidelman the most fully realized version
of Malamud's schlemiel figures. In this collection of stories
Fidelman resembles the hero of the picaresque novel and the
Bildungsroman in the variety of his experiences. Eventually, he
learns that he cannot reject either life or art and remain
whole: both must be accepted.

6   FIELD, LESLIE A., and FIELD, JOYCE W., eds. Bernard Malamud:
      A Collection of Critical Essays. Englewood Cliffs, N.J.:
      Prentice-Hall, 179 pp.
      Twelve essays comprise the substance of this collection
and focus on the thematic continuity of Malamud before and after
The Fixer. They include "Introduction--Malamud, Mercy and
Menschlechkeit" by Leslie and Joyce Field (1975.8); "An
Interview with Bernard Malamud" by Leslie and Joyce Field (1975.7);
"Bernard Malamud and the Jewish Movement" by Sheldon Norman
Grebstein (1973.11) "Bernard Malamud's Ironic Heroes" by Sanford
Pinsker (1971.35); "The Syncretism of Bernard Malamud" by Sam

1975

Bluefarb (1975.2); "Literary Blacks and Jews" by Cynthia Ozick
(1972.30); "Malamud's Head (Rembrandt's Hat)" by Renee
Winegarten (1973.50); "The Promised End: Bernard Malamud's The
Tenants" by John Alexander Allen (1971.1); "Portrait of the
Artist as Schlemiel (Pictures of Fidelman)" by Leslie Field
(1975.5); "Malamud's Trial: The Fixer and the Critics" by
Gerald Hoag (1970.10); "In the Heart of the Valley: Bernard
Malamud's A New Life" by Richard Astro (1975.1); "From Bernard
Malamud, with Discipline and with Love (The Assistant and The
Natural)" by William Freedman (1970.6).
 The essays of Leslie and Joyce Field, Bluefarb, Leslie
Field, and Astro are published here for the first time. The
editors supply a bibliography of primary and secondary sources,
pp. 170-79.

7 FIELD, LESLIE A., and FIELD, JOYCE W., eds. "An Interview
   with Bernard Malamud." In Bernard Malamud: A Collection of
   Critical Essays. Edited by Leslie A. Field and Joyce W.
   Field. Englewood Cliffs, N.J.: Prentice-Hall, pp. 8-17.
  An edited and summarized interview based on an exchange of
letters between Malamud and the Fields. Malamud touches on some
of the following subjects: his interest in myth; the emotional
connection of The Fixer to the Holocaust; his famous metaphorical statement that "all men are Jews"; the minimal
influence of Chagall on his work; the relation of art to life;
knowledge of Yiddishkeit versus reader sensibility; Arthur
Fidelman and Italy; his creation of passionate, individualized
characters, rather than stereotypes; and his interest in reading
biography.

8   . "Introduction: Malamud, Mercy, and Menschlechkeit."
   In Bernard Malamud: A Collection of Critical Essays. Edited
   by Leslie A. Field and Joyce W. Field. Englewood Cliffs,
   N.J.: Prentice-Hall, pp. 1-7.
  Comments on the state of Malamud studies, the governing
themes and symbols in Malamud's fiction, his use of the
schlemiel figure, the moral dimension of the fiction, the
variety of critical approaches to his writing, the inherent
Jewishness of his materials, and Malamud's fundamentally
optimistic view of civilization.

9 FRIEDENTHAL, MARTIN HOWARD. "Heroes for Our Time: The
   Novels of Bernard Malamud." Ph.D. dissertation, St. John's
   University, 288 pp.
  Through Malamud's novels, the hero becomes a complete
human being in his capacity for compassion and suffering. The
introductory chapter defines the nature of Malamud's hero, and a
chapter on each of Malamud's six novels examines the hero's
role. See Dissertation Abstracts International, 37
(1977):5827A.

10   FUKUMA, KIN-ICHI. "Bernard Malamud and Jewish Conscious-
       ness." Kyushu American Literature, no. 16 (May):40-43.
           Jewish consciousness is reflected in those Malamud
       protagonists who undergo a personal redemption. It may be taken
       on, as it is for Frank Alpine in The Assistant, or rediscovered,
       as is the case with Yakov Bok in The Fixer.

11   GUTTMAN, ALLEN. "Literature, Sociology, and 'Our National
       Game.'" Prospects: An Annual Journal of American Cultural
       Studies 1:119-37.
           Examines, in part, the mythic origins of baseball and
       briefly discusses Malamud's The Natural as a fusion of baseball
       history and the rites of spring.

12   HAAS, RUDOLPH. "Bernard Malamud: 'Angel Levine.'" In Die
       amerikanische Kurzgeschichte. Edited by Karl Heinz Göller
       and Gerhard Hoffmann. Dusseldorf: August Bagel Verlag, pp.
       307-17.
           This story furnishes material for the discussion of the
       modern Job problem. Using the biblical account of Job as his
       point of departure, Malamud transforms it into a drama of Jewish
       existence in New York City. Stylistically, "Angel Levine" is in
       the mode of Chagall, but the form, in its closed, tight struc-
       ture, resembles a musical composition in six parts, and is
       characterized by a rising and falling rhythm.

13   HELMCKE, HANS. "Bernard Malamud: 'Take Pity.'" In
       Amerikanische Erzahlliteratur: 1950-1970. Edited by Frieder
       Busch and Renate Schmidt-von Bardeleben. Munich: Wilhelm
       Fink Verlag, pp. 207-17.
           Although most studies deal with "Take Pity" on the level
       of fantasy, Malamud's ambiguity, involving the interplay between
       realism and fantasy, has not been fully discussed. Helmcke
       asserts that the uniqueness and profundity of the story reside
       in its lingering ambiguity concerning time and place. The moral
       drama involving the giving and the taking of pity is thus
       anchored in temporal and timeless dimensions.

14   HERGT, TOBIAS. "Bernard Malamuds 'A Choice of Profession':
       Interpretation einer Kurzgeschichte mit Anregungen zu ihrer
       Behandlung in Oberstufenunterricht." Die Neureren Sprachen
       24 (October):443-53.
           Malamud's "A Choice of Professions" is an effective tool
       in teaching German secondary students about human nature in the
       modern world, the basic structure of the short story, and the
       cultural differences between Germany and America. Cronin, the
       protagonist, is a clear illustration of a man who is lacking in
       insight into his own nature. Regarding the profession of

1975

teaching as though it were a religious vocation, Cronin is
incapable of applying the humanistic values of this profession
to life: he rejects one of his students because of her former
life as a prostitute. In its unity of place, time, plot, and
effect, the story opens up for discussion the basic elements of
fiction. As a glimpse of American students and teachers,
Malamud's narrative portrays styles of life essentially foreign
to the German cultural milieu.

15   KNOPP, JOSEPHINE ZADOVSKY. "Jewish America: Bernard
      Malamud." In The Trial of Judaism in Contemporary Jewish
      Writing. Urbana: University of Illinois Press, pp. 103-25.
         Demonstrates that Malamud, unlike Philip Roth, incorporates
      in his fiction traditional Jewish values that are still
      meaningful. Such Malamud heroes as Frank Alpine and Yakov Bok
      morally evolve to a knowledge of mentshlekhayt already embodied
      in such a figure as Morris Bober. In order to gain access to
      it, Alpine and Bok must first undergo a testing process which
      brings them to a new relationship with Judaism and "the moral
      message of the Old Testament."

16   KOMIZO, YOKO. "On Frank's Conversion in Malamud's The
      Assistant." Kyushu American Literature, no. 16 (May):47-49.
         Explores the meaning of Frank Alpine's conversion to
      Judaism carried by the last sentence of the novel and concludes
      that it sanctifies his ongoing commitment to suffering and moral
      growth, the twin conditions of the Jewish experience.

17   LINDBERG-SEYERSTED, BRITA. "A Reading of Bernard Malamud's
      The Tenants. Journal of American Studies 9, no. 1 (April):
      85-102.
         The Tenants recapitulates many of the themes, techniques, and
      conventions of Malamud's earlier work, and two of these elements
      are of particular note. The partial exchange of identities by a
      Jew and a black furnishes a new twist to Malamud's use of the
      doppelgänger motif, while the sustained grammatical shifts from
      past to present tense add to the novel's surrealism. The
      possibility of redemption seems elusive as Harry Lesser and
      Willie Spearmint ruthlessly struggle against each other in
      behalf of their art.

18   "Malamud, Bernard." In World Authors, 1950-1970: A
      Companion Volume to Twentieth Century Authors. Edited by
      John Wakeman. New York: H.H. Wilson, pp. 917-20.
         The first half of this chapter uses Malamud's own
      autobiographical account of the notable incidents of his
      personal life. The second half supplies a book by book critical
      sketch of his work, adds additional biographical facts to those
      which Malamud supplies, and concludes with a list of primary and
      secondary sources.

19   MESHER, DAVID [R.]. "The Remembrance of Things Unknown:
      Malamud's 'The Last Mohican.'" Studies in Short Fiction 12,
      no. 4 (Fall):397-404.
         "The Last Mohican" reveals themes and techniques found in
      Malamud's first three novels and is a useful perspective on his
      work in general. Of special importance in this story is the use
      of the doppelgänger motif, the vehicle by which one character
      introduces another to self-knowledge. When Fidelman begins to
      identify with his Jewish double, Susskind, he has, in essence,
      gone beyond self-acceptance to a recognition of his affiliation
      with all mankind.

20   PEDEN, WILLIAM. The American Short Story: Continuity and
      Change, 1940-1975. Boston: Houghton Mifflin Co., pp.
      116-21.
         Idiots First (1963), Pictures of Fidelman (1969), and
      Rembrandt's Hat (1973) are illustrative of Malamud's fictional
      variety. Peden's book is a revised and enlarged edition of
      1964.24.

21   PRADHAN, S.V. "Spinoza and Malamud's The Fixer." Indian
      Journal of American Studies 5, nos. 1-2 (January-July):37-52.
         In the Assistant and The Fixer, St. Francis and Baruch
      Spinoza become the respective guardian angels of Malamud's
      heroes, Frank Alpine and Yakov Bok. In both novels, the
      rejection or acceptance of these sage figures becomes a
      structural principle of the plot. Although other critics have
      recognized the influence of Spinoza on Yakov Bok, they have
      ignored the ironic use to which Spinoza has been put, for Bok
      first comprehends his philosophy superficially and only later
      grasps its essence. Illustrative of his growth is his change
      from an apolitical man to a political man, seeing himself within
      history and committed to changing it.

22 · ROTH, DAVID SIDNEY. "The Strongest Link: A Study of the
      Family in the Fiction of Three Major Jewish-American
      Novelists, 1945-1970." Ph.D. dissertation, Kent State
      University, 265 pp.
         Discusses the family in Roth, Malamud, and Bellow and the
      erotic, political, and religious pressures that affect it. In
      all three writers, duty rather than love becomes the basis for
      preserving the appearance of family unity, but ultimately duty
      proves to be destructive rather than fostering cohesion. See
      Dissertation Abstracts International 35 (1975):6157A.

23   ROTH, PHILIP. "Imagining Jews." In Reading Myself and
      Others. New York: Farrar, Straus & Giroux, pp. 215-46.
         Reprint of 1974.17.

1975

24   RUDIN, NEIL. "Malamud's 'Jewbird' and Kafka's 'Gracchus':
        Birds of a Feather." <u>Studies in American Jewish Literature</u>
        1, no. 1 (Spring):10-15.
            Kafka and Malamud's use of a blackbird to depict human
        suffering suggests hitherto neglected connections between these
        writers. Underlying this initial point of contact between them
        is their responsiveness to a Jewish cultural and literary
        tradition. Kafka and Malamud affirm love and responsibility as
        the only means of surviving in a painful and inscrutable world.

25   SCHATT, STANLEY. "The Torah and the Time Bomb: The Teaching
        of Jewish American Literature Today." <u>CLA Journal</u> 18, no. 3
        (March):434-41.
            Uses Malamud's <u>The Assistant</u> and <u>The Magic Barrel</u> to
        illustrate the qualities of affirmation that are at odds with
        the nihilism of contemporary students. The function of Jewish
        teachers must go beyond repudiating the stereotyped literary
        image of the passive Jew; they must have their student confront
        the "significance of Malamud's statement that all men are Jews."

26   SCHMIDT-VON BARDELEBEN, RENATE. "Bernard Malamuds <u>The</u>
        <u>Assistant</u>." In <u>Amerikanische Erzählliteratur: 1950-1970</u>.
        Edited by Frieder Busch and Renate Schmidt-von Bardeleben.
        Kritische Information 28. Munich: Wilhelm Fink Verlag, pp.
        57-74.
            Reviews the novel from several vantage points: its
        departure from the fifties literature of social protest, the
        symbolic use of landscape, the psychological splitting of
        characters, and the impact of Yiddish inflections on the reader.

27   SINGER, BARNET. "Outsider versus Insider: Malamud's and
        Kesey's Pacific Northwest." <u>South Dakota Review</u> 13, no. 4
        (Winter):127-44.
            Considers Malamud's <u>A New Life</u> and Kesey's <u>One Flew Over</u>
        <u>the Cuckoo's Nest</u> as two of the best expressions of contemporary
        regionalism. An outsider to the region, Malamud supplies
        especially fresh perceptions of Oregon's character between 1958
        and 1963. As an insider, Kesey's intense involvement with
        Oregon is expressed almost mythically in the salmon fishing trip
        scene of his novel. Common to both writers, however, is a
        subversive tone directed to the prevailing ethos of the place.

28   STERN, DANIEL. "The Art of Fiction: Bernard Malamud."
        <u>Paris Review</u>, no. 61 (Spring):40-64.
            In response to a request from the <u>Paris Review</u> for an
        interview just after publishing <u>The Fixer</u>, Malamud agreed to
        give one when he reached the age of sixty. Stern's interview
        was conducted on 26 April 1974 as part of the celebration of

Malamud's sixtieth birthday. Included in Malamud's comments are remarks on his early life in Brooklyn, his philosophy of composition, sources for his fiction, and the future of the novel.

29   SWEET, CHARLES A., Jr. "Unlocking the Door: Malamud's 'Behold the Key.'" Notes on Contemporary Literature 5, no. 5 (November):11-12.
      In this story Malamud establishes a series of parallels to T.S. Eliot's The Waste Land, but for Malamud's hero, Carl Schneider, redemption is not intimated.

30   VANDYKE, PATRICIA. "Choosing One's Side With Care: The Liberating Repartee." Perspectives on Contemporary Literature 1, no. 1 (May):105-17 passim.
      Malamud's story, "The Jewbird," is a form of tendentious comedy in which the scurrilous aggressor becomes the butt of his own hostile humor. When Cohen, the assimilated Jew, fails to receive Schwartz as a representative of the traditional Jew--through the recognition of Schwartz's essential suffering--he reveals his own lack of Jewish authenticity. Indeed, the humor of the story comes full circle as Schwartz's most pertinent identity becomes that of an anti-Semite.

*31   WILHELM, CHERRY ANN. "The Moral Fable and the Fiction of Bernard Malamud." M.A. thesis, University of the Witwatersrand.
      Source: Grau, p.103, 1981.6.

32   WINN, H. HARBOUR, III. "Malamud's Uncas: 'Last Mohican.'" Notes on Contemporary Literature 5, no. 2 (March):13-14.
      Malamud ironically juxtaposes Cooper's noble savage, Uncas, with his own Arthur Fidelman. At stake in both cases is the denial of one's racial identity. While Cooper's story involves a tragic elevation, Malamud's furnishes comic deflation.

33   WITHERINGTON, PAUL. "Malamud's Allusive Design in A New Life." Western American Literature 10, no. 2 (Summer):115-23.
      S. Levin is an embodiment of the new Adam, a pioneer of the spirit, practicing a Thoreauvian life as he immerses himself in nature. Through his connection with women, he eventually becomes acquainted with Hawthorne's fallen world. "When Levin slips into the Puritan pattern that trapped Hawthorne's characters and the ideal of love turns into the ideal of guilt, the allusions become very explicit and very conscious."

1975

34   ZLOTNICK, JOAN. "Malamud's The Assistant: of Morris, Frank,
      and St. Francis." Studies in American Jewish Literature 1,
      no. 2 (Winter):20-23.
          Asserts that St. Francis represents the ethical values of
      love and suffering embodied in Morris Bober and at the center of
      the Jewish experience. Thus Frank's spiritual romance with St.
      Francis is converted into a symbolic and literal union with
      Morris, his Jewish role model.

1976

1   ANGOFF, CHARLES. "How 'Jewish' are Jewish Writers in
      America?" Tradition 16, no. 2:24-34.
          Considers Malamud's Jews lacking in authenticity because
      of his cold, cerebral treatment of them. "He misses . . . that
      marvelous combination of ebulience, transcendent morality,
      spiritual anarchism, the cosmic daring, the deep, all-enveloping
      warmth of heart that is Jewishness."

2   AVERY, EVELYN GROSS. "Rebels and Victims: The Fiction of
      Richard Wright and Bernard Malamud." Ph.D. dissertation,
      University of Oregon, 180 pp.
          Compares characters and themes in the works of Richard
      Wright and Bernard Malamud and perceives that the characters of
      the former are rebels and those of the latter are victims. The
      conclusion assesses the nature of black and white confrontation.
      "Self-contempt and helplessness suffered by both victims and
      rebels translate into acts of love by the former, hatred by the
      latter." See Dissertation Abstracts International 37
      (1977):5822A. Revised for publication: 1979.4.

3   BERTHIER, P. Review of Les locataires [The Tenants]. Études
      345 (October):423.
          A violent, darkly humorous, and prophetic novel in which
      Harry Lesser and Willie Spearmint, respectively, represent
      Europe and Africa in conflict. Spearmint fights to assert his
      racial blackness, as well as his American blackness, in this war
      of cultures.

4   FABE, MARILYN MICHELE. "Successful Failures: Guilt and
      Morality in the Novels of Bernard Malamud." Ph.D.
      dissertation, University of California, Berkeley, 214 pp.
          Argues that Malamud's moral code, involving the redemptive
      power of suffering, is really problematic, and has been taken
      for granted by critics who fail to detect the latent hostility
      of his characters to that code. When Malamud is at his best,
      there is a tension between the moral efforts of his characters
      and his own subtle attempts to sabotage them. His fiction rings

false, however, when he lets himself identify with those who
suffer. See <u>Dissertation Abstracts International</u> 38
(1977):787A.

5   FINK, GUIDO. "Il colore sul vuoto: James e Malamud a
       Firenze." In <u>America-Europe: A circolazione delle idee</u>.
       Edited by Tiziano Bonazzi. Bologna: Società Editrice Il
       Mulino, pp. 11-34.
          Examines James and Malamud in relation to the
international theme. Fink centers his discussion on James's
"The Madonna of the Future" and Malamud's "The Pimp's Revenge"
in <u>Pictures of Fidelman</u>, narratives which share similar plots.
Both idealists, Theobald in James's tale and Fidelman in
Malamud's, search for the Florence of the Renaissance. Thus
Theobald is never able to execute his masterpiece and Fidelman's
work amounts to nothing more than a scrawl and is finally
destroyed. More realistic than either Theobald or Fidelman,
Hawthorne's Miriam becomes a productive artist but only through
performing as a copyist.

6   FREESE, PETER, ed. "Bernard Malamud, 'The Last Mohican'
       (1958)." In <u>Die amerikanische Short Story der Gegenwart</u>.
       Berlin: Erich Schmidt Verlag, pp. 205-14.
          Discusses Malamud's unique handling of the international
theme as it is developed through the character of Arthur
Fidelman. Ambivalent about his Jewish identity, Malamud's hero
tries to escape from his own cultural past and start life anew,
determined to sever all connection with the past. Such a
repudiation, however, is also an index of his failure to
comprehend both the glory and misery of Western civilization
reflected in the art of Giotto. Eventually, Fidelman comes to
recognize the supremacy of life over art.

7   FURTH, PIERRE-PASCAL. Review of <u>Les locataires</u> [<u>The</u>
       <u>Tenants</u>]. <u>Europe--Revue Litteraire Mensuelle</u> 54, nos. 571-72
       (November-December):216-17.
          <u>The Tenants</u> is a novel about the destruction of two men,
one white and one black, who inhabit the same tenement and who
behave as though they were warring parts of one personality.
The complexities of Malamud's narrative style suggest the knotty
relationship of his characters, but Malamud is deft in his
handling of them.

8   GEALY, MARCIA BOOHER. "The Hasidic Tradition in the Work of
       Bernard Malamud." Ph.D. dissertation, Ohio State University,
       173 pp.
          Hasidism, in varying degrees, plays a part in all of
Malamud's work including his latest short stories. The concerns
of Hasidism--inner redemption, the relationship between stranger

1976

and community, teacher and pupil--are themes reflected in such diverse works as The Natural, The Assistant, A New Life, The Fixer and The Tenants. See Dissertation Abstracts International 37 (1976):963A.

9   HASSAN, IHAB. "Bernard Malamud." In Contemporary Novelists: Contemporary Writers of the English Language. Edited by James Vinson. New York: St. Martin's Press, pp. 820-24.
     Offers a concise biographical, bibliographical, and critical survey of Malamud's work from The Natural through The Tenants. Hassan's assessment is that Malamud is not really experimental, that his moral imagination is a bit too steadfast, and that his genius is limited.

10   HATVARY, GEORGE E. "The Endings in Malamud's The Tenants." Notes on Modern American Literature 1, no. 1 (Winter):item 5.
     Argues that Malamud experiments with four different endings in The Tenants as a way of speculating on the meaning of life, the meaning of art, and the relationship of art and life to each other.

11   HOWE, IRVING. World of Our Fathers. New York: Harcourt, Brace, Jovanovich, pp. 595-96.
     Asserts that Malamud is a mysterious writer in his ability to render a Yiddish ethos in his fiction without having a clearly discernible relationship to Yiddish culture. When his stories fail, the failure is a result of a forced Jewishness and an excess of sentiment, the consequence of making "Jewishness . . . a program rather than an experience."

12   KEGAN, ROBERT. The Sweeter Welcome, Voices for a Vision of Affirmation: Bellow, Malamud, and Martin Buber. Needham Heights, Mass.: Humanitas Press, 169 pp.
     Attempts to show connections between the neo-Hasidic vision of Martin Buber and the fiction of Malamud and Bellow. Kegan's own experiences in the Lubavitcher Hasidic community of Crown Heights, Brooklyn, is interlaced with the more formal discussions of these writers and serves as a gloss for the experiences presented in the novels. Malamud and Bellow "deal with our movement toward inner and outer wholeness, with the person becoming bigger than the sum of his parts."

13   KELLMAN, STEVEN G. "The Tenants in the House of Fiction." Studies in the Novel 8, no. 4 (Winter):458-67.
     Although The Tenants seems, at first, to be an apocalyptic vision of America in the 1960s, it soon moves away from contemporary reality into its own private world where literary allusiveness becomes a substitute for a sustained realistic illusion. Kellman asserts that the incompleteness of Harry

Lesser as man and artist mirrors the incompleteness of the novel itself--that is, its failure to focus either on the tensions of contemporary life or to examine the relations of art to life.

14   KUDLER, HARVEY. "Bernard Malamud's The Natural and other Oedipal Analogs in Baseball Fiction." Ph.D. dissertation, St. John's University, 305 pp.
        Suggests that Malamud was the first American novelist to recognize that the game of baseball contained inherently Oedipal materials. Using character models from Sophocles' Oedipus Rex in The Natural, Malamud dramatizes baseball as a metaphorical duel between a father figure and his symbolic son. This novel, however, is not an isolated instance in which father conflict and mother fixation resonate. The Assistant, The Magic Barrel, and A New Life carry forward Malamud's Oedipal motifs, while other contemporary novels about baseball also use similar Oedipal patterns. See Dissertation Abstracts International 37 (1977):5829A.

15   HOAG, GERALD. "Malamud's The Tenants: Revolution Arrested." Perspectives on Contemporary Literature 2, no. 2 (November):3-9.
        Three major concerns of Malamud are represented in The Tenants: psychic development, the social revolution, and the relationship of the artist to his contemporaries. Unlike Yakov Bok in The Fixer, Harry Lesser and Willie Spearmint of The Tenants fail to grow in any of these areas. This novel undercuts the optimism of the earlier work.

16   LONG, MARY. "Interview: Bernard Malamud." Mademoiselle 82 (August):235.
        Recalls the advice Malamud furnished on how to put talent to use. Organization is the central ingredient for success in writing, and that quality demands unrelenting discipline. The other ingredient is narration, the ability to tell a story that will lead to illumination. Failure is often to be expected and demands a sense of humor. If a writer can laugh at his own comic situation, he will be able to overcome the obstacles that writers inevitably face.

17   MORSCO, GABRIELLA. Review of Il capello di Rembrandt. Spicilegio Moderno, no. 5, pp. 173-73.
        In this collection, Malamud's continued experiments with techniques are really attempts to explore the possibility for man's greater ethical enrichment and increased self-consciousness. To this end Malamud shifts from symbolism to documentary and from fantasy to naturalism, or he may use a sustained organic metaphor throughout a particular work. In "Rembrandt's Hat," for example, a simple hat, an emblem of hope and failure, becomes a narrative device for establishing a

1976

relationship between two hypersensitive artists.

18   RAO, D. LAKSHMANA. "The Search for Identity in Bernard
      Malamud's The Natural." Trivini: Journal of Indian
      Renaissance 44 (January-March):79-86.
          Roy Hobbs's sense of identity is limited at the outset of
      the novel, but he begins to achieve an authentic sense of self
      when he repudiates Dr. Knobb. With that emerging identity,
      however, comes an excessive egotism, an obstacle to further
      growth. Roy's contact with Iris Lemon stimulates another move
      toward psychic wholeness as he demonstrates a capacity for
      involvement with others. Only when he begins to accept his past
      does he reach his full psychic potential and becomes capable of
      a new life.

19   RIESE, UTZ. "Bernard Malamud: Die Mietier. Weimar Beitrage
      23, no. 4:145-55.
          Malamud's The Tenants is anchored in the traditional
      proletarian novel of the thirties, but its setting, a decaying
      city landscape, goes beyond realism to symbolize the decay of
      human relationships. Estranged from socially productive goals,
      Harry Lesser fails to realize that his love of humanity is in
      conflict with love of himself, narcissistically expressed
      through his art. Willie Spearmint, on the other hand, moves
      closer to political engagement.

20   ROGOFF, LEONARD WILLIAM. "Revelations of Bernard Malamud."
      Ph.D. dissertation, University of North Carolina at Chapel
      Hill, 373 pp.
          Central to Malamud's vision is reconciliation which
      embraces "religion, race, nationality, sexual gender or artistic
      persuasion." When reconciliation comes to his protagonists, it
      arrives unexpectedly, often through the mystery of a sudden
      revelation. See Dissertation Abstracts International 37
      (1977):5126A-27A.

21   ROTH, PHILIP. "Jüdische Phantasien und Phantasien über
      Jüden." Translated into German by Christa Maerker. Akzhente
      13, no. 5 (October):447-74.
          Discusses The Assistant, The Fixer, and Pictures of
      Fidelman as part of a general commentary on the use of fantasy
      by Jewish-American writers and fantasies about Jews. Malamud's
      imaginative and moral conception of the good Jew and the bad
      Gentile would be artistically weak in the fiction of most
      writers, but his allegorical handling of it is always
      compelling. Perhaps the reader's attraction to Malamud is due,
      in part, to the intensity with which suffering features in his
      fiction, for it is possible to become fascinated by characters
      who achieve an apotheosis through undergoing humiliation and
      brutality. There are differences in the treatment of suffering,

however, in these works. In The Assistant, it is embraced; in
The Fixer, it is resisted only in the realm of fantasy; and in
Pictures of Fidelman it is subsumed under the rubric of love.

22   SCHWARTZ, HELEN J. "Malamud's Turning Point: The End of
        Redemption in Pictures of Fidelman." Studies in American
        Jewish Literature 2, no. 2 (Winter):26-37.
        In the first four chapters of this book, Fidelman's
priority of art over life leads to symbolic death, but
eventually Fidelman embraces life over art and is thereby reborn
as both man and artist. In the last two chapters his comic
deflation as hero seems to be an erosion of the moral seriousness we
have come to expect from Malamud, a decline that foreshadows
the wasteland vision of The Tenants.

23   SHARMA, D.R. "Malamud's A New Life: The Drama of
        Becoming." In Studies in American Literature in Honour of
        William Mulder. Edited by Jagdish Chander and Narindar S.
        Pradham. New Delhi: Oxford University Press, pp. 134-53.
        While S. Levin may serve as a spokesman for Malamud's
humanistic values, the essential drama of A New Life consists in
Levin's attempt to enact these values in the world of Cascadia.
It is primarily through his problematic relationship with
Pauline Gilley that he tries to impose order and meaning in his
new life. Levin's commitment to her, with all its encumbrances,
does not bring immediate happiness but rather feelings somewhere
between grace and resignation.

24   _____. "Pictures of Fidelman: From Art to Life." Panjab
        University Research Bulletin 7, no. 1:31-42.
        The characteristic tone in this collection is comic, but
Arthur Fidelman, although a comic character, should not be
considered a schlemiel as some critics have suggested. Such a
stereotype blurs our recognition of Fidelman's complexity as a
character who is capable of psychological and moral regener-
ation. Through Fidelman, Malamud documents man's ability to
maintain his integrity in spite of victimization.

*25   YOKOTA, KAZUNORI. "On Bernard Malamud's 'The Last
        Mohican.'" Chu-shikotu Studies in American Literature
        12:32:37.
        Source: Modern Language Association International
Bibliography (1979), 1:222.

                              1977

1   ADACHI, FUMI. "The Solitary Clowns: Bernard Malamud's A New
        Life." In American Literature in the 1950's: Annual Report
        1976. Tokyo: American Literature Society of Japan, pp.
        76-82.

1977

Half of the novel is a satire on academic life and a
reflection of the topical issues affecting America in the
fifties--the Cold War, McCarthyism, and the Korean War; the
other half is a lyrical love story reminiscent of F. Scott
Fitzgerald but often narrated with Malamud's special humor.

2   ALTER, ISKA SHEILA. "The Man's Dilemna: Social Criticism in
     the Fiction of Bernard Malamud." Ph.D. dissertation, New
     York University, 344 pp.
        Explores the impact of the cultural value system on the
     individual in Malamud's fiction, as he tries to affirm the
     personal values of honesty, responsibility, and love. The
     novels examined in this study are The Natural, The Assistant, A
     New Life, The Fixer, and The Tenants. In all of them the heroes
     face the task of responding in ethical ways to the corrupting
     and dehumanizing forces in society. The decreasing frequency of
     women in Malamud's fiction is an indication that their tradi-
     tional nurturing role is no longer efficacious, but man's
     ethical struggle must continue if he is to consider himself
     human. See Dissertation Abstracts International 38
     (1978):6128A. Revised for publication: 1981.1.

3   ASTRO, RICHARD, and BENSON, JACKSON J., eds. The Fiction of
     Bernard Malamud. Corvallis: Oregon State University Press,
     190 pp.
        The following papers in this collection were delivered at
     a symposium on Bernard Malamud sponsored by the Department of
     English at Oregon State University: "An Introduction: Bernard
     Malamud and the Haunting of America" by Jackson J. Benson
     (1977.4); "Bernard Malamud: 1976. Fictions within Our Fictions"
     by Ihab Hassan (1977.15); "The Malamud Hero: A Quest for
     Existence" by W.J. Handy (1977.13); "Malamud's Yiddish-Accented
     Medieval Stories" by Peter L. Hays (1977.16); "Bernard Malamud
     and the Marginal Jew" by Leslie Field (1977.11); "Through a
     Glass Darkly: Bernard Malamud's Painful Views of the Self" by
     Ben Siegel (1977.36); "The Many Names of S. Levin: An Essay in
     Genre Criticism" by Leslie Fiedler (1977.10); "A Checklist of
     Malamud Criticism" by Donald Risty (1977.33).

4   BENSON, JACKSON J. "An Introduction: Bernard Malamud and
     the Haunting of America." In The Fiction of Bernard
     Malamud. Edited by Richard Astro and Jackson J. Benson.
     Corvallis: Oregon State University Press, pp. 13-42.
        Summarizes the most fruitful approaches to Bernard Malamud
     offered at a symposium at Oregon State University. Included in
     this essay are the views of Ihab Hassan, Leslie Field, Peter L.
     Hays, and Ben Siegel. For Benson, the most illuminating
     perspective on Malamud is the American romantic tradition in
     which psychological and moral allegorization of character is a

central feature. Siegel's observations on Malamud's "doublings, his images and visions, his hauntings" amplifies Benson's own critical thinking.

5   BORNHAUSER, FRED. Review of Idiots First. In Survey of Contemporary Literature. Rev. ed. Edited by Frank N. Magill. Vol. 6. Englewoood Cliffs, N.J.: Salem Press, pp. 3612-14.
     Perceives the unity of Malamud's fiction to be the Jewishness of the author's vision: a synthesis of his culture and his own soul which colors his writing both about Jews and non-Jews. As Malamud's fifth book, Idiots First sustains the high level and vitality of his art.

6   BOYCE, DANIEL F. Review of Pictures of Fidelman. In Survey of Contemporary Literature. Rev. ed. Edited by Frank N. Magill. Vol. 9. Englewood Cliffs, N.J.: Salem Press, pp. 5852-56.
     In bringing together these disparate stories under the rubric "exhibition," Malamud achieves a novelistic unity where none had been before. Progressively, Arthur Fidelman loses sight of his artistic goals as he fails to heed the warnings of his associates. Obsessed with form, he degenerates into a copyist until he comes to the realization that a deep involvement in painting would offer him an unwelcome insight: that his true nature is parasitic. His metaphorical death as an artist is suggested in his creation of a work that depicts holes in the ground. Malamud's view of Fidelman remains ambiguous at the conclusion.

7   CANHAM, LAUREL. "Matrix and Allegory in Selected Malamud Short Stories." Linguistics in Literature 2, no. 3 (Fall):59-91.
     Because of their lexical density "Take Pity," "The Silver Crown," "The Mourners," and "Angel Levine" are fruitful texts for linguistic analysis. A study of vocabulary and morphology, references to days and dates, definition of names, changes of tense, and external matrices increase our awareness of Malamud's depth as a writer.

8   ENGLEBERT, ERNST. Die Bedeutung der Bibel im Romanwerk Bernard Malamuds. Mainzer Studien zur Amerikanistik, edited by Hans Galinsky, vol. 5, Frankfurt-am-Main: Peter Lang, 255 pp.
     The salvation of man is the central theme running through Bernard Malamud's fiction, as well as the central theme of the Old and New Testaments. It seems quite understandable that Malamud should be influenced by the Bible in his use of language, analogues, images, and motifs. Malamud, through his

1977

fiction, brings the Bible up to date, although man remains the
same: flawed and in need of redemption.

9   FIEDLER, LESLIE [A.]. "Malamud's Travesty Western." Novel:
     A Forum on Fiction 10, no. 3 (Spring):212-19.
          A slightly abridged text of 1977.10. The article, with
     the exception of the title and the first four paragraphs, is
     identical to the original text.

10   _____. "The Many Names of S. Levin: An Essay in Genre
     Criticism." In The Fiction of Bernard Malamud. Edited by
     Richard Astro and Jackson J. Benson. Corvallis: Oregon
     State University Press, pp. 149-61.
          Compares Malamud's A New Life to Kesey's One Flew Over the
     Cuckoo's Nest and finds only the latter a true western in its
     mythic vision "of transitory and idyllic love between two males
     in the wilderness." A New Life, on the other hand, lacks any
     vision of the West as a mythic alternative to the restrictions
     and conventions of civilized life. Malamud's novel is most
     successful when S. Levin's comic suffering as a schlemiel is
     developed. As a defender of the Liberal Tradition, S. Levin
     becomes humorless and unsufferable. Abridged: 1977.9.

11   FIELD, LESLIE [A.]. "Bernard Malamud and the Marginal Jew."
     In The Fiction of Bernard Malamud. Edited by Richard Astro
     and Jackson J. Benson. Corvallis: Oregon State University
     Press, pp. 97-116.
          The Jew and Jewishness are central to Malamud's fiction,
     and yet there is still much debate as to what they really mean.
     After examining the many attempts of other commentators to
     arrive at their essence, Field asserts that these concepts can
     only have current meaning in the light of the European Holocaust
     and the rebirth of the state of Israel. Since Malamud's fiction
     ignores these two major events of the Jewish history, Malamud
     falls "within the loose tradition of that special breed of
     hyphenated Jewish writer."

12   GOLDSMITH, ARNOLD. "Nature in Bernard Malamud's The
     Assistant." Renascence 29, no. 4 (Summer):211-23.
          A close study of The Assistant reveals that its nature
     imagery is associated with almost every character in the novel
     and serves a variety of functions beyond the mythic level. The
     daily events experienced by Malamud's characters are mirrored by
     dismal images of fall, winter, and even spring. Summer exists
     only retrospectively as part of an irretrievable past in the
     consciousness of Morris and Helen Bober.

13   HANDY, W[ILLIAM] J. "The Malamud Hero: A Quest for Exis-
     tence." In The Fiction of Bernard Malamud. Edited by

Richard Astro and Jackson J. Benson. Corvallis: Oregon State University Press, pp. 65-86.

Although on the surface Malamud's naturalism resembles Dreiser's, Malamud is possessed of a larger vision of life. In Malamud's world characters are capable of change because of their involvement in human relationships whose dynamics promote an awakening. Such is the case in The Fixer, The Assistant, and A New Life, novels in which the Malamud hero is led to a more purposive life.

14   HARRIS, TONI. Review of The Magic Barrel. In Survey of Contemporary Literature. Rev. ed. Edited by Frank N. Magill. Vol. 7. Englewood Cliffs, N.J.: Salem Press, pp. 4631-34.

This is a collection notable for its insights into character and its variety of ethnic and vocational types. Harris observes that in five stories--"The First Seven Years," "The Mourners," "Take Pity," "The Loan," and "The Lady of the Lake"--Malamud's moral vision is developed through dramatic incident rather than rhetoric.

15   HASSAN, IHAB. "Bernard Malamud: 1976. Fictions Within Our Fictions." In The Fiction of Bernard Malamud. Edited by Richard Astro and Jackson J. Benson. Corvallis: Oregon State University Press, pp. 43-64.

It is difficult to consider Bernard Malamud in the light of such categories as modernism and postmodernism when his traditional humanism seems so alien from them. It is just as difficult to classify Malamud in the context of modern Jewish fiction when our sense of what constitutes such a literature is no longer clear. Hassan suggests that in a cosmic frame the Wandering Jew may now express the mysterious predicament of the human race itself.

16   HAYS, PETER L. "Malamud's Yiddish-Accented Medieval Stories." In The Fiction of Bernard Malamud. Edited by Richard Astro and Jackson J. Benson. Corvallis: Oregon State University Press, pp. 87-96.

Asserts that Malamud was acquainted with medieval literature and echoes much of its chivalric element. In his fiction such characters as Frank Alpine, S. Levin, and Arthur Fidelman suffer predicaments similar to those of Lancelot and Gawain. The basic quest pattern in which they are involved is carried over into Malamud's plots. Moreover, the narratives themselves are reminiscent of the age-old tradition of the oral tale.

17   HOFFER, BATES. "The Magic in Malamud's Barrel." Linguistics in Literature 2, no. 3 (Fall):1-26.

1977

Denies that the story involves the redemption of either
Leo Finkle or Stella Salzman. In desiring Stella, a prostitute,
for his wife, Leo has in various ways broken the Ten
Commandments and thereby increases his distance both from God
and man. The ambiguity surrounding his spiritual conversion in
the tale, as well as Malamud's conclusion, disappears once the
narrative is perceived as an allegory organized around the
five-part structure of the Torah, a context which reveals Finkle
as a "great Law-Breaker."

18   HOFFER, BRUCE, ed. Introduction to "Malamud's Barrel of
      Magic" [A Symposium]. Linguistics in Literature 2, no. 3
      (Fall):i-ii.
          Regards much of the criticism of Malamud's fiction as
cliché-ridden. In order to provide a fresh approach to his
fiction, the articles in this collection offer close textual
analyses "before drawing conclusions about what Malamud is
doing. . . ."

*19   ICHIKAWA, MASUMI. "Bernard Malamud's The Fixer. Chu-shikotu
      Studies in American Literature 13:51-64.
          Source: Modern Language Association International
Bibliography (1979), 1:222.

20   JOHNSON, DAN. Review of Rembrandt's Hat. In Survey of
      Contemporary Literature. Rev. ed. Edited by Frank N.
      Magill. Vol. 9. Englewood Cliffs, N.J.: Salem Press, pp.
      231-35.
          Malamud's characters engage in fierce confrontations.
Occasionally they may achieve a certain wisdom from their
ordeal, but Malamud is primarily concerned with representing the
pain allotted to all human beings.

21   KALINA DE PISZK, ROSITA. "Bernard Malamud: El precio de la
      pasividad en El Ayudante." In Káñina (San José, Costa
      Rica):51-60.
          Establishes points of contact between Malamud and writers
of Yiddish and Hasidic tradition, especially Sholom Aleichem.
While Sholom Aleichem's Tevye responds to the adversity of life
with humor and cutting wit, the suffering of Morris Bober in
Malamud's The Assistant is grimly endured. Even though
Malamud's setting is located in North America, Morris Bober
remains psychologically and symbolically within a shtetl which
he is incapable of transcending.

22   KLIEMANN, KRISTIN. "A perspective on Malamud's 'Idiots
      First.'" Linguistics in Literature 2, no. 3 (Fall):27-40.
          Finds the story an allegory based on the Old Testament
representation of Hell as a place of darkness, shadows, and
physical divisions. In Malamud's narrative the protagonists

142

seem to function in darkness, mingle with shadowy figures, and
continually move from place to place across the city. Qeteb, a
demon of Old Testament Hell, seems to be embodied in Malamud's
Ginzburg, a figure who periodically appears to Mendel in
different guises and places.

23   KUMAR, SHIV P., "Marionettes in Taleysim: Yiddish
      Folkfigures in Two Malamud Stories." Indian Journal of
      American Studies 8, no. 1 (July):18-24.
      Malamud acknowledges that in a general way his Jewishness
has had an important influence on his fiction. Indeed, his
knowledge of Yiddish literature and culture must certainly
account for characters in his fiction who resemble Yiddish folk
figures other than the generally recognized schlemiel. The
luftmensch, the schnorrer, and the shadkhn also figure in his
work. The acquisitive Susskind fulfills the role of schnorrer
in "The Last Mohican." Pinye Salzman of "The Magic Barrel"
resembles the luftmensch in his calculation and scheming; but he
also fulfills the characterization of the shadkhn in his
shrewdness and tact.

24   MANN, HERBERT DAVID. "Bernard Malamud and the Struggle to
      Connect." Ph.D. dissertation, State University of New York
      at Binghamton, 281 pp.
      Relating to another is the most difficult task faced by a
Malamud character, but his continued persistence is a sign that
he remains spiritually alive. The heart of the matter is summed
up by Ludovico in Pictures of Fidelman who observes that "the
basis of morality is recognizing one another's needs and
cooperating." See Dissertation Abstracts International 38
(1977):2128A.

25   MANSKE, EVA. Review of Der Gehilfe [The Assistant].
      Zeitschrift fur Anglistic and Amerikanistik 25, no. 3:272-73.
      Malamud is a sensitive and critical observer of the
disturbed relations between the individual and society.
Although he represents the American dream turned into nightmare,
he establishes no platform for social change.

26   MEETER, GLEN. Review of The Tenants. In Survey of
      Contemporary Literature. Rev. ed. Edited by Frank N.
      Magill. Vol. 11. Englewood Cliffs, N.J.: Salem Press, pp.
      7463-66.
      This novel has curiously failed to stir as much
controversy as Styron's The Confessions of Nat Turner, and
perhaps the most plausible explanation lies in Malamud's
technique: the conscious use of stereotypes to which realistic
detail is subordinated. The result is a narrative that moves
toward a universal statement. Through creating characters who

are diametrically opposite to each other in color, Malamud
symbolizes a fundamental conflict inherent in mankind. The
Tenants may be sadder than Styron's book, but it is also less
depressing "because Malamud lifts the squalor of the present to
the level of myth, and dignifies suffering by letting us share
it with heroes of the past."

27   MESHER, DAVID R. "Malamud's Jewish Metaphors." Judaism 26,
      no. 1: 18-26.
          In The Assistant suffering and selflessness are the
central referents to Jewish identity, but in The Fixer, these
referents, while still valid, have undergone some modification
as they are reflected in the figure of Yakov Bok. As Malamud's
representative Jew, Bok's militancy emerges as an added metaphor
for Jewishness.

28   PALLY, ERWIN. "From Realism to Romance in Six Novels by
      Bellow, Updike, and Malamud." Ph.D. dissertation, University
      of Massachusetts, 262 pp.
          Argues that these novelists were more effective in the
fifties in synthesizing realism and romance than they were in
the sixties. In The Assistant (1957), for example, Malamud's
successful fusion of myth with comedy is ultimately a way of
complementing realism with romance. See Dissertation Abstracts
International 38 (1977):266A-67A.

29   PETERSON, TRICIA. "The Levels of Allegory in 'The Loan.'"
      Linguistics in Literature 2, no. 3 (Fall):41-57.
          Considers "The Loan" an allegory of the story of Moses,
and cites various points of contact between Malamud's
characters and plot of the biblical narrative. Kobotsky
emerges as Moses; Leib corresponds to Aaron, the ruler of the
twelve tribes of Israel, and Bessie fills the role of his wife.
The flight of Malamud's characters from Germany to America
recalls the Israelites in their escape from Egypt. Malamud's
deviation from the Moses story serves to establish the darkness
of his own vision: the helplessness and futility of modern
Judaism.

30   PHILLIPSON, JOHN S. Review of The Fixer. Best Sellers 26
      (15 September):20.
          Observes that this is a deeply religious book about one
man's willingness to take on suffering in behalf of justice and
mankind. The capacity of some Christians for great cruelty must
be a numbing experience for other Christians.

31   Review of The Assistant. In Survey of Contemporary
      Literature. Rev. ed. Edited by Frank N. Magill. Vol. 1.
      Englewood Cliffs, N.J.: Salem Press, pp. 416-17.

The novel is successful both as a morality play and as a model of realism, especially since the subject, the conversion of one man by another to goodness, is inherently difficult. This work is prophetic of Malamud's future success.

32   Review of A New Life. In Survey of Contemporary Literature. Rev. ed. Edited by Frank N. Magill. Vol. 8. Englewood Cliffs, N.J.: Salem Press, pp. 5264-66.
      This academic novel is largely comic and satiric, but Malamud's achievement in this mode does not measure up to the work of Mary McCarthy or Randall Jarrell. S. Levin, the hero, is, however, more than a comic bungler: "he represents sensibility and good will in a world given largely to insensitive and selfish preoccupations." A New Life will give uninitiated readers a pleasurable and uncomplicated introduction to Malamud's fiction.

33   RISTY, DONALD. "A Checklist of Malamud Criticism." In The Fiction of Bernard Malamud. Edited by Richard Astro and Jackson J. Benson. Corvallis: Oregon State University Press, pp. 163-90.
      This checklist is divided into three sections: (1) books on Malamud's work; (2) general books containing discussion of Malamud's work; (3) articles and reviews containing discussion of Malamud's work.

34   ROBINSON, WILLIAM R. Review of The Fixer. In Survey of Contemporary Literature. Rev. ed. Edited by Frank N. Magill. Vol. 4. Englewood Cliffs, N.J.: Salem Press, pp. 2657-61.
      The novel mirrors the rebellion of the sixties and is an innovation in Malamud's fiction in its use of a historical setting. In coming to grips with the absurdity of his existence, Yakov Bok begins to show as much stubbornness as other contemporary existential heroes. Unlike his other fiction, Malamud's The Fixer is committed to the radical changing of society. "As a Jew, Malamud was born to regard history as the dimension within which man's promises were to be fulfilled, and as a liberal he regards progress in time to be the necessary road to relief of man's earthly ailments."

35   ROTH, PHILIP. "Le Juif imaginaire." Translated into French by Harry Blake. Tel Quel, nos. 71-73 (Autumn):76-94.
      Malamud's fiction is characterized by recurring stereotypes: those of the ethical Jew and the sensual and immoral Gentile. The fiction of other writers would inevitably be reduced to triteness were they to furnish such simplistic character constructs; yet Malamud's fiction is somehow convincing, as illustrated by The Assistant, when he uses them as part of an allegorical design. A less benevolent writer might

1977

have ignored Frank Alpine's conversion to Judaism and used this incident as a covert attempt to exact revenge.

36   SIEGEL, BEN. "Through a Glass Darkly: Bernard Malamud's Painful Views of the Self." In The Fiction of Bernard Malamud. Edited by Richard Astro and Jackson J. Benson. Corvallis: Oregon State University Press, pp. 117-47.
        Dreams, fantasies, mirrors, and manuscripts have been employed by Malamud as sources of self-knowledge. In association with these fictive elements is the double figure, the agent of the hero's suffering, compassion, and self-scrutiny--in short, his larger humanity.

37   TAKADA, KEN'ICHI, and SUGAHARA, HIDEO. "Bernard Malamud: The Necessity of Returning to Reality." In American Literature in the 1950's: Annual Report 1976. Tokyo: American Literature Society of Japan, pp. 60-75.
        Malamud's heroes live in an atmosphere of hopelessness, oppressed as they are with the conditions of the present and the spectre of the past. Yet unlike the cloistral world of Anderson or Melville, entrapment in Malamud's becomes paradoxically the catalyst for a new life.

*38   VARELA, LOURDES Y. "Man, Society and Literature." In Literature and Society: Cross Cultural Perspectives: Eleventh American Studies Seminar, October 1976, Los Baños, Philippines. Edited by Roger J. Bresnahan. N.p.: U.S. Information Service, pp. 84-94.
        Source: Modern Language Association International Bibliography (1978)1:156; unverified.

1978

1   BANTA, MARTHA. Failure and Success in America: A Literary Debate. Princeton: Princeton University Press, pp. 158-59.
        Considers the grace which touches Frank Alpine in Malamud's The Assistant similar to that which filters down to the main characters in James's The Wings of the Dove.

2   BARNES, BETTYE. "Malamud's 'Black is My Favorite Color': A Structural Analysis." Linguistics in Literature 3, no. 3 (Fall):71-83.
        Lends itself to a structural analysis and establishes charts of the lexical density connected to the following theme: vision and knowledge versus darkness. Nat Lime is thus associated with darkness, Charity with light, and Nat's mother with knowledge. Barnes argues that the symbolic structure of the story supports an unresolved Judeo-Christian conflict.

3   DAVIS, PETER G. "2 'Malamud' Operas of Blitzstein Given."
       New York Times, 18 January, p. C17.
            Prior to his death, Marc Blitzstein was at work on "Tales
       of Malamud," two one-act operas based on short stories by the
       author. Leonard Lehrman brought these works, "Idiots First" and
       "Klara," to fruition, and they were performed in March 1967 in
       Bloomington, Indiana, and, more recently, at the Madison Avenue
       Baptist Church in New York City. The first is a poignant and
       impressive work, structured into thirteen brief scenes. While
       Blitzstein's music "is in a chromatically dissonant idiom," it
       is always moving. The second, a story involving the attempted
       seduction of an old student by the wife of his former teacher,
       seems strained and artificial.

4   del FATTORE, JOAN. "The Hidden Self: A Study of the Shadow
       Figure in American Short Fiction." Ph.D. dissertation,
       Pennsylvania State University, 217 pp.
            Malamud's "Idiots First" uses the shadow self as the
       vehicle for examining man's potential for good or evil.
       Malamud's use of this Jungian archetype differs from that
       evident in James's "The Beast in the Jungle" and "The Jolly
       Corner," Katherine Anne Porter's "Noon Wine," Flannery
       O'Connor's "The Artificial Nigger," Edgar Allan Poe's "William
       Wilson," John Barth's "Petition," and Shirley Jackson's "The
       Lottery." See Dissertation Abstracts International 39
       (1979):6127A.

5   FIELD, LESLIE [A.]. "Malamud--Dubin's Discontent." Studies
       in American Jewish Literature 4, no. 1 (Spring):77-78.
            Represents Dubin as a middle-aged sexual schlemiel in the
       four parts of Dubin's Lives printed serially in the New Yorker,
       Playboy, and the Atlantic.

6   GEALY, MARCIA [BOOHER]. "A Reinterpretation of Malamud's The
       Natural." Studies in American Jewish Literature 4, no. 1
       (Spring):24-32.
            Claims that Roy Hobbs's quest for himself is illuminated
       by Jewish tradition. In Hasidism, for example, a quest for God
       is tantamount to a search for self-knowledge. Moreover, Hobbs
       reminds us of the penitent beggar or fool found both in Hasidic
       literature and Malamud's later short fiction.

7   GITTLEMAN, SOL. "Chapter VII: The Flight of Malamud's
       Shlemihls." In From Shtetl to Suburbia: The Family in
       Jewish Literary Imagination. Boston: Beacon Press, pp.
       156-64.
            Malamud is perhaps the earliest of contemporary Jewish-
       American novelists to concern himself with the problem of Jewish

1978

self-consciousness in young American Jews. His fictional Jews
are versions of the shtetl schlemiel and luftmensh figures, but
in the new world they are caught between their desire to lose
their Jewish identity and their inability to do so. The stories
in which these figures appear end on a note of qualified
optimism, as a young Jew encounters a figure of his rejected
past who becomes the agent for his reconciliation with that
past. Gittleman briefly comments on "The Lady of the Lake,"
"The Last Mohican," and "The Magic Barrel."

8   HABICH, ROBERT D. "Bernard Malamud: A Bibliographical
       Survey." Studies in American Jewish Literature 4
       (Spring):78-84.
          Selectively and concisely chronicles the development of
Malamud studies since the publication of The Natural in 1952 and
supplies especially useful comments on the following: Malamud's
fiction in other media, the lack of authoritative texts,
Malamud's publishers, and the location of Malamud's papers. He
concludes that current criticism has returned to the topics that
Fiedler and Kazin explored twenty years ago: Malamud's use of
myth, his metaphysical Jewishness, his concern for the human
heart. At this point Malamud's work needs to be measured
against that of Faulkner and Hemingway.

9   HELTERMAN, JEFFREY. "Bernard Malamud." In Dictionary of
       Literary Biography. Vol. 2, American Novelists since World
       War II. Edited by Jeffrey Helterman and Richard Layman.
       Detroit: Gale Research Co., pp. 291-304.
          Offers a brief but illuminating biographical and critical
introduction to the author, including a list of awards and major
works. Helterman comments on Malamud's relation to Bellow and
Roth, his Jewishness, and the literary influences affecting his
work. Brief analyses of The Natural, The Assistant, The Magic
Barrel, A New Life, Idiots First, The Fixer, Pictures of
Fidelman, and Rembrandt's Hat follow. Also furnished are
references to uncollected periodical publications, a concise
bibliography of secondary sources, and two photographs of
Malamud.

10   HERGT, TOBIAS. "Vom Gehiflen zum Helfer: Das Thema der
       Mitmenschlichkeit in Bernard Malamuds The Assistant."
       Neusprachliche Mitteilungen aus Wissenschaft und Praxis
       31:76-81.
          The sickness in American society is represented by the
plight of poor Jews in a non-Jewish neighborhood, and in their
suffering Malamud probes the myth of the American dream,
revealing that it is a grim hoax. Students in the German
Federal Republic will have to decide for themselves if they have
embraced a similar dream.

*11   ICHIKAWA, MASUMI. "Bernard Malamud's The Assistant: An
       Interpretation through His Short Stories." Chu-shikotu
       Studies in American Literature 14:19-33.
            Source: Modern Language Association International
       Bibliography (1979), 1:222.

12   KAPP, ISA. "Malamud's Cantata for Middle Age." New Leader
       61 (24 December):3-5.
            Dubin's Lives is one of the most insightful and detailed
       chronicles on modern marriage to be found in contemporary
       fiction. Malamud's acute eye is capable of capturing the com-
       plexity of his wife Kitty, as well as the texture or ordinary
       life in all of its sensuous reality. Despite the extended
       attention given to marriage and erotic pursuits, Malamud's real
       obsession is with old age. For all its excellence, there is a
       somber quality hanging over the novel which undoubtedly derives
       from Malamud's obsessive concern with approaching death.

13   KELLMAN, STEVEN H. "Malamud in France." Comparative
       Literature Studies 15, no. 3 (September):303-15.
            In exploring the impact of Malamud on the French public in
       general and the French Jews in particular, Kellman finds
       reactions mixed. Malamud's fiction has been regarded as
       significant enough to be published by two of France's most
       distinguished houses, Gallimard and Seuil, yet Malamud's work
       has never appeared on French lists of best-sellers. Indeed
       references to it in French periodicals are infrequent and
       brief. Jacques Cabau in volume 12 of Larousse's twenty-volume
       Grande Encyclopédie (Paris: Larousse, 1974, p. 7513) considers
       Malamud one of the most important and best-known writers of the
       Jewish renaissance. While mainstream critics tend to concur,
       French Jewish critics seem less sympathetic to his work.

14   KERNER, DAVID. "A Note on the Source of 'The Magic
       Barrel.'" Studies in American Jewish Literature 4, no. 1
       (Spring):32-35.
            Claims that "The Magic Barrel" has its source in the old
       Yiddish joke, "A Shidach fun Libe" (A love match). Both the
       drift of the joke and the punch line have their analogues in
       Malamud's tale. Thematically, tradition versus enlightenment is
       at the heart of both narratives.

15   MALIN, IRVING. "The Fixer: An Overview." Studies in
       American Jewish Literature 4, no. 1 (Spring):40-50.
            Offers a detailed summary of the key incidents of the
       novel, concluding that Yakov Bok is neither "the fixer nor the
       Jew" but ultimately a "quirky" human being who transcends
       labels.

1978

16   MANN, HERBERT [DAVID]. "The Malamudian World: Method and
        Meaning." Studies in American Jewish Literature 4, no. 1
        (Spring):2012.
             The Malamudian world has a distinct identity from book to
        book and is sustained by a recurring series of motifs: physi-
        cal ascent, bird imagery, running, time relationships, and
        doppelgängers, among others. Mann illustrates the operation of
        these motifs in various stories and novels and concludes that
        they support the general theme of connection between men, the
        basis of Malamud's moral vision.

17   MESHER, DAVID R. "Names and Stereotypes in Malamud's The
        Tenants." Studies in American Jewish Literature 4, no. 1
        (Spring):57-68.
             Argues that Malamud uses expressive names and stereotypes
        to establish identity and carry themes. This technique is es-
        pecially important here because of the gradual metamorphosis of
        the main characters into racial stereotypes wholly antagonistic
        to each other. Minor as well as major characters are rendered
        stereotypically: Levenspiel, the slum landlord; Irene, the re-
        bellious Jewish daughter; Willie Spearmint-Bill Spear, ghetto
        Negro turned black militant; and Harry Lesser, tenant and
        lessor, occupant and metaphorical landlord.

18   O'BRIEN, JILL LOUISE. "The Humanism of Bernard Malamud in
        Four Selected Novels." Ph.D. dissertation, University of
        Illinois at Urbana-Champaign, 420 pp.
             The "humanism" of Bernard Malamud has never been thor-
        oughly identified nor examined. Chapter 1 of this study offers
        a number of perspectives from which to assess the humanistic
        content of The Natural, The Assistant, A New Life, and The Fixer
        in the subsequent chapters. O'Brien's humanistic points of re-
        ference include the hero's goals, his ethical and aesthetic mo-
        tivations, his interdependence with society, and his relation to
        the universe. See Dissertation Abstracts International 40
        (1979):858A-59A.

19   ORIARD, MICHAEL V. "The Athlete Hero and Domestic Ideals."
        Journal of American Culture 1, no. 3 (Fall):506-19.
             Discusses fiction concerning heroes in sports, including
        The Natural, for its impact on democratic society. While Roy
        Hobbs offers society a potential renewal, the decadence of
        American society in the twentieth century is inimical to his
        very existence.

20   RAY, LAURA KRUGMAN. "Dickens and 'The Magic Barrel.'"
        Studies in American Jewish Literature 4, no. 1
        (Spring):35-40.
             Establishes various points of contact between Leo Finkle
        and Pip of Great Expectations, and regards the contexts in which

150

they appear as mutually illuminating. For both figures court-
ship serves as an initiation experience leading to a new
self-awareness, and in each case a father figure, Salzman and
Magwitch, respectively, leads the hero to a knowledge of love
where it is least expected.

21   Review of Dubin's Lives. Kirkus Reviews 46 (15 December):
        1978.
        The loneliness and pain of middle age in this novel are
relieved by the impressiveness of Malamud's artistic
performance, but like most autobiographical novels, this book is
uneven in its impact despite Malamud's charmingly ironic prose.

22   RUBIN, STEVEN J. "Malamud and the Theme of Love and Sex."
        Studies in American Jewish Literature 4, no. 1
        (Spring):19-23.
        Recognizes the interplay between the physical and the
spiritual in Malamud's fiction, and considers this relationship
Lawrentian in its ineffable mystery. Ultimately, Malamud's
treatment of the sexual relationship is more richly human in its
tragedy and comedy than its fictional equivalents in Bellow and
Roth.

23   _____. "Malamud's Fidelman: Innocence and Optimism
        Abroad." Notes on Contemporary Literature 8, no. 1
        (January):21-3
        Unlike other Jewish writers, Malamud often portrays sex in
fiction as a source of creativity and pleasure. Idiots First
and Pictures of Fidelman are illustrative. Ironically, the
character of Fidelman is redeemed by a homosexual rather than a
heterosexual lover. Through his sexual relationship, Fidelman
achieves a new aesthetic and physical wisdom.

24   SAPOSNIK, IRVING. "Insistent Assistance: The Stories of
        Bernard Malamud." Studies in American Jewish Literature 4,
        no. 1 (Spring):12-18.
        Claims that Malamud's fiction urges the necessity of human
assistance, while at the same time dramatizing the difficulties
that prevent it from occurring. Such works as "Man in the
Drawer" in Rembrandt's Hat and The Tenants contain double
endings and reflect the tension between optimism and pessimism
that has crept into Malamud's vision of man.

25   SHARMA, D.R. "The Tenants: Malamud's Treatment of the
        Racial Problem." Indian Journal of American Studies 8, no.
        2 (January):2-22.
        The Tenants should not be regarded as a sport in Malamud's
canon despite its topical subject matter of Jew confronting
black. The racial conflict of the book is, in fact, an

1978

extension of Malamud's major thematic concern: man's alienation
from what is central to his own humanity, his abilty for
compassion and love. As stereotypes of the Jew and the black,
respectively, Harry Lesser and Willie Spearmint stand for the
extremes of mankind, the superhuman and the subhuman, and as
such they represent a radical departure from the aggregate of
humanity. With these untractable characters, Malamud arrived at
an artistic and spiritual impass, and appropriately he ends the
book on the reiteration of the word "mercy" which amounts to a
request for divine intervention.

26   SHERES, ITA. "The Alienated Sufferer: Malamud's Novels from
        the Perspective of Old Testament and Jewish Mystical
        Thought." Studies in American Jewish Literature 4, no. 1
        (Spring):68-76.
            The story of Abraham's sacrifice of Isaac is reflected in
        Malamud's fiction from The Natural through The Tenants.
        Abraham's radical separation from his place of origin insisted
        on by God is repeated in Malamud through his hero's psycho-
        logical or social isolation. Both figures experience a
        revelation and redemption through suffering, although in
        Malamud's world God's hand is not immediately visible.

27   SMELSTOR, MARJORIE. "The Schlemiel as Father: A Study of
        Yakov Bok and Eugene Henderson." Studies in American Jewish
        Literature 4, no. 1 (Spring):50-57.
            Both Malamud's Yakov Bok and Bellow's Henderson move from
        a condition of lovelessness to love through the acceptance of
        paternal responsibility. In each case, the hero begins the
        novel as self-centered, responsive only to his own needs. When he
        is called upon to act as a parent, the dynamics of fatherhood
        redeem him from the absurdity of his existence as schlemiel.

28   WALDEN, DANIEL. "Malamud's World: An Introduction."
        Studies in American Jewish Literature 4, no. 1 (Spring):1-2.
            Reviews Malamud's position as an American writer, noting
        that his distinction lies in his ability to transmit the
        essential vision of Judaism detached from form and ritual.
        While regarded as a major writer, Malamud's continued output
        prevents a final determination of his overall worth until all of
        his work has been written.

1979

1   AHOKAS, PIRJO. "Two Immigrations: Singer's 'The Joke' and
        Malamud's 'The German Refugee.'" American Studies in
        Scandinavia 11:49-60.

Although both stories share common points of contact, the
importance of their similarities and differences remain largely
unexamined. While each story is concerned with the fate of a
European Jew who has come to America, Singer and Malamud
significantly depart from each other in their treatment of this
figure. Singer's American narrator remains unchanged in his
chronicle about the European Jew who dies after discovering his
own lifelong self-deception; Malamud's American narrator,
relating a similar story, is transformed by his own account.
"He inherits and assimilates part of the European Jew's
experience."

2   ALLEN, GAY WILSON. Review of Dubin's Lives. Georgia Review
    33, no. 3 (Fall):726-30 passim.
        Allen's observations on Malamud's novel are part of an
untitled review essay dealing with the pitfalls of writing
biography. Malamud's novel is especially illuminating in this
connection: first, through revealing the biographer's
identification with his subject and his inevitable loss of
objectivity; and second, in its creating the illusion of truth
as a substitute for the real thing.

3   AMIEL, BARBARA. "Tired Blood, Banana Diets, and the Mid-life
    Crisis." Maclean's 92 (19 March):54.
        The ordinary details of everyday life in Dubin's Lives
serve Malamud as the vehicles for expressing universal themes,
taking the reader well "beyond [Dubin's] . . . banana diets and
hotel trysts." Malamud readers who have been waiting for this
novel to appear will not be disappointed.

4   AVERY, EVELYN GROSS. Rebels and Victims: The Fiction of
    Richard Wright and Bernard Malamud. Port Washington, N.Y.:
    National University Publications, Kennikat Press, 116 pp.
        Explores the role of the black rebel in Wright and the
Jewish victim in Malamud. The study is comprised of the
"Introduction" and five chapters. Chapter 1, "Rebels and
Victims," observes that Wright's rebels fulfill themselves
through violence and Malamud's victims through suffering and
self-sacrifice. In chapter 2, "Genesis," the importance of
tradition to each writer is examined: Wright was anxious to
discover a meaningful past while Malamud, in contrast, inherited
a culture that offered him support in the midst of disaster.
Chapter 3, "Father, Sons and Lovers," perceives Wright's protagonists as psychologically arrested and Malamud's heroes involved
in a process of maturation, culminating in a role of paternal responsibility. Chapter 4, "The Promised Land," discusses the negative and positive aspects of the city, respectively, on
Wright's blacks and Malamud's Jews. In chapter 5, "A Bitter-
sweet Encounter," the complexity of black and Jewish interaction
is traced through recent history and in the literature of these

1979

two writers, revealing "admiration, affection, and attraction as well as envy, hostility, and revulsion." A bibliography of primary and secondary sources is supplied, pp. 111-13. Revision of 1976.2.

5   BELL, PEARL K. "Heller & Malamud, Then & Now." Commentary 67, no. 6 (June):71-75.
    Compares Joseph Heller's use of Jewish materials in Good as Gold to Malamud's handling of the Jewish immigrant experience in The Magic Barrel and The Assistant, concluding that Heller lacks Malamud's imagination and authority. While Heller turns his Jewish milieu into vulgarity, Malamud conveys an authentic sense of the Jewish experience which in his work has "the fixed quality of a fable." His Fidelman, Levin, and Lesser may break with their past, but in contrast to Heller, Malamud captures the psychological impact of the past on their present. In examining William Dubin of Dubin's Lives, Malamud becomes too narrowly absorbed in documenting the sexual and artistic problems of his largely narcissistic character. Unfortunately, this novel represents a reduction of Malamud's humanistic vision.

6   BURCH, BETH, AND BURCH, PAUL W. "Myth on Myth: Bernard Malamud's 'The Talking Horse.'" Studies in Short Fiction 16, no. 4 (Fall):350-53.
    Malamud conjoins Greek myth to Judaic theology in "The Talking Horse" through the characters of Goldberg and Abramowitz. Goldberg is associated with Poseidon, the God of the sea and the God of horses. While Abramowitz is also connected to horse mythology, his name, derivative of Abraham, suggests the dutiful son. At issue in the story is whether the ethics of the centaur or the values of Abraham dominate. The ending is ambiguous.

7   B[UTSCHER], E[DWARD]. Review of Dubin's Lives. Booklist 75 (1 March):1039.
    Endorses Malamud's choice of a biographer as the consciousness for exploring the artist's sensibility. "This is one of Malamud's most sustained and penetrating pieces of fiction."

8   COOPER, ALAN. "Bernard Malamud's Dualities." Jewish Frontier 46, no. 3 (March):25-27.
    Doubleness is at the very heart of Dubin's Lives, and it embraces character, structure, and theme. Dubin's bipartite nature influences his involvement with two distinctly different women; he escapes death twice; he stays at two different hotels; on two occasions he kills the pet cat, one owned by his daughter, the other by his wife. These are simply a few of the examples of the duality which underscores the opposing levels of his existence. "Cut anywhere into the novel and it bleeds a conflict, in Jewish idiom, of a moral consciousness trying . . .

not to suffer the pain of what Cynthia Ozick has called 'disassimilation,' Malamud's metaphor for the problem of freedom."

9   CUSHMAN, KEITH.   Review of Dubin's Lives. Library Journal
       104 (15 January):211-12.
       Regards the novel as another example of Malamud's concern
with redemption. Preoccupied with his own mortality, William
Dubin thinks he has found a new life through the erotic
enjoyment of Fanny Bick. The novel, nevertheless, remains grim
in its suggestion that "the self is a prison from which there is
no escape."

10   DURWOOD, ELISSA.   "On the Road." New Statesman 97 (8
       June):836.
       William Dubin of Dubin's Lives emerges as no more than an
oversexed middle-aged man despite Malamud's attempt to lend
profundity to Dubin's sexual appetites. Malamud's earlier
preoccupation with the value of man has not honestly been
confronted in this novel.

11   EDEL, LEON.   "Narcissists Need Not Apply." American Scholar
       49 (Winter):130-32.
       As a novelist Bernard Malamud is unique in making the
subject of a novel a biographer, and Dubin's Lives is insightful
in its "grasp of the general nature of biography." Virtually a
parable of the biographer's art, the book illustrates the
speculative character of the genre, as Dubin ponders the strange
gyrations of his wife in their garden, only to discover later
their source, an unwelcome bee in her blouse.

12   EVANIER, DAVID.   "Fanny and Duby." National Review 31 (27
       April):570-71.
       The loose threads of Dubin's Lives are not finally tied
together and the ending offers no real conclusion. The novel
does not achieve the economy of Malamud's previous fiction, but
in place of it Malamud creates a kind of poetry, capturing
through imagery and mood the emotional range of Dubin's life.

13   FLOWER, DEAN.   "Picking up the Pieces." Hudson Review 32,
       no. 2 (Summer):293-307.
       Dubin's Lives echoes Malamud's first novel, The Natural,
in its literary allusiveness. References to such writers as
Thoreau, Freud, and Carlyle, among others, abound. In moving
from the ironic observer of life "to an unconscious celebrant of
the Self" within the same novel, Malamud becomes totally
inconsistent. Despite Dubin's sexual self-realization, his
"intelligence and memory" continually bear witness to an older,
more solemn self that serves as his sober alter ego.

1979

14   FRIEDMAN, EDWARD H.   "The Paradox of the Art Metaphor in
        Bernard Malamud's 'The Pimp's Revenge.'" Notes on
        Contemporary Literature 9, no. 2 (March):7-8.
            Arthur Fidelman's painting of "Mother and Son" in "The
        Pimp's Revenge" is a self-referential work which he has great
        difficulty completing because of his ambivalence over his
        mother's death.   In destroying the canvas, he moves closer to
        his own identity: a latent homosexuality expressed in his
        subsequent drawings.

15   GARDNER, JOHN. "Malamud: A Comedy of Ardors." Washington
        Post Book World, 25 February, pp. M1, M3.
            The subject of the middle-age life crisis is developed in
        Dubin's Lives with "almost Melvillian doggedness leaving no
        philosophical or psychological stone unturned." Stylistically,
        Malamud is at his very best when mixes fantasy and realism, but
        he can also lapse into annoying literary language. Although his
        hero is rendered as a self-deluded comic figure, William Dubin's
        attempts at honesty and courage seem to elicit from Malamud an
        almost unqualified endorsement of his hero.

16   GEALY, MARCIA B[OOHER]. "Malamud's Short Stories: A
        Reshaping of Hasidic Tradition." Judaism 28, no. 1
        (Winter):51-61.
            "The Last Mohican," "The Magic Barrel," "Idiots First,"
        "The Jewbird," and "The Silver Crown" are especially revealing
        of Malamud's adaptation of the Hasidic literary tradition.   Some
        of the Hasidic elements in his work include (1) the inward
        journey, (2) an older man giving spiritual tutoring to a younger
        man, (3) the triumph of love, (4) the reality of evil, and (5)
        finally, the transforming potential of the tale itself.
        "Malamud's reworking of Hasidic themes is not unlike Peretz;
        there is the same controlled tension between sacred and profane,
        the same fusion of Jewish past and present." Malamud, however,
        despite his bittersweet irony, possesses a warmth and humor
        lacking in Peretz.

17   GERVAIS, RONALD J. "Malamud's Frank Alpine and Kazin's
        Circumcised Italyener: A Possible Source for The
        Assistant." Notes on Contemporary Literature 9, no. 2
        (March):6-7.
            A vignette in Alfred Kazin's A Walker in the City (1951)
        involving an Italian boy's love for a Jewish girl, his
        conversion to Judaism, and his ritual circumcision may have been
        a source for Malamud's Frank Alpine in The Assistant.

18   GIACHETTI, ROMANO. "Malamud e il vecchio narcisista." La
        Repubblica, 29 May, n.p.

An interview with Malamud on Dubin's Lives that took place in New York City. For Malamud's Dubin, biography becomes a route to his own self-discovery, and his latest subject, D.H. Lawrence, seems to be appropriate for Dubin as a representative man of the seventies who has rediscovered the body. Similar to many of Malamud's other works, the novel is anchored in the detailed and ruminating style of the nineteenth-century novel, and Malamud regards it as a companion piece to his earlier novels.

19   GILMAN, RICHARD.   Review of Dubin's Lives.   New Republic 180
       (24 March):28-30.
           Observes a variety of flaws in Malamud's fiction, but on
       sum Malamud must be regarded as a gifted writer. Dubin's Lives
       is a good example of Malamud's flaws and virtues. Somewhat
       rambling in its narrative, the novel nevertheless rewards the
       reader through "Malamud's mastery of the rhythms of Jewish
       expressiveness." In addition, the subtle modulation of tone
       allows Malamud to capture the Jamesian sense of the "felt life."

20   GRAY, PAUL.   "Lonely Cosmos."   Time 113 (12 February):99
           The reader will respond to Dubin's Lives with more
       admiration than love as he encounters Malamud's major concerns:
       aging, erotic fulfillment, self-examination, and moral
       responsibility. His characters are always convincing even when
       they speak for women's liberation. Depressed by the final
       loneliness that is common to all, Dubin wrestles with his fate
       and seems to take control over his life. Somber though his
       themes may be, Malamud translates them into a pleasurable
       artistic experience.

21   GRUMBACH, DAVID.   "A Biographer's Biography, and an Old
       Fashioned Novel."   Chronicle of Higher Education 17 (20
       February):R7.
           Dubin's Lives is occasionally flawed by coincidence and
       lack of credibility in plot. It is compelling, however, in two
       areas: in the interaction between William Dubin, biographer,
       and his subject, and in the lyricism Malamud introduced in
       sketching his pastoral scenes.

22   HAMANO, NARUO.   "Malamud no jisso: Dubin's Lives (1979) o
       yomu" [The real Malamud].   Eigo Seinen (Tokyo), 125
       (July):166-67.
           In Japanese. These observations are partially the result
       of Hamano's interview with Malamud in Vermont prior to the
       completion of Dubin's Lives. Malamud wanted to express in this
       novel man's yearning for the infinite in contrast to the brevity
       of life. After reading Dubin's Lives, Hamano felt that Malamud
       accomplished his purpose. Dubin's yearning for lasting love
       relationships is undermined by the gradual erosion of love, and

1979

this problem is, in fact, an underlying tension even in such
works as The Assistant, "The Magic Barrel," and A New
Life--narratives in which love is presumably redemptive. As a
reflection of Malamud's own concern with age, Dubin's Lives
incorporates a much more somber vision of man's emotional
longings and ultimate desperation than any found in his earlier
fiction.

23   HAMMOND, JOHN FRANCIS. "The Monomythic Quest: Visions of
      Heroism in Malamud, Bellow, Barth, and Percy." Ph.D.
      dissertation, Lehigh University, 224 pp.
           In each of the four novels discussed, the hero's response
      to the conditions of life carries a different thematic
      emphasis: Malamud's The Natural examines the need for
      responsible action; Bellow's Henderson the Rain King involves
      the acceptance of human limitations; Barth's Giles Goat-Boy
      dwells on the acceptance of the ordinary; Percy's Lancelot,
      however, argues for resistance to the malevolence and
      dehumanization inherent in reality. See Dissertation Abstracts
      International 39 (1979):6130A.

24   HARRIS, ROBERT R. "The Kisses Shouldn't Hurt." Village
      Voice, 29 January, p. 73.
           Malamud's Dubin's Lives has brought together in brilliant
      harmony the various themes which have always fascinated the
      author--"marriage and adultery, the family, self-torment and
      guilt, order and discipline, redemption and suffering . . . ,
      meaningful work and love"--and animated them in the convincing
      rendering of character.

25   HERGT, TOBIAS. Das Motiv der Hochschule im Romanwerk von
      Bernard Malamud und John Barth. Mainzer Studien zur
      Amerikanistik. Frankfurt-am-Main: Peter Lang, 311 pp.
           This study examines Bernard Malamud and John Barth's
      treatment of the university as theme and motif. Noting
      significant differences in their handling of the university,
      Hergt observes that Malamud ties the university to reality and
      uses it as an occasion for moral and social criticism. In
      contrast, Barth establishes the university as a philosophical
      framework within which to develop existential and aesthetic
      themes. The university, either directly or indirectly, figures
      in such Malamud novels as The Natural (1952), The Assistant
      (1957), A New Life (1961), The Fixer (1966), Pictures of
      Fidelman (1969), and The Tenants (1971).

26   HERSHINOW, SHELDON [J.]. "Bernard Malamud and Jewish
      Humanism." Religious Humanism 13, no. 2:56-63.
           Perceives Malamud's moral vision as a synthesis of the
      values which the Judaic, Greek, and Christian traditions share.
      Central to that vision is human suffering which offers, as its
      only justification, the opportunity for promoting nourishing

relationships between human beings. In short, suffering may help one to become humane. Given their long history of suffering, it seems appropriate that Malamud should have made the Jews in his fiction tutors in humanity.

27   HILL, DOUGLAS. "The Examined Life." Books in Canada 8 (April):6-7.
      Dubin's Lives is possibly the richest of Malamud's novels: its language is smooth and straightforward and its subject profound. In its sense of frustration it comes closest to resembling The Assistant. Although redemption for William Dubin remains elusive, his personal suffering never turns into despair. "This is a humane and moving work, of great loveliness."

28   HOWARD, JANE. Review of Dubin's Lives. Mademoiselle 85, no. 5(June):62.
      Dubin's Lives may not be considered a major novel, but its subject, the aging of William Dubin, biographer, is handled with Malamud's usual charm and wisdom. The characterizations of youthful adults tend to be superficial and somewhat disappointing, but Malamud's middle-aged adults are completely credible: "They read. They talk and laugh intelligently. They care about nature, too."

29   HOWE, IRVING. "The Stories of Bernard Malamud." In Celebration and Attacks: Thirty Years of Literary and Cultural Commentary. New York: Horizon Press, pp. 32-34.
      The Magic Barrel provides a wholly unique treatment of the Jewish immigrant world through its speeding up of narrative movement and its compression of language and gesture, but these qualities also suggest an overbearing virtuoso performance. Malamud's stories nevertheless work and are especially convincing in their rendering of "the ethos of Yiddish literature."

30   HUNT, GEORGE. Review of Dubin's Lives. America 141 (8 September):98.
      Dubin's Lives seems less convincing than such earlier works as The Magic Barrel, The Assistant, or The Fixer. The problem lies with the main character, William Dubin, whose emotional shallowness denies him a tragic dimension or credibility in either art or life.

*31   IWAMOTO, IWOWO. Malamud: Geijutsu to seikatsu o motomete [Malamud: Quest for art and life]. Eibei Bungaku Sosho. Tokyo: Sojusha, 208 pp.
      In Japanese. Source: Modern Language Association International Bibliography (1980), 1:248.

1979

32   JACOBS, RITA D. Review of <u>Dubin's Lives</u>. <u>World Literature</u>
       <u>Today</u> 53, no. 4 (Autumn):682-83.
           Malamud is at the top of his form in this novel about an
       aging biographer, probing his own self-consciousness as he
       contemplates the life of D.H. Lawrence. The novel is both
       playful and serious in its depiction of a man caught between the
       love of his wife and the erotic excitement of a young girl.
       "The reader is moved, enlightened, amused and ultimately the
       wiser for having read it."

33   JOHNSTON, ROBERT K. "Malamud's Vision for Humanity."
       <u>Christianity Today</u> 23 (20 July):24-25.
           Malamud's fiction possesses a unity of theme, atmosphere,
       plot, and character, but the tone from work to work varies. One
       critic has observed of <u>The Natural</u> that it is narrated with
       "equal parts Mel Allen and James Joyce." The major sources of
       thematic unity are to be found in Malamud's appropriation of
       Hebraic wisdom and Jewish experience.

34   KALINA de PISZK, ROSITA. "Bernard Malamud: El significado
       de la vida." <u>Káñina</u> (San José, Costa Rica) 3, no. 2:57-62.
           Repudiates the view that Malamud is enigmatic in his
       representation of Judaism. His intentions are clarified when we
       relate his work to the Old Testament and the Talmud since they
       embrace both the nationalistic and the universal elements of
       Judaism. In different periods of Jewish history sometimes the
       nationalistic and at other times the universal elements of
       Judaism were dominant. Both of these strands of Judaism figure
       into such novels as <u>The Assistant</u> and <u>The Fixer</u>, although
       Malamud ultimately emphasizes the universal aspect of the
       religion. The Jews were, in effect, chosen to bring to mankind
       a greater humanity. With such a vision of life, Malamud emerges
       as the Don Quixote of modern literature.

35   KOENIG, RHODA. "Oh, Violence! Please, Violence."
       <u>Alternative: An American Spectator</u> 12 (June):12-14.
           A tough-minded review of <u>Dubin's Lives</u>. Koenig regards
       the novel as a bore and enthusiastic assessments of it as a
       mystery. For the first half of the novel, the plot revolves
       around Dubin's attempt to bed Fanny Bick and to write his D.H.
       Lawrence biography, and these episodes fail to be either funny
       or serious. Book reviewing, especially by academics, fails to
       come to grips with literary failure.

36   KOTRE, JOHN N. Review of <u>Dubin's Lives</u>. <u>Commonweal</u> 106 (7
       December):679.
           William Dubin, biographer, becomes the observer and
       participant in his own identity crisis, and Malamud's references
       to Dubin, changing as they do from first, to second, and to
       third person, underscore our own difficulty in discovering the
       character's essential self.

37   LANDESS, TOM. "Sense and Sensuality." D. Magazine (Magazine
      of Dallas) 6:81-88 passim.
           Reminiscent of Moses Herzog, William Dubin of Dubin's
      Lives is a less pompous and more sensual version of Bellow's
      hero. His sexual preoccupations may be considered not only the
      obsessions of a middle-aged man but an outlet from the moral
      disarray of the early seventies. Unfortunately, Dubin does not
      reflect the depth and humanity that we experience in other
      Malamud heroes or the richness of the Jewish ethos so beauti-
      fully rendered in The Magic Barrel.

38   LASK, THOMAS. "Malamud's Lives." New York Times Book Review
      21 January, p. 43.
           An interview taking place prior to the publication of
      Dubin's Lives. Malamud briefly commented on the following
      topics: "his passion for revision, the dark side of his art,
      the fascination of teaching, the influence of an older
      generation." Through his tragic sense of life Malamud is able
      to find both security and a basis for "joy."

39   LEHMANN-HAUPT, CHRISTOPHER. Review of Dubin's Lives. New
      York Times, 2 February, C23.
           The reader's growing identification with William Dubin
      makes the resolution of his conflict between the need for erotic
      love and the attractions of a stable life a matter of
      significant reader interest. The tensions between intellect and
      instinct remain constant at the end of the novel reinforcing
      Malamud's major theme at the expense of a tidy conclusion to the
      plot. Yet Dubin's Lives may be Malamud's best novel since The
      Assistant, if not his very best.

40   LOCKE, RICHARD. "Malamud's Reach." Saturday Review 6 (17
      March):67-69.
           Malamud's strength as a writer lies in his subtle
      depiction of Jewish life, and in attempting big subjects, he has
      lost his humor and gained pomposity. "If The Fixer aspired to
      Dostoyevskyan extremes of pain and suffering, Dubin's Lives
      reaches for Tolstoyan ripeness and wisdom." Malamud's
      adaptation of D.H. Lawrence pronouncements contributes bombast
      rather than meaningful perceptions to Dubin's Lives. Malamud's
      true stature lies in such works as The Assistant and The Magic
      Barrel.

41   LYONS, BONNIE. Review of Dubin's Lives. Notre Dame English
      Journal 11, no. 2 (April):173-77.
           Regards Malamud's latest novel his best since The
      Assistant. While its minor characters have only varying degrees
      of success, the principal characters, Dubin and Kitty his wife,
      are complex, rich, and highly credible. The great strength of
      the novel must finally be attributed to the eloquence with which
      Malamud expresses his vision of life. Like its predecessors,

1979

> Dubin's Lives shares their central themes: "transformation, growth, death, and rebirth." And once again, a Jew becomes a metaphor for any man who is capable of accepting life in all of its joy, pain, and mystery.

42 MALOFF, SAUL. "Malamud's Lives." Commonweal 106 (27 April): 244-46.

Dubin, the hero of Dubin's Lives, is vampiric and necrophilic in his need to be nourished by the secret sources of vitality of the illustrious dead about whom he writes. It is his literary work, living beyond the author himself, that becomes the vehicle for Dubin's salvation.

43 MASILAMONI, E.H. LEELAVATHI. "Bernard Malamud--An Interview." Indian Journal of American Studies 9, no. 2:33-37.

In this interview Malamud comments on the following topics: the importance of character in fiction; the health of the novel; the impact of World War II and the Holocaust on his work; the role of love from The Natural through The Fixer; and the influences of different religions on his writing.

44 MOSKOWITZ, MOSHE A. "Intermarriage and the Proselyte: A Jewish View." Judaism 28, no. 4 (Fall):423-33.

Doubts that Frank Alpine in The Assistant is a sincere convert to Judaism and argues that his presumed rebirth "via the mohel appears ironic and inconclusive." From the point of view of myth, Alpine's circumcision symbolizes his commitment to the God of Eros, as well as serving as a sign of his outward conversion.

45 PIKE, FRANK. Review of Dubin's Lives. Times Literary Supplement, no. 4003, (7 December):103.

William Dubin, the hero of this novel, is an interesting and rewarding character because of the variety of his feelings and his ability to understand the lives of others. Consequently, this book will engage the mind of adults. "It is difficult to think of a British novelist writing today who could bring this [novel] off without a safety net of defensive ironies."

46 PRESCOTT, PETER. Review of Dubin's Lives. Newsweek 93 (12 February):83.

Identifies one recurring story running through Malamud's fiction, the quest for a new life. Although this book tends to be repetitious in places, William Dubin's introspective probing, rather than Malamud's tediousness, fosters a return to the same obsessive questions concerning love, work, and sex. In this novel human nature is portrayed in all its variety.

47 Review of Dubin's Lives. Atlantic 243, no. 3 (March):132.

This novel presents the most straightforward Malamud narrative since A New Life and possibly achieves a greater impact on the reader than any other novel he has written. While Dubin's Lives does achieve variety "in pace and mood," it lacks a neat conclusion. The ending, however, may be Malamud's way of reflecting the inconclusiveness of life.

48   Review of Dubin's Lives. Choice 16, no. 3 (May):391-92.
        Malamud captures with unusual insight and sensitivity the impact of advancing age on his hero. This novel will illuminate the reader's own reactions to the process of aging.

49   Review of Dubin's Lives. Playboy 26, no. 3 (March):34.
        The torment which William Dubin experiences is rendered so convincingly as to suggest Malamud's own experiences. The book is flawed, however, by the hero's sustained depression and ongoing self-analysis which leave the reader bored.

50   ROSENBERG, L.M. "Fate vs. Accident; Will vs. Desire."
        Southwest Review 64, no. 4 (Autumn):vi-vii; 395-98.
        Dubin's Lives has the makings of a masterpiece, but its promise is never fulfilled. Its solid meaning is complemented by its symbolic cross references to the seasons in nature and human life. Unfortunately, Malamud lets these cross references flounder, along with Dubin's quest for his authentic identity. Moreover, Malamud fails to resolve the central question the novel raises, the meaning of being a man. "What began as a hefty, Tolstoyan study of life in all its facets shifts to a lighter key, becomes a sexual-domestic romance."

51   RUBENSTEIN, ROBERTA. "Search for Self." Progressive 43, no. 6 (June):57-58.
        The materials of Dubin's Lives would resemble soap opera for a less gifted writer than Malamud, but he is able to extract out of them a depth that does justice to the complexities of human life. In Malamud's hands the novel explores "the limits of love and marriage, of familiarity and self-discovery, of self-fulfillment and responsibility, as well as those of biography and fiction themselves."

52   SALE, ROGER. "Dubin's Lives." In New York Review of Books 26 (22 February):19-20.
        Malamud's longest book, and perhaps his best, makes effective use of the novel form, moving leisurely into an exploration of Dubin and his world. Although the book is often heavy with detail, that detail contributes to the impact of Malamud's theme, a man's confrontation with himself and time.

1979

53   _____ . "Hawkes, Malamud, Richler, Oates." In On Not Being
        Good Enough: Writings of a Working Critic. New York:
        Oxford University Press, pp. 30-42 passim.
            These writers are examined in relation to each other for
        the kind of defects revealed in their fiction. While Hawkes's
        Blood Oranges suffers from the gratuitous use of horror,
        Malamud's The Tenants fails to achieve a clear and orderly
        progression of plot. "Malamud's trouble, his fuzziness about
        how to get from his premise to his conclusion, seems more a
        miscalculation than anything else, of a kind that plagues even
        the best writers." His book invites comparison with Saul
        Bellow's Mr. Sammler's Planet for the impass both writers arrive
        at in dealing with blacks. It is still too early to make hard
        judgments about the problems in the work of Mordecai Richler and
        Joyce Carol Oates.

54   SCHOLES, ROBERT. "History as Fabulation: Malamud and
        Vonnegut." In Fabulation and Metafiction. Urbana:
        University of Illinois Press, pp. 200-205.
            An enlarged text of 1966.60.

55   _____ . "A Portrait of the Artist as 'Escape-Goat':
        Malamud's Fidelman." In Fabulation and Metafiction.
        Urbana: University of Illinois Press, pp. 190-92.
            Reprint of 1969.40

56   SHECHNER, MARK. "Jewish Writers." In Harvard Guide to
        Contemporary American Writing. Edited by Daniel Hoffman.
        Cambridge, Mass.: Harvard University Press, Belknap Press,
        pp. 191, 192, 201, 206-212, 232, 233, 287, 390.
            Finds Malamud's vision of ethical responsibility,
        dispensed through allegorical narratives, heavily didactic.
        Such novels as The Natural, The Assistant, and the stories in
        The Magic Barrel are possessed of a referential style and moral
        content that now seem alien to the sensibilities of the modern
        reader. When Malamud writes about disappointment, desperation,
        and loss, he is capable of making his world seem poignantly
        real. His handling of sexual fulfillment seems less certain; it
        is presented either as elusive or illusion.

57   _____ . "The Return of the Repressed." Nation 228 (17
        March):277-78.
            Dubin's Lives represents a climax to the radical changes
        occurring in Malamud's fiction since The Assistant and The Magic
        Barrel. Departing from the ethical vision supplied by Hebrew
        scripture and Yiddish folklore, Malamud now explores the realm
        of contemporary sexuality and self-liberation. Serving as
        William Dubin's shadow self, D.H. Lawrence becomes his tutor in
        erotic love, although the traditional Malamud ethic eventually
        returns with its vision of renunciation and penance. The most

impressive part of the novel "lies in Malamud's command of the
idiom of domestic warfare, the day-to-day details of a marriage
in decline."

58   SHERIDAN, JUDITH RINDE. "Beyond the Imprisoning Self:
Mystical Influences on Singer, Bellow, and Malamud." Ph.D.
dissertation, State University of New York at Binghamton,
221 pp.

These writers are indebted to the traditions of Jewish
mysticism and American transcendentalism. Less mystical than
the others, Malamud receives from these two traditions the
essence of his moral vision, the connections between art and
life, the virtuousness of the simple man, the natural world as
metaphor for humanity, and the value of emotions as a source for
intuitive truth. See Dissertation Abstracts International 39
(1979):7348A-49A.

59   SOLOTAROFF, ROBERT. "Bernard Malamud." In American
Writers: A Collection of Literary Biographies. Suppl. 1,
pt. 2, Vachel Lindsay to Elinor Wylie. New York: Charles
Scribner's Sons, pp. 427-53.

Offers a detailed critical overview of Malamud's fiction
with emphasis on the following topics: the prison motif in the
novels and short stories, Malamud's assertion of traditional
moral values, the technical achievement of his short fiction,
his metaphorical use of the shtetl, his conception of fantasy,
allegory, and myth, the theme of the new life, and an assessment
of the author's accomplishment. A bibliography of Malamud's
novels, collections of short stories, uncollected stories, and
secondary sources is included.

60   STINSON, JOHN J. "Non-Jewish Dialogue in The Assistant:
Stilted, Runyonesque, or Both?" Notes on Contemporary
Literature 9, no. 1 (January):6-7.

Malamud has often been unjustly criticized for apparent
lapses in the use of colloquial language, especially in his
failure to use contractions where appropriate. In this
connection, Ward Minogue's dialogue in The Assistant echoes that
of Damon Runyon's characters whose awkward speech patterns are a
reflection of the deficiencies of the inner man.

61   TOWERS, ROBERT. "A Biographical Novel." New York Times Book
Review, 18 February, pp. 1, 29-31.

Unlike most of his previous work, Malamud's Dubin's Lives
is only remotely concerned with Jewishness; it is also a highly
realistic and the least "fabulous or schematic" narrative since
A New Life. In the first third of the novel, the handling of
the Lawrentian materials is achieved with brilliant humor, but
in the middle section Malamud becomes tired and repetitious.
Malamud's unevenness also extends to his treatment of women,
Fanny Bick and Kitty, Dubin's wife. While the former seems

1979

unconvincing, the latter possesses authenticity. Perhaps the major defect in the novel is Malamud's inconsistent perspective of William Dubin, but despite these flaws the reader will be richly rewarded.

62   TRILLING, LIONEL, ed. Prefaces to the Experiences of Literature. New York: Harcourt Brace Jovanovich, pp. 170-74.
         Reprint of 1967.46.

63   TYLER, RALPH. "A Talk with the Novelist." New York Times Book Review, 18 February, pp. 1, 31-34.
         For Malamud Dubin's Lives "was his attempt at bigness, at summing up what he had learned over the long haul." Despite the inevitable identification of Malamud with his character, William Dubin, the author asserts that Dubin is very much an invention of his imagination and that the thrust of the novel is not really about the fears of aging as much as it is about a three-year crisis in the life of one man. In comparison to his other novels, the texture of reality in this one is much more deeply felt.

64   VENN, GEORGE. "Continuity in Northwest Literature." In Northwest Perspectives: Essays on the Culture of the Pacific Northwest. Edited by E.R. Bingham and G.A. Love. Eugene: University of Oregon Press, pp. 99-118.
         In Malamud's A New Life, meaning for S. Levin is located in history and human relationships rather than place. At the same time the author recognizes the importance of the environment on the self, even though he does not focus on "the . . . environmental questions that concern Gary Snyder."

65   WALDEN, DANIEL. "Bellow, Malamud, and Roth: Part of the Continuum." Modern Jewish Studies Annual III. Joint issue of Yiddish 4, no. 1 and Studies in American Jewish Literature 5, no. 2 (Winter):5-7.
         Surveys the genre of the American Jewish novel from Abraham Cahan to the present. In the case of Malamud, Walden sees Dubin's Lives as a departure from the author's implicit concern with Covenantal Judaism.

66   WOLFE, GEOFFREY. "Malamud's Biographer." Esquire 91 (13 February):17-18.
         William Dubin of Dubin's Lives and Bernard Malamud, its author, are like each other in their growth through their association with their biographical subjects: Dubin, through his work on D.H. Lawrence, and Malamud, in his enlarged vision of fiction, the result of contemplating the character of Dubin.

1980

1   BROWN, MICHAEL. "Metaphor for Holocaust and Holocaust as
     Metaphor: The Assistant and The Fixer of Bernard Malamud
     Reexamined." Judaism 29, no. 4 (Fall):479-88.
         Jewish and non-Jewish writers alike have tended to avoid
     treating the Holocaust as imaginative literature in order to
     avoid trivializing or debasing the enormity of that event.
     While Bernard Malamud has never confronted the Holocaust
     directly, in "The Last Mohican," The Assistant, and The Fixer he
     explores its meaning obliquely. "Malamud suggests . . . that
     the importance of the Holocaust is enlarged when it stands as
     ultimate symbol of inhumanity."

2   DITTMAR, KURT. Partikularistiche Gestaltungstendenzen in der
     zeitgenossischen judisch-amerikanischen Prosaliteratur."
     Amerikastudien 25, no. 1:7-46.
         Offers very brief but important observations on Malamud's
     universalized Judaism, as represented in The Assistant in
     contrast to Cynthia Ozick's recommitment to the essential
     "ethnocultural and theological determinants of Jewish
     identity." Ozick, in essence, repudiates Malamud's famous
     metaphor, that "All men are Jews except they don't know it,"
     regardless of its value in this novel as an allusion to Frank
     Alpine's suffering.

3   FRANK, KATHERINE. "Writing Lives: Theory and Practice in
     Literary Biography." Genre 13, no. 4 (Winter):499-516.
         William Dubin of Dubin's Lives, although a character of
     fiction, possesses valuable insights into the writing of
     biography. For Dubin, as well as the reader, biography becomes
     an affirmation of life in the face of death. Indeed, the
     rationale for the genre is embodied in his following
     reflections: "Everybody's life is mine unlived. One writes
     lives he can't live. To live forever is a human hunger."

4   FRIEDMAN, MELVIN J. "The American Jewish Literary Scene,
     1979: A review essay." Studies in American Fiction 8, no. 2
     (Autumn):239-46 passim.
         Dubin's Lives is Malamud's best novel since The Assistant,
     and it illustrates the innovativeness of contemporary Jewish
     writers in utilizing Christian motifs. Alternating between
     references to Dubin's Jewish past and his deep relationships
     with Christians in the present, Malamud skillfully suggests the
     divisions within his character. Friedman makes brief but useful
     observations about Malamud's other work in relation to that of
     his Jewish contemporaries.

1980

5   "Future of Books Debated." New York Times, 1 February, p.
       C28.
            Bernard Malamud, president of the P.E.N. American center,
       made the opening remarks in a symposium entitled "Can Books
       Survive the Book Business?" The growing number of publishing
       companies in the hands of conglomerates, the inflated prices
       paid for reprint rights by paperback publishers, and the growing
       number of chain bookstores that carry only commercially
       successful titles were, according to Malamud, undermining the
       quality of books now being published.

6   GRAU, JOSEPH A. "Bernard Malamud: A Bibliographical
       Addendum." Bulletin of Bibliography 34 (December):157-66,
       184.
            Grau's article catalogs Malamud's writing since 1968 and
       Malamud criticism since 1975. It is divided into two sections:
       primary and secondary sources. Under primary sources, it lists
       novels and uncollected and collected short fiction published
       since 1968, translations of Malamud's works into other
       languages, and Malamud's appearance in anthologies. Under
       secondary sources Grau includes nonfiction by Malamud,
       criticism, biographical sketches, dissertations, selections of
       foreign criticism, and adaptations of Malamud's fiction to other
       media.

7   HARDER, KELSIE B. "Onomastic Centrality." Literary
       Onomastic Studies 7:33-54.
            It is important to recognize the connection between an
       author's use of names and their metaphorical applications. In
       Dubin's Lives, Malamud uses Thoreau and Lawrence, two of Dubin's
       biographical subjects, to express the tension between his
       celibate and sexual natures. Other names in the novel stimulate
       Dubin into word play and humorous analysis.

8   HELLERSTEIN, KATHRYN. "Yiddish Voices in American English."
       In The State of the Language. Edited by Leonard Michaels and
       Christopher Ricks. Berkeley and Los Angeles: University of
       California Press, pp. 182-201.
            Communication suffers when American vernacular is used to
       narrate fiction that is "conceptually Jewish." Contemporary
       Jewish writers attempt to compensate for this conflict between
       manner and matter by using a combination of American English and
       Yiddish. The result is a dialect that is appropriate in fiction
       when language is crucial in registering the ethos of the char-
       acters. Malamud's dialect reflects the comedy and pathos of
       people who have been shaped by the past but dwell in the
       present, and their condition is reflected in "Talking Horse," a
       parable about the Yiddish language: imprisoned in English, it
       becomes a hybrid, like the half-man, half-beast of the story.

9   HERSHINOW, SHELDON J. Bernard Malamud. Modern Literature
       Monographs. New York: Frederick Ungar Publishing Co., 165
       pp.
       Furnishes a critical survey of Malamud's fiction.
Chapters 1 and 10 supply the book with its thematic frame. The
former focuses on Malamud's moral activism, while the latter
concludes the study with an assessment of his moral and artistic
vision. The intervening chapters examine individual novels and
collections of stories. The Natural weds a narrative about
baseball to Arthurian legend, and through its double level
represents American values in particular and the suffering human
condition in general. The Assistant successfully uses Yiddish
dialect and humor in support of the novel's central theme, the
transformation of Frank Alpine "from moral degenerate" to a man
committed to the acceptance of another's suffering. An academic
novel, A New Life is also "a comedy, a Western adventure, a love
story, and an initiation rite." Malamud's most lucid narrative,
The Fixer, is a novel about existential suffering and spiritual
growth. Pictures of Fidelman belongs to the tradition of the
picaresque novel and the Bildungsroman, the collection of
stories emerging as Malamud's "most accomplished work."
Examining the relations of a Jewish writer to a black writer,
The Tenants explores "the plight of humankind" in America.
Dubin's Lives is highly influenced by D.H. Lawrence and embodies
many of Lawrence's insights in the creation of Dubin. The final
chapter on the fiction recognizes the short stories as brilliant
"comic and seriocomic parables." A bibliography is included,
pp. 151-55.

10   KAKUTANI, MICHIKO. "Malamud Still Seeks Balance and
       Solitude." New York Times, 15 July, p. C7.
       An interview with Malamud revealing the following points
of interest. Because of his private and orderly life, Malamud
has been the source of speculation that he is Philip Roth's
character, Lonoff, in The Ghost Writer. Although Malamud's
direction as a writer crystallized with the advent of the
Holocaust, he is uncomfortable with the label of Jewish writer.
As current president of P.E.N. American center, he is concerned
with the repression of writers in the Soviet Union and South
Africa.

11   KENNEDY, J. GERALD. "Parody as Exorcism: 'The Raven' and
       'The Jewbird.'" Genre 13 (Summer):161-69.
       Persuasively argues that the parodist, by appropriating
and transforming another author's materials for his own
imaginative needs, is released from the influence of the prior
text. Although critical attention to "The Jewbird" has dealt
with the satirizing of Jewish anti-Semitism on one level, on
another "this pogrom" reflects Malamud's own purgative process.
Thus Cohen's struggle to rid himself of Schwartz becomes

metaphorically a reflection of Malamud's need to exorcise the
influence of Poe's "The Raven."

12   KERY, LASLO. "Bernard Malamud in Budapest." Translated by
      J.E. Sollosy. Hungarian P.E.N./Le P.E.N. Hongrois 21:76-79.
      Malamud's work is well known in Hungary, and in this
connection Kery dwells on Malamud's warm relationships with his
literary Hungarian contacts. In preparation for his meeting
with the member of the Hungarian P.E.N., Malamud chose a chapter
from Dubin's Lives and his story "My Son the Murderer" for
translation into Hungarian, and Ádam Réz, one of Hungary's best
translators, was chosen for the assignment. These translations
of Malamud's fiction, and Malamud's new friendship with Réz,
occurred just before Réz's death. Also notable was Malamud's
friendship with Zoltán Zelk, a poet, who had read all the work
of Malamud that had been translated into Hungarian up to that
time.

13   LEVIN, DAVID. "The Lives of Bernard Malamud." Virginia
      Quarterly Review 56, no. 1 (Winter):163-66.
      In Dubin's Lives, Malamud's hero contains within his
characterization elements of the comic that recall Dubin's
counterparts in The Magic Barrel, A New Life, The Tenants, and
even The Natural. Longing for intense erotic fulfillment but
also desirous of an ordered life, Dubin is a typical Malamud
character in his ambivalence and contradictions. "The wit, the
humor, the delightful surprises of Malamud's language bring us a
vitality that deserves our celebration."

14   MALIN, IRVING. "Portrait of the Artist in Slapstick."
      Literary Review 24, no. 1 (Fall):121-38.
      Bernard Malamud has been neglected as a writer concerned
with the relationship of art to life, a theme especially
significant in Pictures of Fidelman. The gradual illumination
of Arthur Fidelman in coming to grips with both modes of
existence is the central issue of this novel. In "The Last
Mohican," Fidelman leaves art criticism for the sake of "his
relationship to real life--to suffering Jews and to
responsibilities." In "Glassblower of Venice," the mediating
influence of Beppo, homosexual lover and "artist," allows
Fidelman to experience the vital connections between art and
life.

15   _____. Review of Dubin's Lives. American Book Review 2, no.
      4 (May-June):8.
      Thoreau and Augustine, invoked in Malamud's epigraphs,
were afflicted by tensions in their own natures, and
appropriately serve as the presiding deities over William Dubin,
a man beset by his own internal conflicts. Malamud, going
beyond the plot, deftly conveys the dualism of his character

through a play on his German name--"du bist?"--and through the
changing seasons, symbolic of Dubin's alternating nature. The
novel presents no clear resolution to the opposing forces within
him.

16   MANEY, MARGARET SCHAEFFER. "The Urban Apocalypse in
      Contemporary American Novels." Ph.D. dissertation, University
      of Miami, 503 pp.
         Bernard Malamud's The Tenants, Nathaniel West's The Day of
      the Locust, Ralph Ellison's The Invisible Man, Hubert Selby's
      Last Exit to Brooklyn, Joyce Carol Oates's Them, and Walker
      Percy's Love in the Ruins combine naturalism, surrealism, and
      the Gothic mode in rendering the city a place of civic and
      spiritual apocalypse. The vision of each novel is discussed in
      detail. See Dissertation Abstracts International 41
      (1980):2111A.

17   MELLARD, JAMES M. The Exploded Form: The Modernist Novel in
      America. Urbana: University of Illinois Press, pp. 152-54.
         Considers Malamud's work an example of "naive-modernist
      fiction." Such fiction is often marked by its use of simple
      people and language and ideas that reflect their imagination.
      Other aspects of Malamud's modernism extend to his playful
      deflation of genre. Such novels as The Natural, The Assistant,
      and The Fixer, while framed respectively in the comic and tragic
      modes, seem at times to be subtle parodies of comedy and
      tragedy.

18   MITCHEL, DAVID J. Review of Dubin's Lives. Biography 3, no.
      2 (Spring):175-77.
         This novel crystallizes the difficulties inherent in
      writing biography, particularly when the biographer's subject
      eludes him. Malamud offers no easy solutions to Dubin's
      professional problems, and the reader must satisfy himself with
      the pleasures of the novelistic experience: "the idiom of
      domestic warfare and the day-to-day details of a marriage in
      decline is masterful."

19   NÁGY, PETER. "Reading American Prose in Budapest." New
      Hungarian Quarterly 21, no. 78 (Summer):177-82.
         Through its plot, sentence rhythms, images, and tension
      Dubin's Lives gives the impression of genius. Malamud's accom-
      plishment is especially impressive because of its seeming art-
      lessness. Although the novel is a compelling psychological
      study of William and Kitty Dubin, it is nonetheless anchored in
      the realism of a particular time and place; the time of the act-
      ion is the close of the Nixon era and its basic setting is the
      New England landscape. The landscape is especially important as
      a symbol "of internal psychological processes" at work in the
      characters. Malamud also proves to be a master of perspective,

1980

allowing his chapter endings to direct the reader's attention to what has preceded and what is to come.

20   PIEILLER, EVELYNE. "Malamud, ou le frisson du vivant."
       Quinzaine Littéraire, no. 338 (16-31 December):5
           A review of Dubin's Lives (retitled in French, La Vie
       multiple de William D.) and Rembrandt's Hat (retitled in French,
       L'Homme dans le tiroir).
           The heroes of Malamud's short stories are deceptively
       normal, but in actuality they are highly stylized and reflect
       the personal vision of the storyteller, a vision that embraces
       fable and magic. The characters are eccentrics dispossessed of
       traditional heroism, but Malamud endows them with stature. His
       new novel introduces a change of style and subject matter to his
       canon. The author tries to convey the life of a writer within
       the boundaries of objective realism until the conclusion, when
       he introduces fantasy. He succeeds in capturing life's
       transience and poignancy.

21   POLT, HARRIET. "Malamud's Lives." Midstream 26, no. 1
       (January):57-58.
           Dubin's Lives lacks the impact of The Assistant and The
       Fixer, novels in which Malamud seems to have a surer grasp of
       the underlying archetypal patterns and themes. Despite
       Malamud's denial of the autobiographical elements in Dubin's
       Lives, the novel may reveal more about his professional
       insecurity than he cares to admit.

22   VEDRAL, JOYCE LAURETTA. "Guilt and Atonement in the Novels
       of Bernard Malamud." Ph.D. dissertation, New York
       University, 334 pp.
           In The Natural, A New Life, and The Tenants, Malamud's
       protagonists are compelled to atone for guilt resulting from
       childhood or adult experiences, but atonement from novel to
       novel may be constructive or destructive. Vedral develops a
       six-part methodology for analyzing the nature of guilt and
       atonement in fiction. See Dissertation Abstracts International
       41 (1980):2608-9A

23   VICKERY, JOHN B. "The Scapegoat in Literature: Some Kinds
       and Uses." In The Binding of Proteus: Perspectives on Myth
       and the Literary Process. Edited by Marjorie W. McCune,
       Tucker Orbison, and Philip M. Withim. Lewisburg, Pa.:
       Bucknell University Press; London: Associated University
       Press, pp. 264-78.
           Comments on Yakov Bok of The Fixer as a scapegoat figure,
       observing that he moves from a passive, sacrificial victim to a
       more active role as legal prisoner whose indictment must be
       proved.

1981

24   WANIEK, MARILYN NELSON. "The Schizoid Implied Authors of Two
      Jewish American Novels." Melus 7, no. 1 (Spring):21-39
      passim.
          Most ethnic writers reveal their own sense of marginality
      in relation to mainstream American society and their subculture
      through the change in their authorial voice. Bernard Malamud is
      a case in point. In The Assistant Malamud's narrative account
      of Morris Bober alternates between affectionate mockery and
      respect for his values. Malamud's shifting perspective of Bober
      is carried by a change in voice that is "variously straight and
      ethnic."

25   WILLIAMS, MARY C. Review of Dubin's Lives. In Magill's
      Literary Annual 1980. Edited by Frank N. Magill. Vol. 5.
      Englewood Cliffs, N.J.: Salem Press, pp. 213-55.
          About guilt and pain, this novel is also suggestive of
      mythical renewal through its two-year cyclical pattern of
      seasons culminating in the spring. In attempting to cope with
      the lives of others, William Dubin discovers a new self. He is,
      however, largely introspective, but his problems engage the
      reader's sympathy and lend the book its appeal.

                             1981

1   ALTER, ISKA [SHEILA]. The Good Man's Dilemma: Social
      Criticism in the Fiction of Bernard Malamud. AMS Studies in
      Modern Literature, no. 5. New York: AMS Press, 214 pp.
          Revision of 1977.2. Expands the earlier study of
      Malamud's fiction to include a chapter on Dubin's Lives, a novel
      regarded as a tragicomedy. Its central theme, the conflict
      between instinct and intellect, is reflected in the structure of
      the plot and in the tensions of personal relationships.

2   BARBER, JAMES, and SATTELMYER, ROBERT. "The Natural and the
      Shooting of Eddie Waitkus." Midwestern Miscellany 9:61-67.
          Eddie Waitkus of the Philadelphia Phillies must be
      considered the major source for Malamud's Roy Hobbs. The
      shooting of Hobbs by Harriet Bird corresponds in many details to
      the shooting of Waitkus in 1949 by Ruth Ann Steinhagen, a
      nineteen-year-old girl who had tricked Waitkus into visiting her
      hotel room. The motives for the shooting were subsequently
      explained in Time and Newsweek which Malamud made use of in
      developing the plot of The Natural. Malamud's adaptation of the
      Waitkus-Steinhagen material is completed with Hobbs's collapse
      in Memo Paris's bedroom, but his novel also serves as a
      prophetic epilogue to Waitkus's eventual obscurity.

1981

3   BILIK, DOROTHY SEIDMAN. "Malamud's Secular Saints and Comic
       Jobs." In <u>Immigrant Survivors: Post-Holocaust Consciousness
       In Recent Jewish American Fiction</u>. Middletown: Wesleyan
       University Press, pp. 53-60.
          Malamud is unique among contemporary writers for the
       number of immigrants and Holocaust survivors he brings into his
       fiction. Although he does not confront the Holocaust directly,
       he evokes "a post-Holocaust sensibility": partially through the
       quasi-surrealistic character and setting and partially through
       the use of a metaphorical language that tries to communicate
       what lies beyond expression. Malamud's distance from the actual
       horror of the Holocaust is also aesthetic; the suffering of Job
       or saintlike victims is colored by a comic and ironic vision.
       Bilik uses <u>The Assistant</u>, <u>The Fixer</u>, <u>The Magic Barrel</u>, and
       <u>Idiots First</u> as examples of works that incorporate the
       post-Holocaust sensibility.

4   BROYARD, ANATOLE. "Being a Character." <u>New York Times Book
       Review</u>, 22 November, p. 55.
          Part of an interview with Bernard Malamud. The author did
       not regard himself as the model for Lonoff in Philip Roth's <u>The
       Ghost Writer</u>, although he admitted that some of William Dubin of
       <u>Dubin's Lives</u> is indeed Malamud. "Without invention," he
       observed, "biographical details remain merely strings of
       uncooked spaghetti."

5   DICKSTEIN, MORRIS. "The World in a Mirror: Problems of
       Distance in Recent American Fiction." <u>Sewanee Review</u> 89, no.
       3 (Summer):386-400 passim.
          In order to escape the formalism of the fifties, much
       recent fiction has taken on the personal note of autobiography.
       This desire to personalize literature is reflected in Malamud's
       <u>Dubin's Lives</u>. Suffering from the same problems of other recent
       autobiographical novels, Malamud's novel fails to establish a
       sufficient distance between the author and his hero. Malamud's
       proximity to William Dubin, biographer, inhibits him from making
       sufficiently perceptive observations about his character. As an
       added consequence, the novel lacks the humor and rich colloquial
       language of Malamud's earlier fiction. "The book is symptomatic
       of the narrowness that can afflict writers writing abut writers
       as surrogates for themselves."

6   GRAU, JOSEPH. "Bernard Malamud: A Further Bibliographical
       Addendum." <u>Bulletin of Bibliography</u> 38, no. 2
       (April-June):101-4.
          This bibliographical list of Malamud items, including
       reviews, criticism, and biography was intended for an earlier
       bibliographical article on Malamud (1980.6), but was excluded
       for lack of space. "Miscellany," designated for section II.B of

that article, was eliminated completely from it and is published
here along with several new citations.

7   HALIO, JAY L. "Fiction About Fiction." <u>Southern Review</u>,
n.s. 17, no. 1 (January):225-34 passim.
      Examines the work of some recent novelists who seem to be
writing fictionalized autobiography. <u>Dubin's Lives</u> is about the
inherent loneliness and isolation of a writer like Malamud who,
late in life, moves from detached contemplation to the immediacy
of erotic experience with all of its inevitable complications.
Despite its celebration of nature and physical passion, the
novel is essentially grim and lacks the optimism even of such
sombre books as <u>The Assistant</u> and <u>The Fixer</u>.

*8   INADA, TAKEHIKO. "Malamud no kaishun" [Malamud's redemption].
In <u>Bungaku Kukan 5. Shosetsu no Uchi to Soto</u>. Tokyo:
Sojusha, pp. 143-59.
      In Japanese. Source: <u>Modern Language Association
International Bibliography</u> (1981), 1:227.

9   LIDSTROM, ROBERT. "Malamud's <u>The Natural</u>: An Arthurian
Quest in the Big Leagues." <u>West Virginia University
Philological Papers</u> 27:75-81.
      The game of baseball is used in the novel as symbolic
vehicle through which to represent a moral and psychological
initiation into manhood independent of time and place. Like the
hero of Arthurian legend, Roy Hobbs must pass through a series
of tests and temptations until he is pure enough to achieve his
own version of the Grail. In its mythical dimensions, the
national sport becomes an arena in which inner struggles are
dramatized.

10   PARA, JEAN-BAPTISTE. Review of <u>La vie multiple de William
D.</u> [Dubin's Lives], translated by Olga Feodorov. Review of
<u>L'homme dans le tiroir</u> [Man in the drawer], translated by
David Guinsbourg. <u>Europe-revue Litteraire Mensuelle</u> 59, no.
623:338.
      Finds the novel disappointing in comparison to the
collection of stories (which is called <u>Rembrandt's Hat</u> in
English, from a story in the book). The novel, like its own
hero, fails to arrive at development. The collection, on the
other hand, is highly successful in its blending of tension,
textual density, symbolism, and humor, and the mediocre lives
that Malamud depicts are redeemed through the quality of his
art.

*11   RIVARD, YVON. Review of <u>Vie multiple de Will</u> [Dubin's
Lives]. <u>Liberté</u> (Canada) 23:128.
      Source: <u>Arts & Humanities Citation Index</u> (1982); 2, col.
5927.

1981

12   SCHMIDT-VON BARDELEBEN, RENATE. "Bernard Malamuds 'The Lady
      of the Lake': Judisch-amerikanische Selbstarstellung und
      britisch-englische Literaturtradition." In Geschichtlichkeit
      und Neuanfang im sprachlichen Kunstwerk: Studien zur
      englischen Philologie zu Ehren von Fritz W. Schulze. Edited
      by Peter Erlebach, Wolfgang G. Muller, and Klaus Reuter.
      Tübingen: Gunter Narr Verlag, pp. 257-51.
          Bernard Malamud adapted Sir Walter Scott's The Lady of the
      Lake as a model for his own story of the same name and used it
      as the basis for probing into the complex problem of
      American-Jewish identity. The theme of true versus false
      identity is at issue in both the story and the poem. While
      class hatred motivates behavior in Scott's poem, in Malamud's
      story the motivating force lies in the self-conscious Jewish
      identity of Levin-Freeman and Isabella del Dongo, which elicits
      different responses in each character. In setting, detail, and
      structure these works also share close points of contact.

13   STAFFORD, WILLIAM T. "The Black/White Continuum: Some
      Recent Examples in Bellow, Malamud, and Updike." In Books
      Speaking to Books: A Contextual Approach to American
      Fiction. Chapel Hill: University of North Carolina Press,
      pp. 73-102.
          Regards Bellow's Mr. Sammler's Planet, Malamud's The
      Tenants, and Updike's Rabbit Redux as novels that reflect the
      relations of black and white in the 1960s. One may view The
      Tenants as a recapitulation of racial and aesthetic strife in
      American history, and the eventual impass in black and white
      relations resulting from their mutually just claims.

14   STOREY, MICHAEL L. "Pinye Salzman, Pan, and 'The Magic
      Barrel.'" Studies in Short Fiction 18, no. 2 (Spring):
      180-83.
          Argues that references to Salzman associate him with Pan,
      the goat-God. Like Pan's daughter, Iynx, Salzman's daughter,
      Stella, is a woman of strong physical passion. Cognizant of
      Finkle's ascetic nature, the marriage broker sees in Stella an
      appropriate complement to it. Contrary to appearances, Salzman
      artfully orchestrates Leo Finkle's interest in and courtship of
      Stella.

1982

1   ALTER, ROBERT. "A Theological Fantasy." New Republic 187
      (20-27 September):70.
          God's Grace is the most explicitly Jewish book Malamud has
      ever written: his hero, Calvin Cohn, formerly a rabbinical
      student, consciously uses Hebraic teaching in his postnuclear
      holocaust world in order to create the environment for the prac-

176

tice of ethical Judaism. Malamud's fable becomes a platform for confronting the inscrutable nature of God and the unpredictable nature of man, as well as offering a prophetic warning to his readers. "The moral message is unexceptionable, but the vehemence with which the brutish counterforce to kindness and pity is imagined at the end is disquieting."

2   BAUMGARTEN, MURRAY. City Scriptures: Modern Jewish
        Writing. Cambridge, Mass.: Harvard University Press,
        pp. 15-16, 24-25, 40-44 and passim.
            American and European Jewish writers have brought the
        inflections of Yiddish and Jewish culture to contemporary
        literature as a way of confronting and articulating the problem
        of identity for the modern Jew. In The Fixer Malamud's Yakov
        Bok serves as a prototype for this figure--even the modern
        Jewish intellectual--who begins by repudiating and then
        reidentifying with his culture. Through its counterpoint of
        Yiddish and English rhythms and through character conflict, "The
        Jewbird" also reflects the tension between nostalgia for
        tradition and desire for assimilation.

3   BRAGG, MELVYN. "Rabbi Crusoe." Punch 283 (27 October):691.
            A great admirer of Malamud's fiction, Bragg considers
        God's Grace inadequate to its intention. Malamud has tried to
        synthesize nuclear holocaust, the historical Holocaust, and the
        concept of being chosen into one narrative, but the enormity of
        the task is too great. The result is a lack of balance and
        coherence. Had Malamud been in control of his materials, he
        would have spent more time developing his Crusoe-like satire, as
        well as the impact of Calvin Cohn's death.

4   BYER, JAMES JOHN. "Dubin's Lives and Bernard Malamud's
        Earlier Works: The Use of Repetition." Ph.D. dissertation,
        University of Kansas, 227 pp.
            Excluding the introduction, this study contains seven
        chapters in which repetition as a basic element in Malamud's
        fiction is examined. Such repetition consists of the evocation
        in Dubin's Lives of characters, phrases, and incidents appearing
        in earlier works of Malamud. "Overall, this study stresses the
        importance of the past in Malamud's fiction and in his
        creativity. While to Malamud's characters the past represents
        limitations, to Malamud himself the past is the context within
        which he finds the freedom to create." See Dissertation
        Abstracts International 43 (1983):2665A.

5   EPSTEIN, JOSEPH. "Malamud in Decline." Commentary 74, no. 4
        (October):49-53.
            Reviews Malamud's career and his relation to Jewish
        American writers past and present, observing that Malamud

1982

differs from them in his concern with the ethical implications
of being a Jew. Epstein concludes that God's Grace, Malamud's
latest novel, is artistically and intellectually thin, lacking
the depth of the fiction prior to The Tenants and Dubin's Lives.

6   FITZPATRICK, SEAN. Review of God's Grace. Best Sellers 42,
        no. 8 (November):90.
        Finds it difficult to identify the object of Malamud's
satire in God's Grace: "It is one more slender novel about a
not-very-religious-but-not-secularized, ineffectual,
self-doubting Jewish intellectual of fondly liberal aspiration,
full of ironic coincidences and non-sequiturs."

7   FREMONT-SMITH, ELIOT. "Malamud Tackles the Word." Village
        Voice, 7 September, p. 35.
        God's Grace invites comparison to such works, for example,
as Lord of the Flies or Robinson Crusoe, but Malamud does not
really add anything new to the genre in which he is working; the
result is a feeling of ennui. The difficulty with God's Grace
is that it centers on the implausible feat of talking chimps and
the equally implausible feat of cohabitation between man and a
lower order of primate culminating in an offspring. "Maybe
Malamud in this enterprise misplaced his magic."

8   FULLER, EDMUND. "After the Holocaust: A Sombre and Funny
        Fable." Wall Street Journal, 13 September, p. 30.
        Considers God's Grace as possibly Malamud's most lasting
work and compares it to Walter M. Miller, Jr.'s "A Canticle for
Leibowitz" and Russel Hoban's "Ridley Walker," other apocalytpic
fables; Malamud's is regarded as the most radical. At first,
the title of the novel, as well as the title of the last
chapter, "God's Mercy," seems sardonic. Yet a careful rereading
may soften one's initial responses. The possibility of mercy is
indeed suggested in this "inventive, reflective, tragicomic,
ultimately reverential fable. . . ."

9   GARCHIK, LEAH. "Malamud's Sense of Despair. San Francisco
        Chronicle, 5 September, pp. 1, 9.
        An interview with Bernard Malamud and a review of God's
Grace. Malamud has been preoccupied with the question of man's
relation to his creator since he began writing, and nowhere has
it been addressed more directly than in his latest novel. In
combining fantasy, philosophy, and animal fable, he has engaged
in a daring fictional experiment in behalf of the gravity of his
subject, nuclear annihilation. Whether God or man is responsible for the destruction of almost all living things is left
for the reader to decide. "[Malamud] succeeded in doing exactly
what he intended to do: not exactly to chastize the human race,
but to sound a warning. . . ."

178

1982

10   GIACHETTI, ROMANO. "Così Malamud inventò Dio." <u>La</u>
      <u>Repubblica</u>, 30 September, n.p.
      An interview with Bernard Malamud concerning his latest
novel, <u>God's Grace</u>. Malamud does not want to believe that his
civilization is close to the end. His narrative becomes a
parable through which both the author and the reader can ponder
the mysterious nature of a God who gives man, his favorite
creature, the power of self-destruction. Malamud desires that
this cosmic mystery, central to his novel, lure the reader back
to human elementals. From the artistic point of view, Malamud's
strategy is filled with risk.

11   GOLLIN, RITA K. "Malamud's Dubin and the Morality of
      Desire." <u>Papers on Language and Literature</u> 18, no. 2
      (Spring):190-207.
      <u>Dubin's Lives</u> probes more fully than any other Malamud
novel the relation between desire and morality. As in the
earlier novels, desire is rendered as a negative experience if
it is the product of selfishness and a positive experience if it
is mutually rewarding. "In Retirement" and "The First Seven
Years" are examples of the former and the latter. In this
novel, Malamud dramatizes desire and morality at a new level of
complexity. While Dubin's passions remain at the end of the
novel important components of his life, they are now put into
proper balance with commitment and responsibility. The ending
"suggests that Dubin has now learned to understand women not
only as daughters, wives, or lovers, but as equals."

12   GORZKOWSKA, REGINA. "The Poor Slav Devil of Malamud's <u>The</u>
      <u>Assistant</u>." <u>Polish Review</u> 27, nos. 3-4:35-44.
      Suggests that the novel should be read against the devil's
apprenticeship motif of slavic folklore for a new perspective.
In essence the motif involves a peasant who has been wronged by
a minor devil. Lucifer is moved to pity by the peasant's unjust
suffering and requires the devil to return to earth in order to
serve the peasant until he is pardoned by him. As a result of
his association with the peasant, the devil partially absorbs
the human nature of his host, but he does not actually steal his
soul as in other variants of the motif. Malamud's rendering of
this motif includes its element of compassion. "Frank's reentry
into humanity and his conversion to Judaism through his complete
identification with Morris is a psychological transposition of
the soul snatching motif. . . ."

13   GREENWELL, BILL. Review of <u>God's Grace</u>. <u>New Statesman</u> 104
      (29 October):31.
      This novel is a departure from Malamud's other work, and
its pleasure lies in Malamud's absurd treatment of man and
animal after a nuclear holocaust. "This is better read as a
madcap endlessly inventive spoof. . . ."

1982

14   HOWES, VICTOR. "The Apocalypse According to Malamud."
        Christian Science Monitor, 10 September, p. B3.
            Bernard Malamud's God's Grace is about beginnings and
        endings: the day the world ends through a nuclear holocaust is
        also the day that it is reborn. "Malamud tells with humor and
        grace of a . . . tragicomic parable, somewhat east of sci-fi,
        somewhat west of allegory."

15   KAKUTANI, MICHIKO. "As the Author Grows Up." New York Times
        Book Review, 25 July, p. 24.
            Malamud comments on the difficulties facing the maturing
        and successful writer. Diminished energy and enthusiasm, as
        well as a too comfortable sense of accomplishment, become
        obstacles that interfere with a high level of creativity. There
        are compensations, however. "What you may lose in complexity of
        words, you make up in understanding."

16   LEICHUK, ALAN. Review of God's Grace. New York Times Book
        Review, 29 August, pp. 1, 14-15.
            In his latest novel Malamud once again proves to be a
        writer of fables. A dialogue with God and the hero, Calvin
        Cohn, a paleontologist, establishes the religious and
        philosophical issues of the narrative. As the last human
        survivor of a nuclear holocaust, Cohn finds himself reenacting
        the Book of Genesis in the company of assorted surviving
        subhuman primates. This plot engagingly presents one of
        Malamud's absorbing preoccupations, the question of human
        survival in a mysterious universe.

17   LEONARD, JOHN. Review of God's Grace. New York Times, 23
        August, p. C18.
            Regards the novel as too heavy handed. Its various
        symbolic resonances and its many tricks of plot are excessive.
        "It is hard for me to accept a chimpanzee as the Lady of the
        Lake, and when Isaac sacrifices Abraham, I find myself tired of
        masks on clowns, of father and of sons."

18   MALOFF, SAUL. "God's Grace." Commonweal 109 (5 November):
        593-94.
            Despite the inherent "cuteness" in this didactic fable,
        God's Grace "is a thoroughly serious novel, and a beautifully
        imagined one," possessed of a tragic vision.

19   NAKANO, MIYO. "Malamud no egaku shremir teki ningen ni
        tsuite: The Assistant no baai [On Malamud's presentation of
        schlemiels: The case of The Assistant]." In Phoneix o
        motomete: Eibei shosetsu no yukue [Search of Phoenix:
        Future of English-American novels]. Tokyo: Nan'undo, pp.
        399-412.
            Source: Modern Language Association International
        Bibliography (1982), 1:219.

20   PRESCOTT, PETER. "The World According to Cohn." <u>Newsweek</u>
       100 (6 September):70.
          The fantasy out of which <u>God's Grace</u> emerges has never
been more effective anywhere in Malamud's fiction. Through this
narrative vehicle, his theme of a new life reappears, this time
after a nuclear holocaust, but the old life, represented by
several rebellious and depraved chimpanzees, gradually reasserts
itself and destroys the Eden established by Calvin Cohn. The
novel "is precisely what fantasy for adults ought to be: at
first charming, then affecting, and finally deeply moving."

21   PRINGLE, MARY BETH. "(Auto)biography: Bernard Malamud's
       <u>Dubin's Lives</u>." <u>International Fiction Review</u> 9, no. 2
       (Summer):138-41.
          Speculates on why Malamud consciously establishes
connections between himself and that of his character, William
Dubin, while attempting to maintain some distance from him.
Pringle suggests that Malamud's involvement with and detachment
from his character is intended to serve as a model for his
reader. While Malamud sees himself in William Dubin, he also
stands back from his character in order to identify him as
Everyman. The reader is invited to respond to Dubin in similar
fashion.

22   RAWSON, CLAUDE. "Bananas." <u>London Review of Books</u> 4, no. 21
       (November-December):9-10.
          <u>God's Grace</u> draws on a variety of sources: Malamud's God
is appropriately the nonpersonal God of the new theology, while
the plot draws on <u>Robinson Crusoe</u> and <u>Gulliver's Travels</u>. In
this context Malamud explores human behavior in relation to
animal behavior in order to suggest the uncertain boundary lines
between the two. This intention is supported by Malamud's
comparison of human and lesser primate mating habits, the
meaning of bananas for Calvin Cohn and Buz, and Malamud's
treatment of cannabalism. "It [cannabalism] is done by
creatures not in every way human, and secondary uncertainties
are introduced as to whether or not it is the humanoid or the
bestial element in them which is responsible." Unfortunately,
Malamud's ultimate vision involving the nature of man and of
animal fails to emerge with clarity.

*23   Review of <u>God's Grace</u>. <u>Listener</u> 108, no. 4:23.
          Source: <u>Book Review Index</u> 19, no. 2 (1983):97;
unverified.

24   REYNOLDS, STANLEY. "Goys and Dolls." <u>Punch</u> 282 (19
       May):821-22.
          In noting the recent publication of <u>Rembrandt's Hat</u> by
Chatto & Windus, Reynolds refers to Malamud as "the American
Chekhov."

1982

25   RICHLER, MORDECAI. "Chumps and Chimps." New York Review of
      Books 29 (18 November):28-30.
         Confesses to an uncertainty about Malamud's intentions in
      God's Grace, and concludes that the darkness of his vision is
      not given appropriate formal expression. The novel suggests
      that Malamud is in decline.

26   SAPOSNICK, IRVING S. "Bellow, Malamud, Roth . . . and
      Styron?" Judaism 31, no. 3 (Summer):322-32.
         Those who have read Malamud's fiction as an undeviating
      affirmation of redemptive suffering have failed to recognize
      Malamud's own ambivalence if not his own outright rejection of
      it. Unlike The Assistant, in which Frank Alpine assumes the
      role of his suffering surrogate father Morris Bober, William
      Dubin of Dubin's Lives refuses to reenact in his own life the
      passivity and helplessness of his father and merely remain
      "Charlie-the-waiter's son." Even in The Assistant, in Helen
      Bober's speech at her father's funeral, and extending through
      Malamud's later fiction, the view that suffering is pointless is
      forcefully expressed.

27   "School Libraries and Free Ideas." Christian Science
      Monitor, 30 June, p. 24.
         The banning of The Fixer from the shelves of a Long Island
      school library by the local school board became an issue in the
      U.S. Supreme Court. The question of whether the book has
      redeeming social value, despite its elements of vulgarity, was
      regarded as an issue appropriate for the jurisdiction of a lower
      court.

28   SHAPIRA, ANN. "Planet of the Apes + 1." Nation 235 (16
      October):374-76.
         In making God responsible for a cosmic holocaust, because
      of dissatisfaction with his own creation, Malamud sets the stage
      in God's Grace for exploring once again what it means to be
      human. In this context, both human beings and talking
      chimpanzees harbor the very same obsessions--appetites for meat,
      sex, spirituality, and power--and traditional distinctions
      between one creature and another gradually disappear. Calvin
      Cohn's Jewish ethos, his occasional Yiddishisms, and other forms
      of linguistic inventiveness add a comic element to the starkness
      of Malamud's vision. In God's ambivalence about his own
      creation, Malamud's novel seems to be self-reflexive, alluding,
      it seems, to the insufficiency of the author's own vision.

29   SINCLAIR, CLIVE. "The Falling-out in Paradise." Times
      Literary Supplement, no. 4152 (29 October):1188.
         Although God's Grace is said to be an innovation in
      Malamud's fiction, The Tenants foreshadows the civil war we
      encounter in his latest novel. Indeed, Morris Bober and S.

Levin look toward Calvin Cohn in their attempt to redeem those whose souls are in need of saving. "By turning living chimps into fiction Malamud has, paradoxically, made them more alive. The weak link in this evolutionary chain is actually homo sapiens, Calvin Cohn himself." Failing to have a particularized past, Malamud's hero possesses less authenticity than his ape charges.

30   SUPLEE, CURT. "God, Bernard Malamud, & the Rebirth of Man." Washington Post, 27 August, pp. F1, F8.
      A review of God's Grace combined with an interview with Bernard Malamud in Bennington, Vermont. This is a novel nourished by biblical parallels, anthropological reading, and themes from the author's earlier novels. In conception the book is Miltonic; in its language and tone, often comic. The idea for his most recent work was specifically suggested by two of Malamud's animal fables, "The Jewbird" and "Talking Horse," although a fictional rendering of judgment day had been a preoccupation of his for some years. According to his friend John Hawkes, Malamud's attempt at writing a fable in a period of postmodern cynicism was both risky and courageous. Referring to his literary counterparts, Malamud agreed with Lionel Trilling's early assessment: that he is much closer to writers in American literature, for example, to the work of Hawthorne, than he is to any other group of writers. At this stage in his career, Malamud is confident about the strength of his work.

31   SZONYI, DAVID. Review of God's Grace. Hadassah 64, no. 1 (August-September):27-28.
      In its evocation of Jewish ritual, lore, and themes, this novel is reminiscent of The Fixer, but it does not possess the unmistakable optimism of the latter. God's Grace ends with an inverted reference to Genesis; in this context, a father is murdered by sons without any instance of divine intervention. The novel is limited by an undynamic narrative and its thin emotional quality. Malamud darkly suggests that God himself may have drawn the blueprint for destroying "His most flawed creature."

32   UPDIKE, JOHN. "Cohn's Doom." New Yorker 58 (8 November): 167-70.
      A novelist who writes according to personal vision rather than fashion, Malamud takes his place among the more disciplined American novelists since World War II. Like his other novels, God's Grace involves a calculated risk, and it is a radical departure from the domesticity of his previous novel, Dubin's Lives, to the abstraction of fable. While Malamud's vision is essentially dark, it remains so within the orthodox framework of a biblical vision. Its allegory, attached as it is to Calvin Cohn's Jewish ethos, seems confusing, especially in the light of

1982

the historical Holocaust. "As a cosmic fable, 'God's Grace'--a tender retelling of Noah's shame and a comic sketch of final horror--is a muddle, but therein lies its mercy."

33   ZIEGELMAN, LOIS A. "Ginzburg Revisited." Modern Language Studies 12, no. 4:91-93.
       "Idiots First" communicates on the level of the earthly and the level of the supernatural, and both levels are synthesized in the conclusion. The three human obstacles to Ginzburg's paternal efforts in behalf of his son, the pawnbroker, philanthropist, and the Rabbi's wife, are symbolically amalgamated into Ginzburg, "the tribal personification of the Angel of Death."

1983

1   ALTER, ROBERT. "Ordinary Anguish." New York Times Book Review, 16 October, pp. 1, 35-36.
       The Stories of Bernard Malamud offers a collective illustration of the essential Malamudian hero appearing in the author's fiction for over thirty years. He is often a Job-like sufferer, bereft of family ties, possibly an immigrant who speaks with Yiddish intonations. The most impressive stories in this collection evoke compassion for the characters through an economy of language and feeling that is reminiscent of Hemingway. Although not all of the stories achieve the same level of quality, they are nevertheless the products of a unique imagination. "It can be said that only Bernard Malamud could have written them."

2   BENEDICT, HELEN. "Bernard Malamud: Morals and Surprises." Antioch Review 41, no. 1 (Winter):28-36.
       A review of God's Grace, an assessment of Malamud's fiction, and an interview with the writer. As a fable about nuclear war, Malamud's new novel represents yet another experiment in a career marked by a variety of fictional subjects and techniques. As in so many of his stories and novels, a dark subject is once again rendered partially comic. Benedict goes on to distinguish between Malamud's Jewish and non-Jewish fiction, discusses his relation to other contemporary Jewish writers, and considers his connection to Jewish culture and tradition. Malamud continues to shy away from questions concerning autobiographical elements in his fiction, is now more confident about himself as a writer, and has become increasingly pessimsitic about the nature of man.

3   BRIGANTI, CHIARI. "Mirrors, Windows and Peeping Toms: Women as the Object of Voyeuristic Scrutiny in Bernard Malamud's A New Life and Dubin's Lives." Studies in American Jewish Literature, no. 3:151-65.

Contends that voyeurism seems to be a behavioral trait of
all the characters in A New Life and is a symptom of their
inadequacy. S. Levin, however, eventually frees himself of it
and becomes an actor instead of remaining merely an observer.
William Dubin of Dubin's Lives, like S. Levin, also observes the
lives of others, but he remains imprisoned in his subjectivity,
unable to commit himself to an active and clearly defined role
in the lives of others. Briganti sees both novels as examples
of the patterns which voyeurism takes in Malamud's other work.

4   BRYANT, EARLE V. "The Tree-Clock in Bernard Malamud's
     'Idiots First.'" Studies in Short Fiction 20, no. 1
     (Winter):52-54.
     The previous interpretations of this story involving a
tree reversing its branches, although sound, do not get to the
heart of the matter. The position of the branches constitutes a
symbolic clock intended to call to the attention of Mendel "that
time is running out." That he comprehends the message of the
tree is indicated by his moan when he notices that the branches
have reversed their position. Thus the seemingly occult
incident in the park is organically related to the theme of the
story, "that soon the Iceman cometh."

5   BURGESS, ANTHONY. "Saying Kaddish for Man." Inquiry
     Magazine 6, no. 2 (January):36-37.
     A whimsical novel of great skill, God's Grace has its
counterparts in such works as Orwell's Animal Farm, Golding's
Lord of the Flies, Defoe's Robinson Crusoe, and Swift's
Gulliver's Travels. Perhaps the culmination of these other
works, God's Grace offers a vision of human nature through fable
rather than diagnosis. As Calvin Cohn's simian charges take on
human qualities, they also begin to display a viciousness never
found in animals. As a Jew, Malamud is in a unique position to
recognize man's destructive potential: "the Holocaust behind
him, and before him the ghastly truth that Israelis can behave
like Nazis." His talent for mixing realism and fantasy has
never been more fully realized.

6   COALE, SAMUEL C. "Marriage in Contemporary American
     Literature: Mismatched Marriages of Manichean Minds."
     Thought 58, no. 228 (March):111-21.
     Like other postmodern fiction, Dubin's Lives presents sex
as a mesmerizing preoccupation. Although Malamud's story is
centered in adultery, it is also in its way religious, as
illustrated in William Dubin's attempt to merge his soul with
the landscape and the season. Nevertheless, both sex and the
natural world prove to be only temporary refuges against the
"insecurities, uncertainties [and] unanswered questions of his
marriage."

1983

*7   Di VEROLI, ELENA MORTARA. "Bernard Malamud." In I
       contemporanei: Novecento americano. Edited by E. Zolla.
       Rome: Lucarini, pp. 581-616.
           Source: Professor Giovanna Franci-Zignani, University of
       Bologna, Italy; unverified.

8   GILBERT, HARRIET. "Making It." New Republic 105 (21
       January):26.
           Pictures of Fidelman is narrated in taut, economical prose
       which contributes to the depth and power of the work. "With wit
       and imaginative vision, the author explores the destruction that
       creation entails."

9   GRAY, PAUL. "Heroism without Sentiment." Time 122 (17
       October):92.
           The Stories of Bernard Malamud reminds us again that the
       author is more successful in this genre than in the novel.
       Malamud gives his sympathy to his many stubborn, eccentric, and
       defeated figures, and "these stories reveal a gentleness in
       [his] . . . art that was not always clear before."

10   HELLER, KAREN. "Malamud's Long View of Short Stories." USA
       Today, 19 August, p. 30.
           According to the author, his best stories will be
       appearing in Stories of Bernard Malamud, to be published by
       Farrar, Straus & Giroux in October 1983. After completing God's
       Grace, a daring novel involving talking simians who survive a
       nuclear holocaust, Malamud is back at work on the short story, a
       genre in which he feels most comfortable. While recognizing the
       need for freedom and experimentation, he contended in this
       interview that most young authors find it difficult to submit
       themselves to a literary discipline.

11   KING, FRANCIS. "Perfectionist." Spectator 250 (15
       January):22-33.
           A belated review of Pictures of Fidelman recently reissued
       in a Collected Edition of Bernard Malamud's Works by Chatto &
       Windus. King concludes that this episodic novel is marked by
       its various styles and moods, its manic humor, and its
       exasperation at the failure of life and art to blend with each
       other.

12   L'HEUREUX, JOHN. Review of The Stories of Bernard Malamud.
       New York 16 (17 October):94.
           The richest of Malamud's stories are included in this
       collection, and they offer alternately surprise, illumination,
       and redemption. "What immediately strikes the reader is how
       quickly and completely Malamud compels our belief in the reality
       of his fictional world . . . ."

13   LYONS, GENE. "A Chosen People." <u>Newsweek</u> 102 (17
        October):86-87.
            Praises "Man in the Drawer" and "The Last Mohican" as the
        best work in <u>The Stories of Bernard Malamud</u>, but does not find
        the others in this collection as successful. These stories now
        seem dated since they were originally published, and their
        didacticism more strident than that in the novels.

14   MALAMUD, BERNARD. [Introduction to] <u>The Stories of Bernard</u>
        <u>Malamud</u>. New York: Farrar, Straus & Giroux, pp. vii-xiii.
            Reprint of 1983.15.

15   _____. "The Making of a Writer: Pleasures of the Fast
        Payoff." <u>New York Times Book Review</u>, 28 August, pp. 3, 19.
            Malamud's first goal was to discover his own voice and
        identity as a writer. After accepting a teaching position at
        Oregon State College in 1949, his thoughts began to dwell on his
        immigrant father and his own relations to Jews; both
        preoccupations were to feature in his subsequent writing. Even
        at the outset of his career, Malamud alternated between writing
        novels and short stories, but the latter gave him special
        delight because of the immediacy with which they conveyed their
        drama. The writing of fiction has, in general, been a source of
        satisfaction and meaning to Malamud: first, through the
        imaginative pleasure of allowing him to interact with his
        characters; second, through the value that his narrative art
        places on human life. Although Malamud has taught creative
        writing courses, he believes that such courses have limited
        value beyond a year. A young writer must become self-reliant
        and independent early. Reprinted: 1983.14.

16   MITGANG, HERBERT. "Arts Medals Presented." <u>New York Times</u>,
        18 May, p. C14.
            The American Academy and Institute of Arts and Letters
        awarded Bernard Malamud its Gold Medal in Fiction. "Mr. Malamud
        was cited for 'his variations on themes from Scripture' handled
        with 'dignity, humor, and honor.'"

17   OZICK, CYNTHIA. "Literary Blacks and Jews." In <u>Art and</u>
        <u>Ardor: Essays by Cynthia Ozick</u>. New York: Alfred A. Knopf,
        pp. 90-112.
            Reprint of 1972.30; 1975.6.

18   QUART, BARBARA KOENIG. "Women in Bernard Malamud's
        Fiction." <u>Studies in American Jewish Literature</u>, no.
        3:138-50.
            The men in Malamud's novels are unable to commit
        themselves to or sustain loving relationships with women,
        "despite the intense passion, lust, yearning directed at . . .

1983

[women]." Vocation takes precedence over love, and often
physical imperfections in women tend to keep men at a
psychological distance from them. The Assistant, The Fixer, A
New Life, and Dubin's Lives are discussed.

19   WADE, ROSALAND. Review of God's Grace. Contemporary Review
      242, no. 1404 (January):47.
         This novel does not add anything new to the reader's
awareness of the fragility of civilization. The interest it
stimulates comes from its radical departure from Malamud's other
work.

20   YARDLEY, JONATHAN. "Bernard Malamud: An Artist in
      Command." Washington Post Book World 13 (16 October):3.
         The Stories of Bernard Malamud reveals the author's
amazing ability to mix suffering and joy, opposing qualities
which are reflected in the twenty-five stories of this
collection. "Coming as it does on the heels of the disastrous
God's Grace, [this volume] reaffirms Malamud's high and honored
place among contemporary American writers."

Index

32, 35-37, 39, 41-42,
45-49, 51-52, 61, 66;
1980.4, 15, 18-21, 25;
1981.10
-seasonal pattern, 1979.50
-sex, 1979.57; 1981.7;
1982.2; 983.6
-tensions, 1979.39
-voyeurism, 1983.3
-women, 1983.3
Ducharme, Robert E., 1970.2;
1971.9; 1973.7; 1974.4
Dupee, Frederick Wilcox, 1964.7;
1965.3
Durwood, Elissa, 1979.10

Edel, Leon, 1979.11
Edelman, Lily, 1966.14; 1970.3;
1973.8
Edelstein, J.M., 1963.8
Ehrmann, Herbert B., 1966.15
Eigner, Edwin M., 1968.4; 1970.5
Eliot, George, Daniel Deronda,
1974.20
Eliot, T.S., 1964.11; 1966.64,
The Waste Land, 1974.15
Elkin, Stanley, 1967.10
Elliot, George P., 1957.3;
1966.16-17
**Ellison, Ralph, The Invisible
Man, 1958.3; 1980.16**
Ellmann, Mary, 1969.10
Elman, Richard, 1961.5; 1966.18
Emerson, Ralph Waldo, 1969.7
Engelbert, Ernst, 1977.8
Epstein, Joseph, 1982.5
Ethical vision in Malamud,
1979.56
Ethnic marginality, 1980.24
Evanier, David, 1979.12
Existentialism, 1965.4; 1968.1;
1973.42

Fabe, Marilyn Michele, 1976.4
Fairytale formula, 1973.18
Family in Malamud, 1975.22
Fanger, Donald, 1966.19
Fantasy forms in Malamud, 1971.53
Farber, Steven, 1969.11
**Farrell, James T., 1962.14,
Studs Lonigan, 1970.20**

Faulkner, Howard John, 1972.7
Featherstone, Joseph, 1967.11
Feinstein, Elaine, 1970.4;
1972.8; 1974.5
Fenton, James, 1969.12
Fictional world of Malamud,
1978.16
Fiedler, Leslie A., 1955.1;
1958.3; 1959.2; 1960.3-4;
1964.7-8; 1968.8; 1977.3,
9-10
Field, Joyce W., 1970.5; 1975.6-8
Field, Leslie A., 1970.5;
1975.5-8; 1977.3-4, 11; 1978.5
Fineman, Irving, 1966.20; 1967.12
Fink, Guido, 1968.5; 1976.5
**Finkelstein, Sidney, 1965.4;
1972.9**
"The First Seven Years," 1972.10
Fisch, Harold, 1971.10
Fitzgerald, Edward, 1952.2
Fitzgerald, F. Scott, 1966.64
Fitzpatrick, Sean, 1982.6
The Fixer, 1966.42, 58; 1968.5;
1971.35; 1975.10; 1980.1, 9,
23; 1981.3; 1982.2, 27; 1983.18
-brudermensch ideal, 1970.27
-character change, 1977.13
-Christian perspective,
1967.21
-compared with Dostoevski's
The Devils, 1970.28
**-compared with Milton's
Samson Agonistes, 1969.22**
-compared with Roth's When
She Was Good, 1967.42
-compared with Samuel's
Blood Accusation, 1966.12,
24, 71; 1967.2, 5
-compared with Styron's
The Confessions of Nat
Turner, 1968.3
-critics of, 1970.10
-death-of-God theology,
1967.21, 1972.22
-existentialism, 1971.17;
1973.42
-father-son motif, 1974.4
-freedom in, 1969.34
-Gentile suffering, 1971.10
-guilt, 1970.22; 1980.22